OBSESSIVE-COMPULSIVE DISORDER AND COMORBIDITY

Obsessive-Compulsive Disorder and Comorbidity

Ruth Gross-Isseroff
and
Abraham Weizman
Editors

Nova Science Publishers, Inc.
New York

For permission to use material from this book please contact us:
Telephone 631-231-7269; Fax 631-231-8175
Web Site: http://www.novapublishers.com

Library of Congress Cataloging-in-Publication Data

Obsessive-compulsive disorder and comorbidity / Ruth Gross-Isseroff and Abraham Weizman (Editors).

p. cm.

Includes bibliographical references and index.

ISBN 1-59454-884-6

1. Obsessive-compulsive disorder--Complications. 2. Comorbidity. I. Gross-Isseroff, Ruth. II. Weizman, Abraham.

[DNLM: 1. Obsessive-Compulsive Disorder. 2. Comorbidity. WM 176 O14265 2006]

RC533.O2643 2006

616.85'227--dc22 2006001270

Published by Nova Science Publishers, Inc. ✢ New York

Dedication

This book is dedicated with love to our parents: Drs. Jeana and Harry Gross & Bath-Sheva and Mendel Weizman

CONTENTS

In: Obsessive-Compulsive Disorder and Comorbidity
Editors: R. Gross-Isseroff and A. Weizman, pp. 1-3
ISBN 1-59454-884-6

Chapter 1

COMORBIDITY OF OBSESSIVE-COMPULSIVE DISORDER

Ruth Gross-Isseroff* and Abraham Weizman
Research Unit, Geha Mental Health Center, Petach Tikva, Israel

INTRODUCTION

The subject of comorbidity in psychiatric disorders has received renewed attention during the last decade. Though definitions of comorbidity vary it is common to assume that the term refers to the co-occurrence of two or more psychiatric disorders as defined by a standard diagnostic criteria (Wittchen, 1996).

Obsessive-compulsive disorder (OCD) is a relatively well defined entity. As many clinicians and basic scientists have noted, it rarely occurs by itself. It is usually accompanied by other psychiatric and/or neurologic disorders. Is the context of the occurrence of OCD relevant to the pathophysiology of the disorder? To its treatment? To prognosis? These questions will be discussed in the present book, and if not providing definitive answers, we hope to, at least, highlight some questions which will undoubtedly be raised in future research efforts.

Depression in its various manifestations and more specifically major depressive disorder is by far the most common disorder to co-occur with OCD (e.g. Dunner, 2001). The epidemiology of this combination of disorders, issues of definition and treatment are discussed in the present volume. One of the major concerns when OCD is accompanied by depression is the diagnostic priority of the two disorders. Is depression secondary? Does the fact that the patient suffers from prolonged OCD induce the state of depression or are the two disorders independent? Or, conversely, does depression predispose the patient to OCD?

Diverse anxiety disorders, such as social anxiety disorder, panic disorder and generalized anxiety disorder are also common in OCD patients (Dunner, 2001). Again, is there a common pathophysiological basis in anxiety disorders that predisposes patients to other anxiety

* Research Unit, Geha Mental Health Center, P.O.B. 102, Petach Tikva 49100, Israel; Phone: 972-3-9258439, Fax: 972-3-9258388, risseroff@clalit.org.il; aweizman@clalit.org.il

disorders? Anxiety disorders have been said to involve an overactivation of the amygdala, while OCD involves an overactivation of the orbitofrontal cortex. It is of interest to note, in the context of comorbidity between these disorders, the neural connections between these two brain regions.

Of special interest is the comorbidity of OCD with schizophrenia (e.g. Poyurovsky et al., 2004). At different points in the history of psychopathology, obsessions were regarded as an extreme form of delusions, thus predisposing OCD patients to schizophrenia. Conversely, at other times it was claimed that the two disorders cannot co-occur and, moreover, that OCD is a defense against the disintegration of schizophrenia. Lately rates of comorbidity of the two disorders have been assessed and have reached as high a value as 15% (Tibbo and Warneke, 1999). Several brain regions are involved in the two disorders as shown by neuroimaging studies (Gross-Isseroff et al., 2003). The treatment of the comorbidity of the two is intriguing.

OCD is part of a spectrum of disorders, including, among others, Tourette syndrome, trychotilomania, compulsive gambling (Jaisoorya et al., 2003; Richter et al., 2003). Is there a predisposition of patients with any one of these disorders to develop the others? Genetic studies point to a possible common mechanism in this cluster of disorders (Cuker et al., 2004).

Some neurologic diseases such as Parkinson's and Sydenham's chorea are sometimes accompanied by OCD. Is the involvement of the basal ganglia the underlying mechanism?

Some brain injuries, either mechanical or as a result of cerebro-vascular eventss are followed by OCD-like symptoms (Grados, 2003). Again, the mechanism and the brain region specificity are not clear.

Beside the obvious clinical challenges posed by the problem of comorbidity, it seems that this problem is much more relevant to basic science than previously thought. Different types of OCD have different patterns of comorbidity and different patterns of heredity (Mataix-Cols et al., 2005). Moreover, age at onset of OCD is correlated with clusters of comorbid disorders and early vs late age at onset appear to have different patterns of comorbidity as well as different patterns of inheritance (Diniz et al., 2004; Millet et al., 2004). Need we stress the importance of these finding to deciphering the genetic basis of the disorder? Thus, comorbidity in OCD seems to have genetic implications, which in turn may be significant in the biological sub-typing of the disorder. These issues, we feel, are far beyond any predictions we would have been able to foresee a decade or two ago.

We hope that the present volume will address some of these issues and help to illuminate them with the cumulative light provided by state of the art research.

We would like to thank all authors for their efforts to meet the challenge we posed them.

References

Cuker A, State MW, King RA, Davis N, Ward DC (2004) Candidate locus for Gilles de la Tourette syndrome/obsessive-compulsive disorder/chronic tic disorder at 18q22. *Am. J. Med. Genet.*, 130, 37-39.

Diniz JB, Rosario-Campos MC, Shavitt RG, Curi M, Hounie AG, Brotto SA, Miguel EC (2004) Impact of age at onset and duration of illness on the expression of comorbidities in obsessive-compulsive disorder. *J. Clin. Psychiatry*, 65, 22-27.

Dunner DL (2001) Management of anxiety disorders: the added challenge of comorbidity. *Depress. Anxiety*, 13, 57-71.

Grados MA (2003) Onsessive-compulsive disorder after traumatic brain injury. *Int. Rev. Psychiatry*, 15, 350-358.

Gross-Isseroff R, Hermesh H, Zohar J, Weizman A (2003) Neuroimaging communality between schizophrenia and obsessive-compulsive disorder: a putative basis for schizo-obsessive disorder? *World J. Bio. Psychiatry*, 4, 129-134.

Jaisoora TS, Reddy YC, Srinath S (2003) The relationship of obsessive-compulsive disorder to putative spectrum disorders: results from an Indian study. *Compr. Psychiatry*, 44, 317-323.

Mataix-Cols D, Rosario-Campos MCd, Leckman JF (2005) A multidimensional model of obsessive-compulsive disorder. *Am. J. Psychiatry*, 162, 228-238.

Millet B, Kochman F, Gallarda T, Krebs MO, Demonfaucon F, Barrot I, Bourdel MC, Olie JP, Loo H, Hantouche EG (2004) Phenomenological and comorbid features associated in obsessive-compulsive disorder: influence of age of onset. *J. Affect. Disord.*, 79, 241-246.

Poyurovsky M, Weizman A, Weizman R (2004) Obsessive-compulsive disorder in schizophrenia: clinical characteristics and treatment. *CNS Drugs*, 18, 989-1010.

Richter MA, Sumerfeld LJ, Antony MM, Swinson RP (2003) Obsessive-compulsive spectrum conditions in obsessive-compulsive disorder and other anxiety disorders. *Depress. Anxiety*, 18, 118-127.

Tibbo P, Warneke L (1999) Obsessive-compulsive disorder in schizophrenia: epidemiologic and biologic overlap. *J. Psychiatry Neurosci.*, 24, 15-24.

Wittchen H-U (1996) Critical issues in the evaluation of comorbidity in psychiatric disorders. *Br. J. Psychiatry*, 168 (*Suppl. 30*), 9-16.

In: Obsessive-Compulsive Disorder and Comorbidity
Editors: R. Gross-Isseroff and A. Weizman, pp. 5-15
ISBN 1-59454-884-6

Chapter 2

OBSESSIVE-COMPULSIVE DISORDER AND MAJOR DEPRESSION: ASSOCIATED AND DIFFERENT

Richard B. Rosse[1,2], Lynn H. Deutsch[2], Abraham Weizman[3], Judy Eller[1] and Stephen I. Deutsch,[1,2*]

[1]Mental Health Service Line, Department of Veterans Affairs Medical Center, NW, Washington

[2]Department of Psychiatry, Georgetown University School of Medicine, NW, Washington

[3]Department of Psychiatry, Sackler School of Medicine, Tel-Aviv University, Israel

ABSTRACT

Overall, the epidemiologic data show that obsessive-compulsive disorder (OCD) and major depression present as concurrent comorbid conditions with a lifetime frequency that is considerably higher than would be expected based on the lifetime rate of occurrence of either disorder alone in the general population. These data and the fact that major depression, OCD alone, and their concurrent comorbid presentation respond, albeit not completely, to pharmacotherapy with serotonin reuptake inhibitors (SRIs) stimulated speculation that OCD and major depression share some common pathophysiological substrate. Clearly, in terms of a neurotransmitter abnormality, serotonin is likely to figure prominently; however, the major serotonergic projections arising from the raphe nucleus are diffuse and elaborate. In fact, PET data evaluating regional glucose utilization, both before and after treatment with a representative SRI (i.e., paroxetine), suggest important differences in the neurobiological substrates for major depression and OCD. Further, OCD and major depression can influence the metabolic responses of depressive and OCD symptoms, respectively, to this treatment intervention. Moreover, some of the regional differences (e.g., high pretreatment rates of glucose utilization in the right putamen in

* Stephen.Deutsch@med.va.gov

OCD) implicate other neurotransmitters in addition to serotonin (e.g., L-glutamate). Finally, behavioral syndromes associated with cocaine dependence and abuse (e.g., "compulsive foraging") could serve as heuristic "models" for exploring the relatedness and differences between OCD and major depression.

Epidemiologic Considerations: High Rates of Comorbidity

The lifetime rates of comorbidity for OCD among patients with bipolar disorder, unipolar depression and any other Axis I disorder were determined from an analysis of the Epidemiologic Catchment Area (ECA) data base (Chen & Dilsaver, 1995). Diagnoses were derived from data obtained with the Diagnostic Interview Schedule and made according to DSM III criteria. In order to make the comorbid diagnosis of OCD in the context of bipolar disorder, unipolar depression and other Axis I disorders, the "hierarchical" rules of the DSM III were suspended; ordinarily, according to DSM III, a diagnosis of OCD would not be rendered in the context of bipolar disorder or unipolar depression. The study sample included 167 persons with bipolar disorder, 796 persons with unipolar depression, and 5,659 persons with other Axis I disorders; all of whom were age 18 or older. The lifetime rates of comorbid OCD among the persons with bipolar disorder, unipolar depression and other Axis I disorders were 21.0%, 12.2%, and 5.9%, respectively. Interestingly, the likelihood of comorbid OCD among persons with bipolar disorder was two times higher than among persons with unipolar depression. The rates of comorbid OCD among persons with affective disorders must be considered high because the estimate of the lifetime rate of OCD in the general population based on the ECA data was 2.6%. Comorbid OCD was associated with higher lifetime rates of suicidal ideation for persons with bipolar disorder and unipolar depression, and a higher lifetime rate of suicide attempts for persons with bipolar disorder. The authors conjectured that the data support an association between bipolar disorder and OCD. A similar association between unipolar depression and OCD is confounded by the possibility that the onset of OCD can precede the initial episode of major depression; thus, OCD could be primary and depression secondary (Chen & Dilsaver, 1995).

Studies show that a high percentage of patients attending primary care clinics have potentially remediable and often unrecognized psychiatric disorders, especially anxiety and depressive disorders (e.g., Von Korff et al., 1987). In fact, it is not uncommon for patients to have mixed symptoms of anxiety and depression and comorbid disorders. In the study by Von Korff et al. (1987), an average of 1.86 of the following diagnoses was assigned to 86 primary care patients: major depression, dysthymia (lifetime diagnosis), panic disorder, generalized anxiety disorder, and obsessive-compulsive disorder.

Major Depression is a common diagnosis in primary care settings; estimates suggest that about 5% of general medical patients attending ambulatory medical settings meet criteria for major depression (Cooper-Patrick et al., 1994). Further, at least twice as many of these general medical patients have at least one depressive symptom. In an analysis of NIMH Epidemiologic Catchment Area (ECA) data, patients with major depression attending general medical clinics (n=387) and specialty mental health clinics (n=172) were compared to each other (Cooper-Patrick et al., 1994). This comparison confirmed the high prevalence of comorbid major depression and OCD; however, a significantly higher percentage of patients receiving care in the specialty mental health clinics (p<0.001) had the comorbid conditions (23.3%) than those in general medical clinics (10.1%). The data could suggest that ascertainment of this comorbidity is less likely to occur outside of specialized mental health clinics; alternatively, it may be that patients with more complicated presentations and greater functional impairment are more likely to be referred for specialty care. In any event, the comorbid presentation of major depression and OCD is not uncommon (Cooper-Patrick et al., 1994).

Because of diagnostic instability and misclassification, the true prevalence of OCD in community and primary care studies may be significantly lower than the estimates of 1% to 3% (Fireman et al., 2001). Importantly, even if the true prevalence that is adjusted for diagnostic instability and misclassification is in the range of 0.3% to 1.0%, a population-based study of the 1-year prevalence of clinically recognized OCD in 1,728,480 persons aged 6 years and older enrolled in a large health maintenance organization (HMO), which serves about 30% of the general population of the San Francisco Bay area and Sacremento, California, showed it to be only 0.084% (Fireman et al., 2001). Even if the lowered estimates of prevalence of OCD in community settings are accepted (i.e., 0.3% to 1.0%), the data from this large HMO study suggest that only a minority of actual OCD cases (8% to 28%) is clinically recognized and receiving effective treatment. Interestingly, below the age of 18 years, OCD was more prevalent among males (male/female ratio was 1.90), whereas in adults, OCD was more common among females (male/female ratio was 0.68). Rates of psychiatric comorbidity, including multiple conditions, were high among the patients diagnosed with OCD: 37% of the adult patients having one and 38% having two or more disorders (Fireman et al., 2001). For the adults, major depression was the most common comorbid condition (56%), whereas for children and adolescents, attention deficit disorder (ADD; 34%) and major depression (33%) were about equally as common. However, among the children and adolescents, comorbid ADD occurred about twice as commonly in males than females (40% vs 19%, respectively). As suggested by the authors (Fireman et al., 2001), comorbid psychiatric diagnoses may be more commonly recognized in clinical settings because they may contribute to greater suffering and impairment and increased likelihood that patients will seek care. Nonetheless, the frequent comorbidity of OCD and major depression suggests that they may be linked through some shared pathophysiological mechanism.

The prevalence of comorbid DSM-III-R anxiety disorders and major depression was assessed cross-sectionally in a well-characterized sample of adult outpatients with major depression (n=255) (Fava et al., 2000). The patients participated in clinical trials and were enrolled in a Depression Research Program. Because comorbidity may have stimulated these patients to seek treatment in a specialty clinic, the investigators recognized that their prevalence estimates were likely to be higher than those assessed in samples of community-dwelling residents; a phenomenon referred to as Berkson's bias. The investigators also sought to examine possible temporal relations between the first presentations of the comorbid conditions and major depression. Lifetime prevalences of DSM-III-R axis I disorders were assessed in the 255 patients (male=77, female=178; mean age=37.5$\pm$10.5 years) with the Structured Clinical Interview for DSM-III-R-Patient Edition (SCID-P). This instrument includes a "chronology module," facilitating the assessment and recording of the onset of disorders and when symptoms were most recently manifest. The prevalence of comorbidity was very high; 50.6% of the patients had at least one current or lifetime anxiety disorder. The percentage of patients with current or lifetime OCD in this sample was 6.3%; 4.7% or 12 patients met criteria for a current diagnosis of OCD (Fava et al., 2000). The temporal occurrence of OCD in this sample was more likely to follow the initial onset of an episode of major depression. In general, patients with any comorbid anxiety disorder were younger when they first presented with their index episode of major depression, compared to patients with major depression alone. Thus, the presence of a comorbid anxiety disorder may result in an earlier age of expression of the depression phenotype; perhaps, this reflects an epistatic interaction between genes contributing to liability for depression and those contributing to liability for anxiety disorders.

In another cross-sectional survey of an OCD specialty clinic sample, 57% of patients fulfilling DSM-III-R diagnostic criteria for OCD had at least one other axis I disorder (Rasmussen & Eisen, 2002). Moreover, in view of the chronic nature of OCD, if one considers lifetime histories of OCD patients, the percentage of them with a comorbid axis I disorder is even higher. Major depressive disorder is the most common comorbidity in adult patients; in a series of 100 patients with primary obsessive-compulsive disorder, the percentages of patients with a current and lifetime diagnosis of major depression were 31% and 67%, respectively (Data from Jenike et al. as cited by Rasmussen & Eisen, 2002). However, the simultaneous onset of OCD and depression occurred in only a minority of patients, the frequency was 8% in a clinic sample of 250 patients diagnosed with OCD according to DSM III (Rasmussen & Eisen, 2002). The majority of patients in this latter sample reported that depression developed after the onset of their OCD symptoms; thus, in these patients depression may be “secondary” to the primary OCD. In any event, the high frequency of comorbid OCD and major depression has stimulated interest into possible mechanisms underlying this comorbid presentation, and the implications of the comorbidity for treatment and outcomes.

Treatment Considerations: More Similar than Different

Serotonin reuptake inhibitors (SRIs) are uniquely indicated for the treatment of patients presenting with both current major depression and current OCD (Hoehn-Saric et al., 2000). Interest in SRIs stemmed from the demonstration of their efficacy in OCD (e.g., Chouinard et al., 1990; Greist et al., 1995), in addition to their demonstration of efficacy for major depression (e.g., Fabre et al., 1995; Lydiard et al., 1997). In a pivotal study, the effectiveness of sertraline, an SRI, was compared to that of desipramine, a non-SRI with predominantly noradrenergic effects, against symptoms of OCD and major depression in patients meeting DSM-III-R criteria for both current disorders (Hoehn-Saric et al., 2000). In this 12-week, double-blind study, 166 patients meeting DSM-III-R criteria for comorbid OCD and major depression were recruited across 16 university sites and randomized to treatment with either sertraline (up to 200 mg/day) or desipramine (up to 300 mg/day). Patients needed to manifest symptoms of both OCD and major depression, meeting threshold severity criteria on the Yale-Brown Obsessive-Compulsive Scale (Y-BOCS) and Hamilton Rating Scale for Depression (HAM-D), and scoring at least 4 (i.e., moderate) on the Clinical Global Impression (CGI) scale for both OCD and major depression. After a one-week, single-blind, placebo washout period, sertraline and desipramine were initiated according to a “flexible” titration schedule. Efficacy or clinical response was defined a priori as a 50% reduction from baseline in the 24-item HAM-D score, and a 40% decrease in the Y-BOCS total score. Further, remission of major depression was defined as a score of 7 or less on the 17-item HAM-D. Data were analyzed conservatively using week 12 end-point data for completers or the "last observation carried forward" in an "intention-to-treat" strategy. 79 patients were assigned to treatment with sertraline (32 male, 47 female), and 85 to treatment with desipramine (34 male, 51 female). Patients in both treatment arms suffered from symptoms of OCD for more than 17 years, whereas the average durations of the current episode of major depression for patients in the sertraline and desipramine groups were 24 months and 29 months, respectively. 84% of the patients (66 out of 79) randomized to sertraline completed treatment, whereas 62% of the patients (53 out of 85) randomized to desipramine did so ($p=0.002$). Patients randomized to sertraline showed a significantly greater adjusted improvement from baseline to week 12 than patients treated with desipramine on the two primary outcome measures of efficacy: the 24-item HAM-D ($p=0.03$) and the Y-BOCS ($p=0.05$). A statistically significantly higher proportion of patients met criteria for clinical response on the Y-BOCS and achieved clinical remission on the 17-item HAM-D (score of ≤ 7) treated with sertraline (48% and 49%, respectively), compared to desipramine (31% and 35%, respectively). The results demonstrated the superiority of sertraline, an SRI, over desipramine, a predominantly norepinephrine reuptake inhibitor, for treating the concurrent presentation of OCD and major depression (Hoehn-Saric et al., 2000). Prior studies of the efficacy of SRIs in OCD excluded patients with the relatively common comorbidity of major depression. The interpretation of these results is somewhat limited because of the absence of a placebo arm; however, rates of improvement were higher than those found with placebo in other treatment studies of OCD. The greater effect of sertraline on symptoms of major depression could imply that major depression in the context of OCD is a more serotonergic condition than presentations of major depression alone. Alternatively, in the event that major depression can arise secondary to OCD, the resolution of symptoms of OCD could have positive derivative therapeutic effects on symptoms of major depression (Hoehn-Saric et al., 2000).

Pathophysiologic Considerations: Differences Emerge

The neuroanatomic substrate for OCD, as revealed by PET studies of unmedicated, nondepressed patients, appears to involve increased glucose metabolism or cerebral blood flow in the orbitofrontal cortex, anterior cingulate gyrus, caudate nuclei, and thalamus (see for review Saxena et al., 2002). The beneficial therapeutic effect of SRIs in OCD may be correlated with decreasing functional activity within circuits encompassing these structures (e.g., orbiotfrontal-basal ganglia-thalamo-cortical circuits). The functional circuitry of major depression, which is a very frequent comorbid condition with OCD, seems to involve diminished activity in the dorsolateral prefrontal cortex and basal ganglia and elevated activity of the ventrolateral prefrontal cortex. Similarly, pharmacological treatment, including SRIs, tricyclic antidepressants, the lithium ion, and electroconvulsive therapy, is associated with normalization of activity (see for review Saxena et al., 2002). In view of the frequent comorbidity of OCD and major depression and the response of the concurrent conditions and either condition alone to SRIs, Saxena and colleagues (2002) studied changes in glucose utilization in response to treatment with paroxetine in patients with OCD alone (n=25), major depression (n=25), and the combined disorders (n=16), and control subjects (n=16). Patients were diagnosed according to DSM-IV criteria; the Y-BOCS, Hamilton Depression Rating Scale, the Hamilton Anxiety Scale, the Global Assessment Scale, and the CGI-Improvement scale were used to rate symptom severity and level of function. Threshold criteria on the Y-BOCS and 17-item Hamilton Depression Rating Scale were used to define and identify patients in the OCD alone, major depression and comorbid conditions. After a baseline PET scan, which measured cerebral glucose utilization with ^{18}F-fluorodeoxyglucose, patients were treated with paroxetine for 8 to 12 weeks prior to rescanning. The control subjects were scanned on baseline and 10 to 12 weeks later without treatment. Patients were titrated and treated, if tolerated, with the target dose of paroxetine of 40 mg/day for the first 8 weeks; thereafter, the dose could be raised to a maximum of 60 mg/day for an additional 4 weeks. By definition, treatment response for the OCD group was a decrease of 25% or more on the Y-BOCS and a CGI rating of "much improved" or "very much improved." For the patients with major depression, treatment response was defined as a 50% decrease in the Hamilton Depression Rating Scale and a CGI rating of "much improved" or "very much improved." Images were analyzed with both an MRI-based region-of-interest (ROI) approach normalized to ipsilateral hemispheric glucose metabolism and statistical parametric mapping. In contrast to the ROI approach, statistical parametric mapping can suggest relations between treatment response and smaller regions of the brain, and is also not biased by a priori hypotheses about possible associations.

Statistical analyses revealed that "diagnosis" interacted significantly with therapeutic response to paroxetine to effect pretreatment to posttreatment changes in the metabolic activity of specific regions (Saxena et al., 2002). Thus, although all of the patient groups were treated similarly, paroxetine did not have the same "functional neuroanatomical" effect in each of the diagnostic groups. The regional changes in glucose utilization depended on the underlying pathophysiology and the degree of symptomatic improvement. The patients with OCD alone showed significant pretreatment to posttreatment metabolic decreases in the right caudate, right putamen, right ventrolateral prefrontal cortex (VLPFC), bilateral orbitofrontal cortex (OFC), and bilateral thalamus. Moreover, patients with OCD alone responding to paroxetine showed right-sided decreases in the caudate, putamen and thalamus. In general, these data supported involvement of orbitofrontal-basal ganglia-thalamo-cortical circuits in the symptoms of OCD, especially in the right hemisphere. Patients with major depression and the concurrent comorbid conditions showed significant pretreatment to posttreatment metabolic decreases in the left VLPFC and left inferior frontal gyrus. These data are consistent with other studies suggesting an association between heightened metabolic activity in the left VLPFC and left inferior frontal gyrus and symptoms of anxiety and depression. Patietns with OCD alone and those with the comorbid conditions, whose OCD symptoms responded to paroxetine, were clearly dissociated with regard to pretreatment to posttreatment changes in the right caudate. Whereas OCD responders showed decreases in the right caudate, the therapeutic response of OCD symptoms to paroxetine in the patients with the comorbid conditions showed increases in glucose utilization in the right caudate. The data suggest that the pathophysiology of major depression influences the altered subcortical metabolism associated with the clinical presentation of OCD.

Although SRIs are indicated for major depression and OCD, the proportions of patients with these diagnoses responding adequately to them is still disappointing (Saxena et al.,

2003). Only about two-thirds of patients with major depression and half of patients with OCD respond adequately. Thus, interest exists in possible biological markers of treatment response, which would guide the rational selection of an appropriate treatment intervention and, perhaps, further elucidate distinctive differences in the pathophysiology of major depression and OCD (Saxena et al., 2003). In order to evaluate potential neurobiological substrates predictive of treatment response to SRIs, specifically paroxetine, and to see if these substrates differ for major depression and OCD, the PET pretreatment regional glucose utilization data for 27 patients with OCD alone, 27 patients with unipolar major depression, and 17 with the concurrent comorbid conditions, who were treated for 8 to 12 weeks with paroxetine, were analyzed (Saxena et al., 2003). Possible linear relations between changes in the severity of both symptoms and function in response to paroxetine and pretreatment metabolic activity in specific brain regions were sought with the Y-BOCS, the Hamiltons Depression Rating Scale, and the Global Assessment Scale; the scales were administered immediately before and after treatment.

Using the ROI approach, the therapeutic response of OCD symptoms and the overall functioning of patients with OCD to paroxetine were significantly associated with higher pretreatment levels of glucose metabolism in the right caudate. There was no association between treatment response to paroxetine and pretreatment glucose utilization in the (right) caudate in major depression (Saxena et al., 2003). Also, the ROI approach revealed that paroxetine treatment-associated improvements in depressive symptoms and functioning were significantly associated with lower pretreatment glucose metabolism in the right amygdala. Further, the ROI approach showed that a complex relation existed between lower pretreatment metabolic activity in the thalamus and paroxetine-associated improvement of depressive symptoms; this relation was shown for the 44 patients with OCD but was not seen with the 27 patients with major depression alone. Thus, the presence of OCD may influence the "depression-specific" metabolic response of the thalamus to paroxetine. Other than higher pretreatment activity in the right caudate, there was no association between the treatment response of OCD symptoms to paroxetine and any brain region.

Statistical parametric mapping revealed potentially interesting associations between the treatment response of depressive symptoms to paroxetine and lower pretreatment glucose metabolism in the left amygdala and left dorsal thalamus, and higher pretreatment glucose metabolism in the midline prefrontal cortex. Interestingly, using statistical parametric mapping, in the 27 patients with major depression alone, there were no significant correlations between treatment-related changes in the Hamilton Depression Rating Scale scores and regional pretreatment glucose metabolic activity. Thus, OCD may influence the metabolic response of depressive symptoms to paroxetine, while major depression itself may not be associated with clear biological markers of treatment response to an SRI.

Crack Cocaine and Drug-induced Models of Depression and OCD

Some have proposed the period of cocaine abstinence after chronic cocaine use as a model of depressive disorder (e.g., Baumann & Rothman, 1998). Depression, sadness and negativity are ubiquitous components of the early stage of cocaine abstinence (e.g.,Weddington et al., 1990; Gawin & Kleber, 1986). The period of acute crack cocaine intoxication (i.e., continual smoking off of a "crack pipe") can last from a few hours to a few days, depending on the availability of a crack cocaine supply or resources to obtain more. The initial phase of cocaine abstinence after a period of hours to days of cocaine intoxication is called by many the "Crash" or "Early Phase" of cocaine abstinence and is classically associated with the symptoms of high craving for cocaine, loss of appetite, agitation, and sadness (that can develop into serious depression). Technically, using the current DSM-IV nosology, this condition would be a Substance-Induced Depressive Disorder. Some biologic marker findings suggest similarities between cocaine withdrawal and depression (e.g., Kowatch et al., 1992) and "...a survey of the literature reveals similarities in the profile of 5-HT [5-hydroxytryptamine] dysfunction between rats withdrawn from cocaine and humans diagnosed with depression (Baumann & Rothman, 1998)."

Additionally, strong associations between OCD and cocaine use have also been noted, based on evidence from studies including:

1) Epidemiology—Crum and Anthony (1993) reported on their Epidemiologic Catchment Area (ECA) study using standard epidemiologic strategies, including conditional multiple logistic regression to estimate the risk of OCD for active cocaine users versus non-users, and unconditional multiple logistic regression to estimate OCD risk for 414 active cocaine users versus 12,892 participants not using cocaine. Both of these epidemiologic strategies yielded consistent results: subjects actively using cocaine were found to be at increased risk for OCD.
2) Phenomenology--Rosse and his associates (1993, 1994a,b) described a post cocaine-use syndrome ("Compulsive Foraging") that may serve as a drug-induced model of idiopathic OCD. Compulsive foraging is associated with and related to:
   a. intense cocaine craving and the irresistible obsessional belief that the addict or others might have accidentally misplaced some useable quantity of crack cocaine and,
   b. the compulsive behavior of searching for these pieces of "misplaced" crack.
   c. OCD-like phenomena have also been associated with other chronic stimulant abuse, such as chronic amphetamine use, where it is called being "hung up"-- the amphetamine addict will repeat an action over and over, such as taking a clock apart and then trying to put it back together again, or cleaning an oven repeatedly.
3) Treatment reports-- Interestingly, the compulsive foraging behavior has been successfully treated with a psychotropic agent of low toxicity (i.e., trazodone) useful in the treatment of OCD (Khouzam, 1995).
4) Biologic Marker studies:
   a. OCD patients have been described as having a greater frequency of reflexive glances (i.e., increased saccadic distractibility) during an antisaccade task than normals (Rosse et al., 1994b).
   b. To further explore a possible relationship between cocaine dependence and OCD, Rosse and associates (1994b) compared the antisaccade task performance of cocaine dependent individuals to a group without neuropsychiatric disorder or substance abuse histories. It was only when the cocaine using group was divided into those endorsing and those not endorsing cocaine-induced compulsive

foraging that statistically significant differences emerged, suggesting some similarity between idiopathic OCD and cocaine-induced compulsive foraging. The cocaine-induced compulsive foraging group had the poorest antisaccade performance.

Depression and OCD and Central 5-HT and Neuropeptide Y (NPY)

Potential links between cocaine use, depression and OCD, may include not only the central 5-HT system (Baumann & Rothman, 1998), but could also include the Neuropeptide Y (NPY) system. This neuropeptide has been implicated in depression (e.g., Widerlov et al., 1998), and cocaine use, which "drives" down NPY levels (Wahlestedt et al., 1991). Further, low central NPY levels are associated with high anxiety, as seen in compulsive foraging, and low appetite, as seen during early cocaine abstinence in spite of low food intake in the prior intoxication period.

Wahlestedt and associates (1991) postulated that the "...[NPY] decrease may relate to the anxiety and depression [syndromes] associated with cocaine withdrawal in humans." Additionally, NPY has been found to promote food foraging and resource checking behaviors across the animal kingdom (e.g., influencing overall posture and behavioral response as the animal struggles to answer questions such as "is this stimulus related to prey or predator?") (Carr et al., 2002). In fact, Sokolowski (2003) argues, "...the molecular and neural components of behaviors [related to NPY] studied in simpler organisms can reveal the building blocks used to assemble more elaborate behavior patterns [even of relevance to humans]." Rosse and his associates (1994a) speculated that the syndrome of compulsive foraging might be related to ancestral brain mechanisms that helped assure that an environment once rich in resources (e.g. food) was fully exploited and foraged before moving into a novel, unknown and potentially dangerous environment in search of resources, as such a move might have been associated with great risk in our evolutionary past. Whether cocaine-induced "drops" of brain NPY levels are etiologically related to the onset of cocaine-induced compulsive foraging, and the agitation, anxiety, depression or low appetite of the early "Crash" will have to await further studies. Moreover, low neuropeptididergic Y (NPY)-mediated neural transmission that is associated with anxiety states and behavioral inhibition, as seen in OCD-anxiety states and depression, could also be associated with NPY receptor alterations, rather than discernable changes in CSF NPY levels.

Conclusions

In any event, although both disorders (i.e., depression and OCD), separately and when combined respond to SRIs, their neurobiological substrates appear to differ from each other. Further, the presence of OCD and major depression may influence in a regionally selective way the pretreatment metabolism and metabolic response of specific depressive and OCD symptoms, respectively, to paroxetine (Saxena et al., 2003). Finally, an examination of the neurotransmitter and neuropeptidergic abnormalities associated with cocaine-related syndromes (e.g., the "Crash" and "compulsive foraging") may clarify the basis of the high lifetime frequency of this concurrent comorbidity.

References

Baumann MH, Rothman RB (1998) Alterations in serotonergic responsiveness during cocaine withdrawal in rats: similarities to major depression in humans. *Biol Psychiatry*, *44*, 578-591.

Carr JA, Brown CL, Mansouri R, Venkatesan S (2002) Review: Neuropeptides and amphibian prey-catching behavior. *Comparative Biochemistry and Physiology Part B*, *132*, 151–162.

Chen Y-W, Dilsaver SC. (1995) Comorbidity for obsessive-compulsive disorder in bipolar and unipolar disorders. *Psychiatry Research*, *59*, 57-64.

Chouinard G, Goodman W, Greist JH, Jenike M, Rasmussen S, White K, Hackett E, Gaffney M, Bick PA. (1990) Results of a double-blind placebo controlled trial of a new serotonin uptake inhibitor, sertraline, in the treatment of obsessive-compulsive disorder. *Psychopharmacol Bull.*, *26*, 279-284.

Cooper-Patrick L, Crum RM, Ford DE. (1994) Characteristics of patients with major depression who received care in general medical and specialty mental health settings. *Medical Care*, *32*, 15-24.

Crum RM, Anthony JC. (1993) Cocaine use and other suspected risk factors for obsessive-compulsive disorder: a prospective study with data from the Epidemiologic Catchment Area surveys. *Drug Alcohol Depend.*, *31*, 281-295.

Fabre LF, Abuzzahab FS, Amin M, Claghorn JL, Mendels J, Petrie WM, Dube S, Small JG. (1995) Sertraline safety and efficacy in major depression: a double-blind fixed-dose comparison with placebo. *Biol Psychiatry*, *38*, 592-602.

Fava M, Rankin MA, Wright EC, Alpert JE, Nierenberg AA, Pava J, Rosenbaum JF. (2000) Anxiety disorders in major depression. *Comprehensive Psychiatry*, *41*, 97-102.

Fireman B, Koran LM, Leventhal JL, Jacobson A. (2001) The prevalence of clinically recognized obsessive-compulsive disorder in a large health maintenance organization. *Am J Psychiatry*, *158*, 1904-1910.

Gawin FH, Kleber HD.(1986) Abstinence symptomatology and psychiatric diagnosis in cocaine abusers. Clinical observations. *Arch Gen Psychiatry*, *43*, 107-113.

Greist J, Chouinard G, DuBoff E, Halaris A, Kim SW, Koran L, Liebowitz M, Lydiard RB, Rasmussen S, White K, Sikes C. (1995) Double-blind parallel comparison of three dosages of sertraline and placebo in outpatients with obsessive-compulsive disorder. *Arch Gen Psychiatry*, *52*, 289-295.

Hoehn-Saric R, Ninan P, Black DW, Stahl S, Greist JH, Lydiard B, McElroy S, Zajecka J, Chapman D, Clary C, Harrison W. (2000) Multicenter double-blind comparison of sertraline and desipramine for concurrent obsessive-compulsive and major depressive disorders. *Arch Gen Psychiatry*, *57*, 76-82.

Khouzam HR, Mayo-Smith MF, Bernard DR, Mahdasian JA. (1995) Treatment of crack-cocaine-induced compulsive behavior with trazodone. *J Subst Abuse Treat.*, *12*, 85-88.

Kowatch RA, Schnoll SS, Knisely JS, Green D, Elswick RK. (1992) Electroencephalographic sleep and mood during cocaine withdrawal. *J Addict Dis.*, *11*, 21-45.

Lydiard RB, Stahl SM, Hertzman M, Harrison WM. (1997) A double-blind, placebo-controlled study comparing the effects of sertraline versus amitriptyline in the treatment of major depression. *J Clin Psychiatry*, *58*, 484-491.

Rasmussen SA, Eisen JL. (2002) The course and clinical features of obsessive-compulsive disorder. In:Davis KL, Charney D, Coyle JT, Nemeroff C, eds. *Neuropsychopharmacology: The Fifth Generation of Progress*. Philadelphia: Lippincott Williams & Wilkins, pp. 1593-1608.

Rosse RB, Fay-McCarthy M, Collins JP Jr, Risher-Flowers D, Alim TN, Deutsch SI. (1993) Transient compulsive foraging behavior associated with crack cocaine use. *Am J Psychiatry*, *150*, 155-156.

Rosse RB, Fay-McCarthy M, Collins JP Jr, Alim TN, Deutsch SI. (1994a) The relationship between cocaine-induced paranoia and compulsive foraging: a preliminary report. *Addiction*, *89*, 1097-1104.

Rosse RB, McCarthy MF, Alim TN, Deutsch SI. (1994b) Saccadic distractibility in cocaine dependent patients: a preliminary laboratory exploration of the cocaine-OCD hypothesis. *Drug Alcohol Depend.*, *35*, 25-30.

Saxena S, Brody AL, Ho ML, Alborzian S, Maidment KM, Zohrabi N, Ho MK, Huang S-C, Wu H-M, Baxter LR, Jr. (2002) Differential cerebral metabolic changes with paroxetine treatment of obsessive-compulsive disorder vs major depression. *Arch Gen Psychiatry*, *59*, 250-261.

Saxena A, Brody AL, Ho ML, Zohrabi N, Maidment KM, Baxter LR, Jr. (2003) Differential brain metabolic predictors of response to paroxetine in obsessive-compulsive disorder versus major depression. *Am J Psychiatry*, *160*, 522-532.

Sokolowski MB. NPY and the regulation of behavioral development. (2003) *Neuron*,*39*, 6-8.

Von Korff M, Shapiro S, Burke JD, Teitlebaum M, Skinner EA, German P, Turner RW, Klein L, Burns B. (1987) Anxiety and depression in a primary care clinic. Comparison of diagnostic interview schedule, general health questionnaire, and practitioner assessments. *Arch Gen Psychiatry*, *44,* 152-156.

Wahlestedt C, Karoum F, Jaskiw G, Wyatt RJ, Larhammar D, Ekman R, Reis DJ. (1991) Cocaine-induced reduction of brain neuropeptide Y synthesis dependent on medial prefrontal cortex. *Proc Natl Acad Sci USA*, 88, 2078-2082.

Weddington WW, Brown BS, Haertzen CA, Cone EJ, Dax EM, Herning RI, Michaelson BS. (1990) Changes in mood, craving, and sleep during short-term abstinence reported by male cocaine addicts. A controlled, residential study. *Arch Gen Psychiatry.*, *47*, 861-868.

Widerlov E, Lindstrom LH, Wahlestedt C, Ekman R. (1988) Neuropeptide Y and peptide YY as possible cerebrospinal fluid markers for major depression and schizophrenia, respectively. *J Psychiatr Res.*, *22*, 69-79.

In: Obsessive-Compulsive Disorder and Comorbidity
Editors: R. Gross-Isseroff and A. Weizman, pp. 17-33
ISBN 1-59454-884-6

Chapter 3

OBSESSIVE-COMPULSIVE DISORDER: COMORBIDITY WITH OBSESSIVE-COMPULSIVE SPECTRUM DISORDERS

Christine Lochner* and Dan J. Stein
MRC Unit on Anxiety Disorders, Department of Psychiatry, University of Stellenbosch, Cape Town, South Africa

ABSTRACT

While the majority of patients with obsessive-compulsive disorder (OCD) suffer from at least one comorbid obsessive-compulsive spectrum disorder (OCSD) in their lifetime, there has been relatively little systematic investigation of the structure and implications of such comorbidity. Nevertheless, it has been suggested that comorbidity with certain OCSDs in OCD may serve to define important OCD subtypes, characterized by differing phenomenology and neurobiological mechanisms. In this chapter, existing literature on the comorbidity of OCD with different putative OCSDs is reviewed. We provide evidence that comorbid OCD spectrums disorders in OCD fall into three different clusters (reward dependence, impulsivity, somatic), which are defined by different clinical features.

INTRODUCTION

The obsessive-compulsive spectrum of disorders refers to a range of conditions where phenomenology and psychobiology overlap with obsessive-compulsive disorder (OCD). There is growing evidence that these are highly prevalent and disabling disorders, but that many respond to interventions that are effective for OCD (Hollander, 1993;Stein, 2000;Stein

* Correspondence: Christine Lochner, PhD. PO Box 19063, Tygerberg, 7505, South Africa. Tel: +27 21 938 9179; Fax: +27 21 933 5790 ; Email: cl2@sun.ac.za

and Hollander, 1993). While most of the literature focuses on the dimensional relationships across OCD and different obsessive-compulsive spectrum disorders (OCSDs), the current chapter will focus on the comorbidity of OCSDs in OCD. We will argue that a consideration of such comorbidity may well contribute to delineating the heterogeneity of OCD. Although OCD can be considered a rather homogeneous disorder in a number of respects, further understanding of its pathogenesis and treatment may well require a better understanding of its different subtypes (Lochner and Stein, 2003).

How to Delineate the OCD Spectrum of Disorders?

An immediate question is how to define the boundaries of the obsessive-compulsive spectrum of disorders. Debate about criteria for inclusion into the obsessive-compulsive spectrum continues, with some authors arguing for a more conservative approach that includes OCD and apparently genetically related conditions such as Tourette's disorder (TD), whereas others have argued for a broader spectrum that may also include somatic disorders (e.g. body dysmorphic disorder and hypochondriasis), eating disorders (anorexia and bulimia nervosa), impulse control disorders (such as pathological gambling and compulsive shopping), stereotypical movement disorders (with or without self-injury), and some personality disorders (including borderline and obsessive-compulsive personality disorder).

Different theoretical and methodological approaches to understanding and investigating the etiology of OCD have led to different approaches to the obsessive-compulsive spectrum. For example, Freud and subsequent psychoanalysts hypothesized that unconscious conflict led to obsessional defenses. In this formulation there was a spectrum from the obsessive-compulsive character, through obsessive-compulsive neurosis, and on to psychosis (Stein and Hollander, 1993). In addition, in a series of studies psychopharmacologists have highlighted the use of "pharmacological dissection", emphasizing that OCD and a number of other apparently related disorders such as body dysmorphic disorder and trichotillomania, respond more robustly to serotonin reuptake inhibitors (SRIs) than to noradrenergic reuptake inhibitors (NRI's) (Stein, 2000). Neuroanatomical research, facilitated by the introduction of advances in structural and functional imaging, has indicated that OCD is mediated by cortico-striatal-thalamic circuitry, and has therefore encouraged a view of the disorder as a 'developmental basal ganglia syndrome' (DBGS) (Palumbo et al., 1997). Indeed, family studies have provided good evidence for a genetically defined spectrum between OCD, TD, and motor tic disorders (Grados et al., 2001;Pauls et al., 1986, 1995). Alternatively, a neuroimmunological perspective has focused on OCD, tics, and other symptoms as symptoms of pediatric autoimmune neuropsychiatric disorders associated with Streptococcus (PANDAS) (Leonard and Swedo, 2001).

Another approach to the OCD spectrum has been to focus less on similarities between different conditions, and more on contrasts across these disorders. Arguably, compulsive and impulsive disorders fall on opposite ends of a dimension of risk/harm avoidance. Typically, people who score high on the "*harm avoidance*" dimension of Cloninger's Temperament and Character Inventory (Cloninger et al., 1994) are hypervigilant and attempt to avoid harm and anxiety or discomfort; conversely, high scorers on "*risk / novelty seeking*" typically want to increase gratification or pleasure and may be prone to impulsiveness. According to this perspective, OCD falls on the compulsive, *harm avoidance* end of the spectrum, with the impulsive disorders (e.g. kleptomania, pathological gambling, pyromania) falling onto the opposite, *risk taking / novelty seeking* impulsive end of the spectrum. Disorders such as TD and trichotillomania may demonstrate both compulsive and impulsive characteristics, and fall somewhere in-between the two poles (Hollander, 1998;Stein and Hollander, 1993).

In the simplest view of OCSDs as either similar to OCD, or as different from OCD, these categories lie on a unidimensional spectrum. Nevertheless, the psychobiology of OCD and related disorders may be too complex to be understood in terms of a single pharmacological mechanism or underlying gene; for example, some subtypes of OCD and some OCSDs may be mediated by dopaminergic systems, while other subtypes of OCD and related OCD spectrum disorders may be mediated by serotonergic neurocircuitry (Lochner and Stein, 2003). Similarly, it may be argued that compulsivity and impulsivity are not simply dimensionally opposed, but rather are *orthogonal* dimensions, i.e. some patients may be *high* on both impulsivity and compulsivity, while others are *low* on both of these constructs. Indeed, in view of the range of different approaches to the OCD related disorders, it can be suggested that it is increasingly appropriate to replace the concept of a spectrum of disorders with one of a *vector space* of obsessive-compulsive disorders. In this chapter we provide some preliminary data to provide a starting point for drawing out this space.

Comorbidity of OCD Spectrum Disorders in OCD

Understanding the vector space of OCD-related disorders may contribute to understanding the heterogeneity of OCD. A number of studies have demonstrated that at least half of OCD subjects met criteria for at least one current putative OCSD, and that more than two-thirds had a lifetime history of at least one comorbid OCSD (du Toit et al., 2001;Richter et al., 2003). Comorbidity of certain OCD-related disorders in OCD seems to point to the involvement of specific pathophysiological mechanisms and may help predict treatment outcomes. Comorbid TD, for example, may point to particular involvement of the dopamine system, and may suggest that augmentation of SRIs with first generation dopamine blockers will be useful.

There has, however, been relatively little systematic investigation of comorbid OCD spectrum disorders in OCD. Tics and certain personality disorders like obsessive-compulsive personality disorder (OCPD) have long been noted to be more prevalent than expected in OCD. (The implications of comorbid tics in OCD are discussed in more detail below.) There has been controversy about whether OCPD predisposes to OCD (as proposed by psychoanalytic theory) or whether OCPD is a consequence of OCD (as OCPD symptoms improve during OCD pharmacotherapy). More recently, as previously mentioned, Du Toit *et al.* (Du Toit et al., 2001) have demonstrated that at least half of OCD subjects met criteria for at least one current putative OCSD, and Richter *et al.* (Richter et al., 2003) suggested that more than two-thirds had a lifetime history of at least one comorbid OCSD. In the Du Toit-sample of OCD patients, the OCSDs with the highest prevalence rates were compulsive self-injury (22.4%), compulsive buying (10.6%), and intermittent explosive disorder (10.6%). In their comparison study, Richter *et al.* (Richter et al., 2003) also found that an OCD group differed significantly from other anxiety disorder groups (social anxiety and panic disorder) in showing a greater number of lifetime OCSDs affecting each individual, and a greater proportion of individuals having a lifetime history of multiple OCD spectrum conditions.

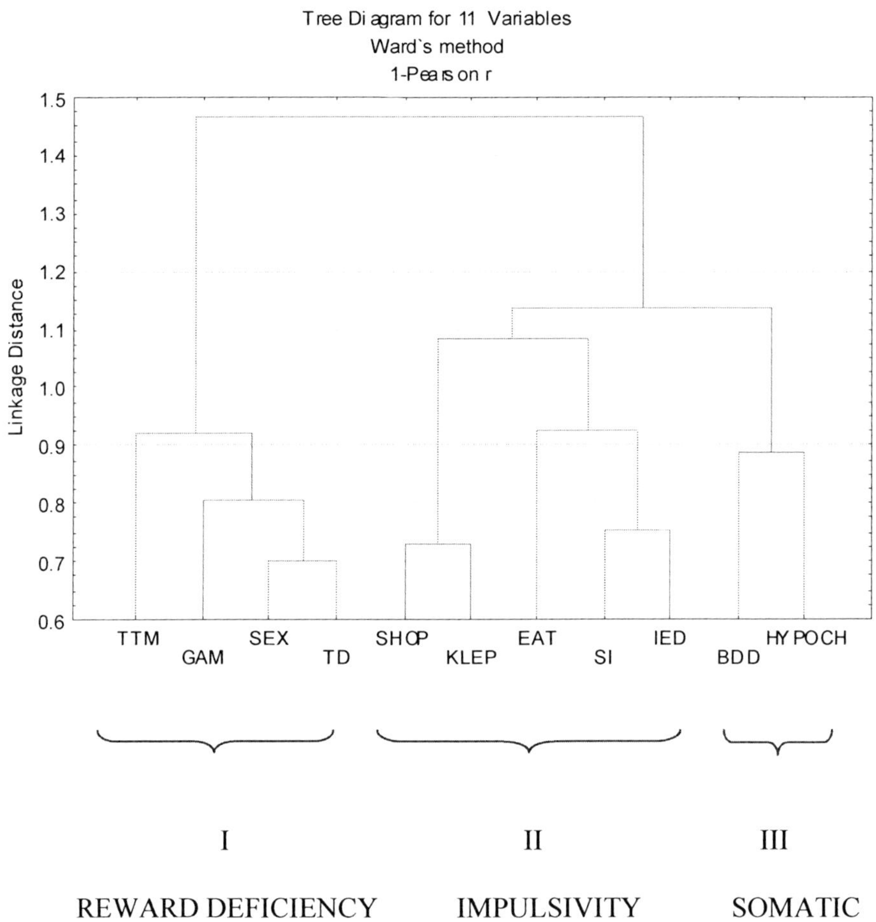

TTM = trichotillomania GAM = pathological gambling SEX = hypersexual disorder TD = Tourette's disorder SHOP = compulsive shopping KLEP = kleptomania EAT = eating disorders SI = self-injury IED = intermittent explosive disorder BDD = body dysmorphic disorder HYPOCH = hypochondriasis

Figure 1. Cluster analysis results: Tree diagram

We recently conducted a cluster analysis of comorbid OCDSs in OCD in an attempt to delineate the hypothesized spectrum of OCD-related disorders (Lochner *et al.*, Comprehensive Psychaitry, vol 46: 14-19, 2005). Cluster analysis of the OCSDs in our sample of 210 OCD patients identified 3 separate clusters at the 1.1 linkage distance level. Based on their most prominent features the three clusters were named: 1.) "Reward deficiency" (including trichotillomania, pathological gambling, hypersexual disorder and TD), 2.) "Impulsivity" (including compulsive shopping, kleptomania, eating disorders, self-injury and intermittent explosive disorder, and 3.) "Somatic" (including body dysmorphic disorder and hypochondriasis). Several significant associations were found between cluster scores and other variables. For example, Cluster I scores were associated with earlier age of onset and the presence of tics, Cluster II scores were associated with female gender and childhood emotional abuse, and Cluster III scores were associated with less insight and with somatic obsessions and compulsions. This structure of OC spectrum disorders is partly consistent with a number of previous theoretical attempts to classify the different OCSDs (Figure 1). We discuss each of these identified clusters in further detail.

THE REWARD DEFICIENCY CLUSTER

Cluster I, subsequently named "Reward deficiency", included trichotillomania (TTM), pathological gambling, hypersexual disorder and TD. A number of authors have emphasized the involvement of the dopaminergic system in OCD patients with comorbid tics (McDougle et al., 1994, 2000) and TD (Singer et al., 1991). There is some evidence that pathological gambling, hypersexual disorder and TTM (Bergh et al., 1997;Hollander et al., 2000;Seedat et al., 2000;Stein et al., 2001;Stein and Hollander, 1992) (all clustered together with TD in Cluster I) may also be mediated by a dysfunctional dopamine system. In addition, it may be suggested that the disorders included in this category are characterized by various behaviours or rituals associated with obtaining pleasure / gratification or relief (i.e. motivated by *reward*). Blum and colleagues (Blum et al., 2000) have argued that a number of OCSDs are characterized by such reward deficiency, pleasure seeking behaviour, and dopaminergic deficits. Indeed, the term "reward deficiency syndrome" has been put forward to account for links between several disorders in which altered dopaminergic function has been posited (Blum et al., 2000) – hence our use of this term to describe Cluster I.

Phenomenology

TD is characterized by motor and one or more verbal tics (described as sudden rapid repetitive non-rhythmic movements, gestures or utterances) beginning before the age of 18 years (American Psychiatric Association, 1994), the performance of which is associated with a reduction in tension or relief. Similarly, the symptoms of TTM, hypersexual disorder (e.g. the excessive preoccupation with non-paraphilic sexually arousing fantasies, urges, or excessive sexual behaviours over time) and pathological gambling may also be seen as involving attempts at achieving gratification or reward.

Furthermore, the incidence of tics and tic disorders in OCD is high (37 – 59%) (Leonard et al., 1992;Pitman et al., 1987). Patients with a primary diagnosis of TD also often report OCD and OC symptoms (12 – 90%) (Como, 1995;Leckman et al., 1994;Leckman et al., 2003). Tics also share some phenomenological similarities with the compulsions of OCD (Como, 1995;Leckman et al., 1994). On the other hand, tics may be distinguished from compulsions: In general, compulsions are typically quite complex and performed in response to an obsession or according to some rigidly applied rules. In contrast, although they may also be *complex*, tics are typically *less* complex than compulsions and not aimed at neutralizing the anxiety associated with the obsessions (American Psychiatric Association, 1994).

There is a large body of evidence suggesting OCD patients with tics and OCD patients without tics differ in a number of ways, with differences observed in the phenomenology, symptom profile, age of onset and gender ratio, and pharmacological treatment response

(Holzer et al., 1994;Leckman et al., 1994;McDougle et al., 1993;Petter et al., 1998;Zohar et al., 1997). For example, in a comparison of patients with OCD alone and patients with both OCD and TD, the former group was more likely to have (1) contamination obsessions and compulsions, (2) fear of not saying the right thing, and (3) BDD, while the latter group (OCD with TD) was more likely to have (1) an obsession with the need for symmetry accompanied by magical thinking, (2) fear of doing something embarrassing or of blurting out an obscenity, (3) intrusive violent or sexual images and thoughts, (4) touching compulsions, (4) blinking or staring rituals, (5) self-injurious compulsions, (6) hoarding, and (7) counting (George et al., 1993). Several other studies have found similar findings – e.g. adolescents with OCD and comorbid tics were more prone to aggressive and sexual images and obsessions than were adolescents without tics (Zohar et al., 1997).

Sensory phenomena may be another important phenotypic measure for grouping patients into an OCD-TD/tics subtype. These phenomena include both bodily and mental sensations: Bodily sensations refer to focal or generalized body sensations (usually tactile, muscular-skeletal/visceral, or both) occurring either before, or during, the patient's performance of the repetitive behaviours. Mental sensations on the other hand include urge only, energy release (i.e. mental energy build-up that need to be discharged), incompleteness, and just-right perceptions. Evidence suggests that these bodily and mental sensations are more frequently found in patients with OCD and TD than in patients with OCD alone (Miguel et al., 2000).

OCD patients with and without tics may also differ in terms of other clinical features. An OCD family study found that younger age of onset of OCD symptoms and possibly male gender in probands were associated with increased tic disorders in relatives (Leckman et al., 2003). Similarly, the association of Cluster I scores with earlier onset OCD; and with harm-related and sexual / religious obsessions and compulsions, is consistent with previous data indicating that OCD with tics is characterized by early age of onset and by these symptom subtypes (Do Rosario-Campos et al., 2001;Eichstedt and Arnold, 2001;Geller et al., 1998;George et al., 1993).

Neurobiology

Tic disorders tend to occur in a specific subgroup of OCD families, suggesting that presence of tic disorders is more likely to indicate a more familial OCD phenotype (Pauls et al., 1995). Consistent with this hypothesis, family studies of OCD probands have revealed tics in at least 17% of adult patients and increased rates of tics in their first-degree relatives (Holzer et al., 1994;Pauls et al., 1995). In addition to genetic or familial transmission, OCD with comorbid tics may also both be seen after neuroimmunological insult

The importance of the genetic contribution to tics is supported by data that tics are more useful than obsessions or compulsions in distinguishing relatives of patients with OCD from relatives of control subjects. Furthermore, regional cerebral blood flow patterns in individuals with OC behaviour in TD families are comparable to their relatives with TD, and differ from individuals with primary OCD but with no family history of tic disorders (Moriarty et al., 1997).

Additional data supporting the existence of an OCD-TD/tic subtype focus on treatment response. A retrospective, case-controlled analysis by McDougle *et al.* (McDougle et al., 1993) found that fluvoxamine alone was less effective in OCD patients with tics than in patients without tics. In a continuation of this study, the researchers (McDougle et al., 1994) found that treatment-refractory OCD patients with comorbid tic disorders (including TD) responded to haloperidol (a first generation dopamine blocker) augmentation of fluvoxamine, whereas this strategy was of little benefit for patients without tics. Other studies have, however, suggested that new generation dopamine blockers are effective in the treatment of refractory OCD patients with or without tics (McDougle et al., 2000).

The release of dopamine in the ventral striatum (nucleus accumbens) plays a crucial role in reward processing (Blum et al., 2000). It can be speculated that the gratification / release symptoms that characterize this cluster of reward deficiency disorders are mediated by dopaminergic dysfunction in ventral striatal circuits. The relationship between putative dopaminergic mediation of OCD symptoms, and possible dopaminergic dysfunction in comorbid reward deficiency disorders deserves further investigation.

The Impulsivity Cluster

Cluster II included compulsive shopping, kleptomania, eating disorders (including anorexia and bulimia nervosa), self-injury and intermittent explosive (IED) disorder, and as these conditions appear to be associated with impaired impulse control, Cluster II was subsequently termed "Impulsivity". Observation of such a cluster is consistent with previous work noting that many patients with OCD manifest impulsive behaviour or comorbid impulse control disorders (Hollander and Rosen, 2000;McElroy et al., 1994;Stein and Hollander, 1993, 1993). Indeed, although OCD has been associated with increased harm or risk avoidance, the role of impulsivity in OCD has received substantial theoretical and clinical interest (Oldham et al., 1996).

Our findings indicated that Cluster II was associated with increased novelty seeking, a temperament trait that is characterized by impulsivity and risk taking behaviour (Cloninger et al., 1993). Previous work has on impulsivity in OCD has primarily used aggressive and auto-aggressive (suicidal) behaviours as an index of impulsivity. For example, it has been suggested that at least a subset of OCD patients has difficulties controlling their anger (Hoehn-Saric and Barksdale, 1983;Manchanda et al., 1979;Millar, 1983). Similarly, consistent with the hypothesis of significant impulsivity in OCD, an epidemiological study showed increased incidence of conduct problems in the childhood history of OCD patients (Hollander et al., 1996).

Impulsivity is a characteristic feature of the OCSDs on Cluster II. For example, kleptomania is classified in the Diagnostic and Statistical Manual of Mental Disorders, 4th edition (DSM-IV) as one of the impulse control disorders, and is characterized by repeated failure to resist impulses to steal objects not for personal use or financial gain (American Psychiatric Association, 1994). Compulsive shopping is also characterized by the presence of repetitive impulsive and excessive buying that leads to personal and familial distress, with impulsivity singled out as one of the main clinical features of this condition (Lejoyeux et al., 1996). Furthermore, previous work has found that OCD patients often present with comorbid eating disorders (Nagata et al., 2000) as well as with self-injurious behaviours (Winchel and Stanley, 1991). Conversely, eating disorders, essentially characterized by a severe disturbance in the person's perception of body shape and weight, may also be characterized by comorbid impulsive symptoms or 'multi-impulsivity' (Eddy and Walbroehl, 1998;Fessler, 2002;Nagata et al., 2000). In addition, in an earlier analysis of our data, we found that one of the OCSDs with the highest prevalence rates was self-injury (i.e. impulse control disorder not otherwise specified) (du Toit et al., 2001). The compulsive self-injurious behaviours seen in patients with OCD included pathological skin picking, TTM, and onychophagia (nail biting).

Also included in this cluster is IED, a condition that is characterized by discrete episodes of aggressive impulses that result in serious assaultive acts toward other people and/or destruction of property (American Psychiatric Association, 1994). Rather little research has been done on IED as defined by these DSM-IV criteria, or on the comorbidity between IED and OCD. The association between OCD and IED-type of behaviour is supported by early analyses that revealed that patients with obsessive-compulsive "neurosis" have impulsive "other-directed" symptoms, such as acting-out hostility (Manchanda et al., 1979;Millar, 1983), arguably resembling aspects of IED.

Phenomenology

In summary, OCD patients with any of the OCSDs included in Cluster II may present with significant impulsiveness or impulse control problems. Indeed, increasing data from comorbidity studies supports the existence of an OCD-Impulsivity subtype. For example, an earlier analysis of our dataset (Du Toit et al., 2001) compared OCD patients with and without comorbid OCSDs, and found evidence for significant comorbidity between OCD and impulse control disorders, e.g. 10.6% of patients also presented with comorbid compulsive shopping and IED. The cluster analysis positioned some of these impulse control disorders (including compulsive shopping, kleptomania and IED) in one cluster, supporting the idea that one spectrum of comorbid OCSDs in OCD is characterized by impulsivity.

It has been suggested that obsessive-compulsive and impulsive symptoms are qualitatively similar in that both involve difficulties delaying or inhibiting repetitive behaviours (Hollander and Wong, 1995). Indeed, there are arguably some similarities in the phenomenology between OCD and disorders of impulse control. For example, both OCD and the impulse control disorders are characterized by intrusive, irresistible urges to commit an act that may or may not be seen as senseless. Also, many patients with either of these conditions frequently experience an increasing sense of tension associated with attempts to resist the behaviour, and temporary relief from anxiety following their engagement in the behaviour.

In addition, our cluster analysis findings suggested an association between the conditions included in this "impulsivity" cluster with female gender and with emotional abuse. This is consistent with previous work linking a subset of OCD patients, as well as eating disorders and self-injurious behaviours in women, to early traumatic experiences (Bogetto et al., 1999;de Silva and Marks, 1999;Fallon et al., 2000;Paul et al., 2002).

Neurobiology

In addition to the phenomenological similarities, there are also some similarities in the neurobiology and treatment response between OCD and disorders of impulse control. Thus, the serotonin system may mediate both impulsive-aggressive as well as obsessive-compulsive symptoms, and SRIs may be useful for both OCD and disorders of impulse control. For example, there are now several controlled studies of SRIs in different impulse control disorders, including borderline personality disorder. Similarly, reductions in impulsivity and hostility have been noted after successful treatment of OCD symptoms with SRIs (Lopez-Ibor, Jr., 1990).

Various medications other than SRIs may, however, also be useful in the treatment of both OCD and impulsivity. First, there is some evidence that anticonvulsant agents are effective in a number of disorders characterized by impulsivity, e.g. binge-eating (McElroy et al., 2003;Shapira et al., 2000) and kleptomania (Dannon, 2003). Second, dopamine blockers, as noted earlier, can be effective in treatment-refractory OCD, and these agents can also be effective in decreasing impulsive symptoms (Klein, 1968;Montgomery and Montgomery, 1982;Soloff et al., 1986).

THE SOMATIC CLUSTER

BDD, characterized by a preoccupation with imagined defects in appearance (American Psychiatric Association, 1994), and hypochondriasis, a disorder characterized by repeated concerns about illness, were included in Cluster III, which we termed "Somatic". Ruminations and rituals that concern health or appearance are the hallmark of somatic-related disorders included in this category, and may include a number of OCSDs, e.g. BDD, hypochondriasis and perhaps olfactory reference syndrome (ORS). There are other obsessive-compulsive related symptoms that can also be conceptualized as revolving around the body, the body functions or appearance – for example eating disorders, TTM, and self-injury – however, these conditions were included in other clusters.

Our finding of an association between Cluster III and somatic obsessions and compulsions was not surprising. Indeed, consistent with a somatic subtype of OCD, many OCD patients report somatic or body-focused concerns and rituals (Simeon et al., 1995). In addition, somatic OCD symptoms are often seen in non-psychiatric healthcare settings. For example, brief psychiatric screening of 92 patients attending a dermatology clinic revealed that approximately one fifth scored positive either for OCD or for a clinically relevant spectrum disorder such as BDD (Fineberg and Roberts, 2001).

Somatic concerns in patients with BDD manifest as obsessive preoccupations with an imagined or minimal defect in physical appearance despite an objectively normal appearance (also described as "imagined ugliness") (American Psychiatric Association, 1994). BDD patients suffer from repetitive, persistent ideas or thoughts about these defects, with consequent compulsive - mostly body focused - behaviours, including constant checking in mirrors, applying make-up to cover-up the "flaw", excessive (hair) grooming, and repeated reassurance seeking from others about their "defect" (Phillips, 1991). Body parts often involved in BDD concerns are the head or facial features (including nose, mouth, skin and hair), body size or symmetry and the sexual organs (penis, breasts) (Hollander et al., 1993).

Hypochondriasis is similarly characterized by excessive somatic concerns. In particular, patients with hypochondriasis have a preoccupation or excessive concern with the fear of having, or a belief that they have an illness (in the absence of objective proof), with subsequent reassurance seeking, compulsive checking behaviours and a relentless pursuit of medical care (American Psychiatric Association, 1994). Again, patients with hypochondriacal concerns may present widely to general medical settings seeking medical assistance for their somatic symptoms.

Olfactory reference syndrome (ORS) is another putative OCD related condition characterized by persistent preoccupations about body odour accompanied by shame, embarrassment, significant distress, avoidance behaviour and social isolation (Pryse-Phillips, 1971). Although ORS was not included in the questionnaire on which the current cluster analysis drew, this condition may arguably be positioned together with other disorders with somatic concerns. ORS is not included in the DSM-IV or the International Classification of Diseases 10th Edition (ICD-10) as a separate category. Nevertheless, it has been argued that ORS represents a unique cluster of symptoms that can be delineated as a separate diagnostic entity (Lochner and Stein, 2003).

Phenomenology

Similarities between OCD and BDD have been described in terms of clinical presentation, comorbidity rates, treatment response profiles, and other features. In particular, the two disorders have similar sex ratios, demographic characteristics, and illness severity (McKay et al., 1997;Phillips et al., 1998;Saxena et al., 2001). In addition, the repetitive and intrusive nature of their body-focused concerns, together with rituals such as checking, also suggest significant overlap between OCD and BDD (Phillips, 1991;Saxena et al., 2001). Some authors have suggested that "obsessive-compulsiveness" or obsessive or compulsive personality traits are a hallmark of BDD. BDD appears to be relatively common among patients with OCD, with rates of BDD ranging from 8% to 38% among patients with OCD (Hollander and Phillips, 1993;Phillips, 1991;Phillips et al., 1998;Pigott et al., 1994;Simeon et al., 1995). That BDD is related to OCD may also be supported by the finding of an elevated rate of BDD in family members of OCD patients compared to those of controls (Bienvenu et al., 2000). Moreover, patients with body dysmorphic concerns frequently have poor insight; previous data have also suggested an association between health concerns and poor insight (Abramowitz et al., 1999). Similarly, our data suggested an association between the somatic cluster of conditions and poor insight.

In addition, some of the somatic symptoms presented by patients with OCD or BDD overlap with the somatic and health related concerns characteristic of hypochondriasis. Similar to OCD and BDD, patients with hypochondriasis may also have elaborate "checking" rituals involving their body resulting in at least temporary reduction in their anxiety levels. Consistent with our finding that hypochondriasis is included in the somatic cluster of conditions, it has been suggested that there is much overlap and relatively high prevalence of hypochondriasis in OCD (Bienvenu et al., 2000;Jaisoorya et al., 2003). Relatively few studies have systematically assessed the prevalence of comorbid hypochondriasis in OCD patients; nevertheless, Pigott *et al.* (Pigott et al., 1994) have found a lifetime prevalence rate of 23% for hypochondriasis in a sample of OCD patients. Recent work has also suggested that hypochondriasis occurred more frequently in OCD than in controls (Bienvenu et al., 2000;Jaisoorya et al., 2003).

ORS symptoms meet DSM-IV criteria for obsessions and compulsions insofar as these are repetitive intrusive thoughts (about body odour and the offence that their body/body odour may cause to others), followed by ritualistic attempts to decrease anxiety (e.g. excessive washing, asking for reassurance etc.). Also similar to some OCD and BDD patients, patients with ORS tend to change their clothes with more than the usual frequency, and often restrict their social and domestic excursions to an extent because of their obsessions and fears (Pryse-Phillips, 1971). In addition, in OCD, BDD, hypochondriasis and ORS, the fixity of and the resistance to the pathological thoughts vary to a large extent, and insight into the excessiveness or irrationality thereof may waver over time. The prevalence of comorbid ORS in OCD patients is unknown. Nevertheless, given the significant overlap between the somatic symptoms that are often characteristic of both disorders, it may be suggested that ORS may in some contexts even be considered as a variant of OCD or BDD. ORS symptoms should arguably be considered for inclusion in OCD checklists such as the Yale-Brown Obsessive-Compulsive Symptoms Checklist (Y-BOCS).

Neurobiology

A somatic subtype of OCD is validated by this cluster analysis – and there is evidence that both OCD and somatic OCD spectrum disorders respond to similar medications (Phillips and Najjar, 2003). In particular, in all of these disorders, a preferential response to treatment with anti-obsessional drugs - particularly SRIs and other agents that act by inhibiting the reuptake of serotonin, e.g. clomipramine, has been suggested. Until recently, approaches to treatment-resistant BDD in particular have received little investigation, but available data indicate that switching to another SRI and several SRI-augmentation strategies may be helpful (Phillips, 2002).

In a family study conducted by Bienvenu *et al.* (Bienvenu et al., 2000), it was suggested that BDD may be co-transmitted with OCD, providing further evidence for a significant neurobiological overlap between these disorders.

For now, there is no evidence that OCD patients of the comorbid somatic subtype have a different or unique neurobiological profile or treatment response compared to other OCD subtypes. It has been suggested that OCD patients with poor or less insight (e.g. our sample of OCD patients of the somatic subtype) may have a different treatment response than patients with better insight (Attiullah et al., 2000), but the relationship between the degree of insight and outcome of therapy remains unclear (Kozak and Foa, 1994). Additional research is needed in order to address this issue.

CONCLUSION

In summary, although further work is required, there is evidence that comorbid OCSDs in OCD fall on different dimensions, and that these can help define the heterogeneity of OCD.

Comorbid TD/tics is one of the obsessive-compulsive related conditions that is frequently presented by patients with a primary diagnosis of OCD. Moreover, the OCD-TD/tics subtype of OCD (part of the "reward deficiency" cluster) probably has the most empirical support, with both familial transmission and treatment data suggesting that the presence or absence of comorbid TD/tics may be a particularly meaningful way of subtyping OCD. For example, there appears to be an association between tics, male gender, early age of onset, and disruptive behaviour disorders in younger OCD patients (Geller et al., 2001). In addition, the apparently high rate of tics and TD in OCD patients and their relatives is consistent with the hypothesis that in some cases, OCD and TD may be alternative manifestations of the same underlying illness or biological defect. Both serotonergic and dopaminergic dysregulation may be important in patients with the tic-related subtype of OCD; in particular, patients with OCD and comorbid tics may preferentially respond to a combination of an SRI and a low-dose neuroleptic.

Secondly, there is evidence for an impulsive subtype of OCD. In particular, a cluster of OCD patients may present with impulse control disorders (e.g. comorbid kleptomania, compulsive shopping and IED) as well as eating disorders and self-injurious behaviours - conditions that are often characterized by impulsivity. Consistent with the idea of an OCD-Impulsivity subtype, both OCD and impulsiveness may fall on a spectrum from ego-dystonic to ego-syntonic, and may both be characterized by repetitive behavioural patterns. Indeed, there is a long history of work demonstrating poor impulse control in some patients with OCD (Gardner and Gardner, 1975;Hoehn-Saric and Barksdale, 1983). SRIs may be useful in the treatment of both OCD and disorders characterized by impulsivity (e.g. case reports of patients with good response to SRIs in patients with kleptomania, self-mutilation, or sexual compulsivity), suggesting that similar mechanisms may mediate both compulsive and impulsive symptoms.

Finally, it has been suggested that there may be a somatic subtype of OCD, characterized by excessive concern about health or appearance. Such a hypothesis is consistent with findings that certain somatoform disorders (especially BDD) and pathologic grooming behaviours are transmitted in families of patients with OCD, and can be considered part of the familial OCD spectrum (Bienvenu et al., 2000). Certainly, BDD may be found in some OCD patients (as can other *somatically* focused disorders such as hypochondriasis). However, there still remains a relative paucity of studies focusing on the neurobiology and pharmacotherapy of BDD and hypochondriasis, and of BDD / hypochondriasis in OCD patients.

This chapter has argued for the existence of valid, reliable and consistent OCD subtypes based on comorbidity between OCD and OCSDs. The TD/tics subtype of OCD (part of the reward deficiency cluster) has received particular attention. Nevertheless, data suggest the existence of other subtypes including an impulsivity subtype, and a somatic subtype. Several significant associations consistent with previous data were found between these subtypes and other clinical and demographic variables; for example, the reward deficiency cluster was associated with earlier age of onset and the presence of tics, the impulsivity cluster was associated with female gender and childhood emotional abuse, and the somatic cluster showed an association with less insight and with somatic obsessions and compulsions. Further empirical exploration of these proposed subtypes is needed to adequately characterize the heterogeneity of OCD and to determine the endophenotypes that characterize this complex condition.

REFERENCES

Abramowitz JS, Brigidi BD, Foa EB. (1999) Health concerns in patients with obsessive-compulsive disorder. *J Anxiety Disord*, *13*, 529-539.

American Psychiatric Association. (1994) *Diagnostic and statistical manual of mental disorders*. Washington DC, American Psychiatric Association.

Attiullah N, Eisen JL, Rasmussen SA. (2000) Clinical features of obsessive-compulsive disorder. *Psychiatr Clin North Am*, *23*, 469-491.

Bergh C, Eklund T, Sodersten P, Nordin C. (1997) Altered dopamine function in pathological gambling. *Psychol Med*, *27*, 473-475.

Bienvenu OJ, Samuels JF, Riddle MA, Hoehn-Saric R, Liang KY, Cullen BA, Grados MA, Nestadt G. (2000) The relationship of obsessive-compulsive disorder to possible spectrum disorders: results from a family study. *Biol Psychiatry*, *48*, 287-293.

Blum K, Braverman ER, Holder JM, Lubar JF, Monastra VJ, Miller D, Lubar JO, Chen TJ, Comings DE. (2000) Reward deficiency syndrome: a biogenetic model for the diagnosis and treatment of impulsive, addictive, and compulsive behaviors. *J Psychoactive Drugs*, *32* Suppl., i-112.

Bogetto F, Venturello S, Albert U, Maina G, Ravizza L. (1999) Gender-related clinical differences in obsessive-compulsive disorder. *Eur Psychiatry*, *14*, 434-441.

Cloninger CR, Przybeck TR, Svrakic DM, Wetzel RD. (1994) *The Temperament and Character Inventory: A guide to its development and use*. Missouri, Center for Psychobiology of Personality, Washington University, St. Louis.

Cloninger CR, Svrakic DM, Przybeck TR. (1993) A psychobiological model of temperament and character. *Arch Gen Psychiatry*, *50*, 975-990.

Como PG. (1995) Obsessive-compulsive disorder in Tourette's syndrome. *Adv Neurol*, *65*, 281-291.

Dannon PN. (2003) Topiramate for the treatment of kleptomania: a case series and review of the literature. *Clin Neuropharmacol*, *26*, 1-4.

De Silva P, Marks M. (1999) The role of traumatic experiences in the genesis of obsessive-compulsive disorder. *Behav Res Ther*, *37*, 941-951.

Do Rosario-Campos MC, Leckman JF, Mercadante MT, Shavitt RG, Prado Hd HS, Sada P, Zamignani D, Miguel EC. (2001) Adults with early-onset obsessive-compulsive disorder. *Am J Psychiatry*, *158*, 1899-1903.

du Toit PL, van Kradenburg J, Niehaus D, Stein DJ. (2001) Comparison of obsessive-compulsive disorder patients with and without comorbid putative obsessive-compulsive spectrum disorders using a structured clinical interview. *Compr Psychiatry*, *42*, 291-300.

Eddy MF, Walbroehl GS. (1998) Recognition and treatment of obsessive-compulsive disorder. *Am Fam Physician*, *57*, 1623-1624.

Eichstedt JA, Arnold SL. (2001) Childhood-onset obsessive-compulsive disorder: a tic-related subtype of OCD? *Clin Psychol Rev*, *21*, 137-157.

Fallon BA, Qureshi AI, Laje G, Klein B. (2000) Hypochondriasis and its relationship to obsessive-compulsive disorder. *Psychiatr Clin North Am*, *23*, 605-616.

Fessler DM. (2002) Pseudoparadoxical impulsivity in restrictive anorexia nervosa: a consequence of the logic of scarcity. *Int J Eat Disord*, *31*, 376-388.

Fineberg N, Roberts A. Obsessive-compulsive disorder: A twenty-first century perspective. In: Fineberg N, Marazziti D, Stein DJ, editors. *Obsessive-compulsive disorder: A practical guide*. London: Martin Dunitz Ltd, 2001. p. 1-13.

Gardner AR, Gardner AJ. (1975) Self-mutilation, obsessionality and narcissism. *Br J Psychiatry, 127*, 127-132.

Geller D, Biederman J, Jones J, Park K, Schwartz S, Shapiro S, Coffey B. (1998) Is juvenile obsessive-compulsive disorder a developmental subtype of the disorder? A review of the pediatric literature. *J Am Acad Child Adolesc Psychiatry, 37*, 420-427.

Geller DA, Biederman J, Faraone S, Agranat A, Cradock K, Hagermoser L, Kim G, Frazier J, Coffey BJ. (2001) Developmental aspects of obsessive-compulsive disorder: findings in children, adolescents, and adults. *J Nerv Ment Dis, 189,* 471-477.

George MS, Trimble MR, Ring HA, Sallee FR, Robertson MM. (1993) Obsessions in obsessive-compulsive disorder with and without Gilles de la Tourette's syndrome. *Am J Psychiatry, 150*, 93-97.

Grados MA, Riddle MA, Samuels JF, Liang KY, Hoehn-Saric R, Bienvenu OJ, Walkup JT, Song D, Nestadt G. (2001) The familial phenotype of obsessive-compulsive disorder in relation to tic disorders: the Hopkins OCD family study. *Biol Psychiatry, 50*, 559-565.

Hoehn-Saric R, Barksdale VC. (1983) Impulsiveness in obsessive-compulsive patients. *Br J Psychiatry, 143*, 177-182.

Hollander E. Introduction. In: Hollander E, editor. *Obsessive-compulsive related disorders.* Washington DC: American Psychiatric Press, 1993. p. 1-16.

Hollander E. (1998) Treatment of obsessive-compulsive spectrum disorders with SSRIs. *Br J Psychiatry* Suppl 1998; 7-12.

Hollander E, Buchalter AJ, DeCaria CM. (2000) Pathological gambling. *Psychiatr Clin North Am, 23*, 629-642.

Hollander E, Cohen LJ, Simeon D. (1993) Body dysmorphic disorder. *Psychiatr Ann, 23*, 359-364.

Hollander E, Greenwald S, Neville D, Johnson J, Hornig CD, Weissman MM.(1996) Uncomplicated and comorbid obsessive-compulsive disorder in an epidemiologic sample. *Depress Anxiety, 4*, 111-119.

Hollander E, Phillips K. Body image and experiences disorders. In: American Psychiatric Press, editor. *Obsessive-compulsive related disorders*. Washington DC: 1993. p. 17-48.

Hollander E, Rosen J. (2000) Impulsivity. *J Psychopharmacol, 14*, S39-44.

Hollander E, Wong CM. (1995) Body dysmorphic disorder, pathological gambling, and sexual compulsions. *J Clin Psychiatry, 56* Suppl 4, 7-12.

Holzer JC, Goodman WK, McDougle CJ, Baer L, Boyarsky BK, Leckman JF, Price LH. (1994) Obsessive-compulsive disorder with and without a chronic tic disorder. A comparison of symptoms in 70 patients. *Br J Psychiatry, 164*, 469-473.

Jaisoorya TS, Janardhan Reddy YC, Srinath S. (2003) The relationship of obsessive-compulsive disorder to putative spectrum disorders: results from an Indian study. *Compr Psychiatry, 44*, 317-323.

Klein DF. (1968) Psychiatric diagnosis and a typology of clinical drug effects. *Psychopharmacologia, 13*, 359-386.

Kozak MJ, Foa EB. (1994) Obsessions, overvalued ideas, and delusions in obsessive-compulsive disorder. *Behav Res Ther, 32*, 343-353.

Leckman JF, Grice DE, Barr LC, de Vries AL, Martin C, Cohen DJ, McDougle CJ, Goodman WK, Rasmussen SA. (1994) Tic-related vs. non-tic-related obsessive-compulsive disorder. *Anxiety, 1*, 208-215.

Leckman JF, Pauls DL, Zhang H, Rosario-Campos MC, Katsovich L, Kidd KK, Pakstis AJ, Alsobrook JP, Robertson MM, McMahon WM, Walkup JT, van de Wetering BJ, King RA, Cohen DJ. (2003) Obsessive-compulsive symptom dimensions in affected sibling pairs diagnosed with Gilles de la Tourette syndrome. *Am J Med Genet, 116B*, 60-68.

Lejoyeux M, Ades J, Tassain V, Solomon J. (1996) Phenomenology and psychopathology of uncontrolled buying. *Am J Psychiatry, 153*, 1524-1529.

Leonard HL, Swedo SE. (2001) Paediatric autoimmune neuropsychiatric disorders associated with streptococcal infection (PANDAS). *Int J Neuropsychopharmacol, 4*, 191-198.

Leonard HL, Swedo SE, Rapoport JL, Rickler KC, Topol D, Lee S, Rettew D. (1992) Tourette syndrome and obsessive-compulsive disorder. *Adv Neurol, 58*, 83-93.

Lochner C, Stein DJ. (2003) Heterogeneity of Obsessive-Compulsive Disorder: A Literature Review. *Harv Rev Psychiatry, 11*, 113-132.

Lochner C, Stein DJ. (2003) Olfactory reference syndrome: Diagnostic criteria and differential diagnosis. *J Postgrad Med, 49*, 328-331.

Lopez-Ibor JJ, Jr. (1990) Impulse control in obsessive-compulsive disorder: a biopsychopathological approach. *Prog Neuropsychopharmacol Biol Psychiatry, 14*, 709-718.

Manchanda R, Sethi BB, Gupta SC. (1979) Hostility and guilt in obsessive-compulsive neurosis. *Br J Psychiatry, 135*, 52-54.

McDougle CJ, Epperson CN, Pelton GH, Wasylink S, Price LH. (2000) A double-blind, placebo-controlled study of risperidone addition in serotonin reuptake inhibitor-refractory obsessive-compulsive disorder. *Arch Gen Psychiatry, 57*, 794-801.

McDougle CJ, Goodman WK, Leckman JF, Barr LC, Heninger GR, Price LH. (1993) The efficacy of fluvoxamine in obsessive-compulsive disorder: effects of comorbid chronic tic disorder. *J Clin Psychopharmacol, 13*, 354-358.

McDougle CJ, Goodman WK, Leckman JF, Lee NC, Heninger GR, Price LH. (1994) Haloperidol addition in fluvoxamine-refractory obsessive-compulsive disorder. A double-blind, placebo-controlled study in patients with and without tics. *Arch Gen Psychiatry, 51*, 302-308.

McElroy SL, Arnold LM, Shapira NA, Keck PE, Jr., Rosenthal NR, Karim MR, Kamin M, Hudson JI. (2003) Topiramate in the treatment of binge eating disorder associated with obesity: a randomized, placebo-controlled trial. *Am J Psychiatry, 160*, 255-261.

McElroy SL, Phillips KA, Keck PE, Jr. (1994) Obsessive-compulsive spectrum disorder. *J Clin Psychiatry, 55* Suppl, 33-51.

McKay D, Neziroglu F, Yaryura-Tobias JA. (1997) Comparison of clinical characteristics on obsessive-compulsive disorder. *J Anxiety Disord, 11*, 447-454.

Miguel EC, do Rosario-Campos MC, Prado HS, do VR, Rauch SL, Coffey BJ, Baer L, Savage CR, O'Sullivan RL, Jenike MA, Leckman JF. (2000) Sensory phenomena in obsessive-compulsive disorder and Tourette's disorder. *J Clin Psychiatry, 61*, 150-156.

Millar DG. (1983) Hostile emotion and obsessional neurosis. *Psychol Med, 13*, 813-819.

Montgomery SA, Montgomery D. (1982) Pharmacological prevention of suicidal behaviour. *J Affect Disord, 4*, 291-298.

Moriarty J, Eapen V, Costa DC, Gacinovic S, Trimble M, Ell PJ, Robertson MM. (1997) HMPAO SPET does not distinguish obsessive-compulsive and tic syndromes in families multiply affected with Gilles de la Tourette's syndrome. *Psychol Med*, *27*, 737-740.

Nagata T, Kawarada Y, Kiriike N, Iketani T. (2000) Multi-impulsivity of Japanese patients with eating disorders: primary and secondary impulsivity. *Psychiatry Res*, *94*, 239-250.

Oldham JM, Hollander E, Skodol AE. *Impulsivity and compulsivity*. Washington, DC: American Psychiatric Press, 1996.

Palumbo D, Maughan A, Kurlan R. (1997) Hypothesis III. Tourette syndrome is only one of several causes of a developmental basal ganglia syndrome. *Arch Neurol, 54*, 475-483.

Paul T, Schroeter K, Dahme B, Nutzinger DO. (2002) Self-injurious behavior in women with eating disorders. *Am J Psychiatry*, *159*, 408-411.

Pauls DL, Alsobrook JP, Goodman W, Rasmussen S, Leckman JF. (1995) A family study of obsessive-compulsive disorder. *Am J Psychiatry*, *152*, 76-84.

Pauls DL, Towbin KE, Leckman JF, Zahner GE, Cohen DJ. (1986) Gilles de la Tourette's syndrome and obsessive-compulsive disorder. Evidence supporting a genetic relationship. *Arch Gen Psychiatry*, *43*, 1180-1182.

Petter T, Richter MA, Sandor P. (1998) Clinical features distinguishing patients with Tourette's syndrome and obsessive-compulsive disorder from patients with obsessive-compulsive disorder without tics. *J Clin Psychiatry*, *59*, 456-459.

Phillips KA. Body dysmorphic disorder: the distress of imagined ugliness. (1991) *Am J Psychiatry, 148*, 1138-1149.

Phillips KA. (2002) Pharmacologic treatment of body dysmorphic disorder: review of the evidence and a recommended treatment approach. *CNS Spectrum*, *7*, 453-460.

Phillips KA, Gunderson CG, Mallya G, McElroy SL, Carter W. (1998) A comparison study of body dysmorphic disorder and obsessive-compulsive disorder. *J Clin Psychiatry*, *59*, 568-575.

Phillips KA, Najjar F. (2003) An open-label study of citalopram in body dysmorphic disorder. *J Clin Psychiatry*, *64*, 715-720.

Pigott TA, L'Heureux F, Dubbert B, Bernstein S, Murphy DL. (1994) Obsessive-compulsive disorder: comorbid conditions. *J Clin Psychiatry*, *55* Suppl, 15-27.

Pitman RK, Green RC, Jenike MA, Mesulam MM. (1987) Clinical comparison of Tourette's disorder and obsessive-compulsive disorder. *Am J Psychiatry*, *144*, 1166-1171.

Pryse-Phillips W. (1971) An olfactory reference syndrome. *Acta Psychiatr Scan*, *47*, 484-509.

Richter MA, Summerfeldt LJ, Antony MM, Swinson RP. (2003) Obsessive-compulsive spectrum conditions in obsessive-compulsive disorder and other anxiety disorders. *Depress .Anxiety*, *18*, 118-127.

Saxena S, Winograd A, Dunkin JJ, Maidment K, Rosen R, Vapnik T, Tarlow G, Bystritsky A. (2001) A retrospective review of clinical characteristics and treatment response in body dysmorphic disorder versus obsessive-compulsive disorder. *J Clin Psychiatry*, *62*, 67-72.

Seedat S, Kesler S, Niehaus DJ, Stein DJ. (2000) Pathological gambling behaviour: emergence secondary to treatment of Parkinson's disease with dopaminergic agents. *Depress Anxiety*, *11*, 185-186.

Shapira NA, Goldsmith TD, McElroy SL. (2000) Treatment of binge-eating disorder with topiramate: a clinical case series. *J Clin Psychiatry*, *61,* 368-372.

Simeon D, Hollander E, Stein DJ, Cohen L, Aronowitz B. (1995) Body dysmorphic disorder in the DSM-IV field trial for obsessive-compulsive disorder. *Am J Psychiatry, 152*, 1207-1209.

Singer HS, Hahn IH, Moran TH. (1991) Abnormal dopamine uptake sites in postmortem striatum from patients with Tourette's syndrome. *Ann Neurol*, *30*, 558-562.

Soloff PH, George H, Nathan RS, Schultz PM, Ulrich RF, Perel JM. (1986) Progress in the pharmacotherapy of borderline personality disorders: A double-blind study of amitriptyline, haloperidol, and placebo. *Arch Gen Psychiatry*, *43*, 691-697.

Stein DJ. (2001) Neurobiology of the obsessive-compulsive spectrum disorders. *Biol Psychiatry*, *47*, 296-304.

Stein DJ, Black DW, Shapira NA, Spitzer RL. (2001) Hypersexual disorder and preoccupation with internet pornography. *Am J Psychiatry*, *158*, 1590-1594.

Stein DJ, Hollander E. (1992) Low-dose pimozide augmentation of serotonin reuptake blockers in the treatment of trichotillomania. *J Clin Psychiatry*, *53*, 123-126.

Stein DJ, Hollander E. (1993) Impulsive aggression and obsessive-compulsive disorder. *Psychiatr Annals*, *23*, 389-395.

Stein DJ, Hollander E. The spectrum of obsessive-compulsive related disorders. In: Hollander E, editor. *Obsessive-compulsive related disorders*. Washington DC: American Psychiatric Press, 1993.

Winchel RM, Stanley M. (1991) Self-injurious behavior: a review of the behavior and biology of self-mutilation. *Am J Psychiatry*, *148*, 306-317.

Zohar AH, Pauls DL, Ratzoni G, Apter A, Dycian A, Binder M, King R, Leckman JF, Kron S, Cohen DJ. (1997) Obsessive-compulsive disorder with and without tics in an epidemiological sample of adolescents. *Am J Psychiatry*, *154*, 274-276.

In: Obsessive-Compulsive Disorder and Comorbidity
Editors: R. Gross-Isseroff and A. Weizman, pp. 35-46
ISBN 1-59454-884-6

Chapter 4

SCHIZO-OBSESSIVE DISORDER

Michael Poyurovsky*

Tirat Carmel Mental Health Center, Tirat Carmel, Israel and Rapapport Faculty of Medicine, Technion – Israel Institute of Technology, Haifa, Israel

Abraham Weizman

Laboratory of Biological Psychiatry, Felsenstein Medical Research Center and Geha Mental Health Center, Petah Tiqva and Sackler Faculty of Medicine, Tel Aviv University,. Tel Aviv, Israel

Ronit Weizman

Tel Aviv Mental Health Center, Tel Aviv and and Sackler Faculty of Medicine, Tel Aviv University, Tel Aviv, Israel

INTRODUCTION

Schizophrenia and OCD have notable areas of conformity on the neurobiological and phenomenological levels. Both affect men and women equally and have a chronic course and similar distribution of age at onset (with a trend towards earlier age of onset for OCD). A significant neurodevelopmental component and overlapping brain areas (prefrontal cortex, anterior cingulate, caudate nucleus and thalamus) have been consistently implicated in both disorders (Tibbo & Warneke, 1999; Gross-Isseroff et al, 2003). According to recent reports, an estimated 7.8 to 25% of patients with schizophrenia also have obsessive-compulsive disorder (OCD) (Fenton et al., 1986; Eisen et al., 1997; Porto et al., 1997; Poyurovsky et al., 1999a, 2001; Bermanzohn et al., 2000). Furthermore, the therapeutic efficacy of antipsychotic agents and selective serotonin reuptake inhibitors (SSRIs) in both disorders suggests a pathophysiological convergence. Nevertheless, schizophrenia and OCD are distinct clinical entities, and an accurate diagnosis of both, in their "pure" and overlapping forms, is necessary to adequately plan treatment, determine prognosis, and investigate etiologies. This chapter

* Correspondence: Michael Poyurovsky, M.D. Tirat Carmel Mental Health Center, 9 Eshkol Street, Tirat Carmel 30200, Israel. Tel: +972-4-8559349; Fax: +972-4-8559330; E-mail: tyrmichael@matat.health.gov.il

highlights some aspects of the current research pertinent to the OCD-schizophrenia interface and suggests further steps to identify clinically and etiologically relevant homogeneous subgroups and their boundaries on the putative schizophrenia-OCD axis.

Characterization of Obsessive-Compulsive Phenomena in Schizophrenia

Prevalence

Although obsessive-compulsive (OC) symptoms were initially thought to occur in only 1.1%-3.5% of patients with schizophrenia (Jahrreis, 1926; Stengel, 1945;Rosen, 1956), Fenton and McGlashan (1986), applying operationally defined behavioral criteria, found a significantly higher rate of OC symptoms in schizophrenia than previously reported (12.8%-25%). The majority of later reports on schizophrenia-OCD co-morbidity utilized rigorous DSM-III-R/DSM-IV criteria for both disorders and the direct Structured Clinical Interview for DSM (SCID) (Bland et al., 1987; Karno et al., 1988; Eisen et al., 1997; Porto et al., 1997; Poyurovsky et al., 1999; Tibbo et al., 2000; Bermanzohn et al., 2000; Kruger et al., 2000; Poyurovsky et al., 2001; Craig et al., 2002; Ohta et al., 2003). However, their estimates of the rate of occurrence of OC phenomena in schizophrenia varied substantially (range 3.8% - 59.2%), depending on several factors: the particular definition used: OCD (Bland et al., 1987; Karno et al., 1988; Eisen et al., 1997; Porto et al., 1997; Poyurovsky et al., 1999; Tibbo et al., 2000; Bermanzohn et al., 2000; Kruger et al., 2000; Poyurovsky et al., 2001; Craig et al., 2002; Ohta et al., 2003) vs OC symptoms (Fenton and McGlashan 1986; Berman et al., 1995; Porto et al., 1997; Dominquez et al., 1999); the patient population studied: inpatients (Fenton and McGlashanl, 1986; Poyurovsky et al., 1999; Craig et al., 2002; Fabish et al., 2001; Ohta et al., 2003; Nechmad et al., 2003) vs outpatients (Berman et al., 1995; Eisen et al., 1997; Dominquez et al., 1999; Fabish et al., 2001; Craig et al. 2002) vs community residents (Bermanzohn et al., 2000; Kruger et al., 2000); and the phase of the schizophrenic illness: first admission (Poyurovsky et al, 1999) vs chronic stage (Lysaker et al, 2000; Craig et al., 2000; Poyurovsky et al., 2001). These studies provide evidence that the rate of occurrence of OC symptoms/OCD in schizophrenia is considerably higher than in the general population (2-3%), indicating a possible pathophysiological linkage between the two disorders. This conclusion was supported by the finding of Eisen and Rasmussen (1993) that about 4% of patients with OCD met the full criteria for schizophrenia.

Clinical Characteristics: Differentiation between OC and Psychotic Symptoms in Schizophrenia

According to the DSM-IV, the main features of OCD are recurrent, persistent and intrusive thoughts, images or impulses (obsessions), and repetitive actions (compulsions) or mental rituals aimed at preventing or reducing the anxiety and distress that arise from obsessions. Obsessive thoughts are recognized by the individual to be unreasonable and excessive. The most prevalent obsessions are aggressive, contamination, somatic and sexual obsessions and the most prevalent comulstions are cleaning/washing, counting, ordering and hoarding; this is true for most cases of OCD in schizophrenia as well (Porto et al., 1997; Tibbo et al., 2000; Poyurovsky et al., 2001; Ohta et al., 2003).

A major challenge in the identification of OC phenomena in schizophrenia is the differentiation of obsessions from delusions and/or formal thought disorders that are characteristic of schizophrenia, and of compulsions from schizophrenic mannerisms and stereotypic behavior. Even patients with "pure" OCD may exhibit varying degrees of insight (Lelliott et al., 1988; Eisen & Rasmussen, 1993), with 5-35% showing partial or no insight (Foa & Kozak, 1995; Catapano et al., 2001; Matsunaga et al., 2002). A small subset even expriences delusional transformation of obsessions (Gordon, 1950; Solyom et al., 1985; Insel & Akiskal, 1986). At the same time, the concept of delusion as a complete loss of insight has been challenged by findings that there are dimensions of delusions (Kendler et al., 1983; Spitzer, 1990; Appelbaum et al., 1999).

Fenton and McGlashan (1986) proposed several behavioral categories of OC symptoms in schizophrenia patients: 1 - repeated behaviors that interfere with daily activities; 2 - indecision/stuckness; 3 - repeated behaviors performed before some goal-directed activity; 4 - repeated behaviors aimed at magically avoiding harm; 5 - obsessive/pedantic speech; 6 - verbal rituals, such as repetition of phrases; 7 - compulsive repetition of acts the patient finds repulsive (e.g., searching through trash cans); 8 - complaints of recurrent, persistent ideas experienced as senseless. Nevertheless, in the majority of their patients (19/21 the OC symptoms were independent of the psychotic symptoms. This finding was confirmed in other studies as well Eisen et al., 1997; Tibbo et al., 2000; Poyurovsky et al., 2001).

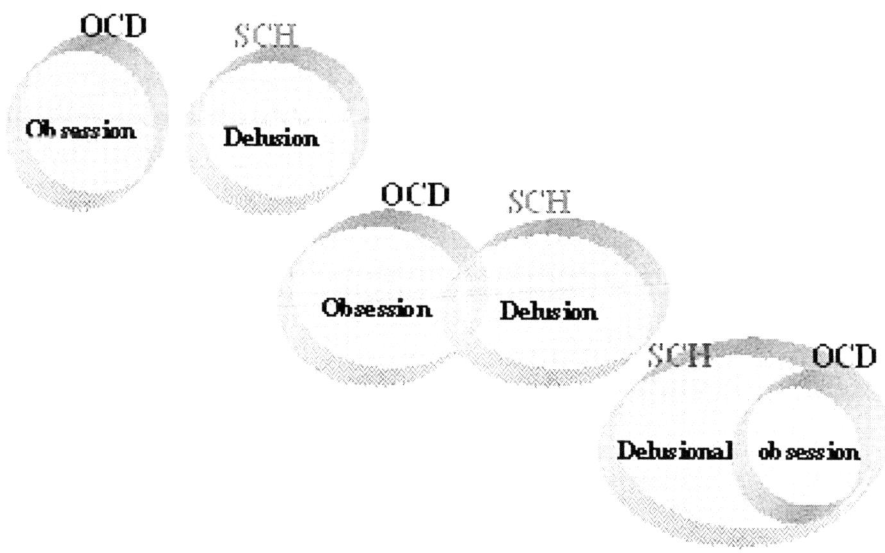

Figure1: Schizophrenia with OCD - Three Sub-Groups

Two major subgroups of schizophrenia patients with OCD were suggetsted: subgroup I – patients with "classic" ego-dystonic obsessions and/or compulsions unrelated to the content of delusions and hallucinations; and subgroup II - patients who in addition to "classic" ego-dystonic OCD symptoms also had OC symptoms that were related to the content of their delusions and hallucinations. Porto et al (1997) described a third subgroup of patients in whom during psychotic exacerbations, OC symptoms were incorporated into the delusional beliefs, but during remission of the schizophrenia, the OC symptoms persisted in a non-delusional form (Figure 1). Patients in all three subgroups met the full DSM-IV criteria for OCD and for schizophrenia. At least at some time during the course of schizophrenia, all had readily detectable OC symptoms with typical content, insight into the nature of their OC symptoms, and marked functional impairment due to the obsessive-compulsive component. This complex OC-delusion/hallucination symptom profile appears to be obsessional in form and psychotic in content, and was termed "obsessive delusions" (Bermanzohn et al. 1997). Obsessive delusions, however, have a similar repetitive, intrusive and distressful nature to typical obsessions (Bermanzohn et al., 1997)

Modulatory Effect of OC Symptoms on Schizophrenia

The effect of OC symptoms on schizophrenic symptomatology remains unclear. Some studies reported a lower seveirty of delusions and formal thought disorders in first-episode schizo-obsessive patients (Poyurovsky et al., 1999), although most found either no difference (Eisen and Rasmussen, 1993; Berman et al., 1998; Hwang et al., 2000; Kruger et al., 2000) or more severe positive symptoms (Kruger et al., 2000; Lysaker et al., 2000). It is possible that OC symptoms exert a "moderating" effect on some positive symptoms during the initial stages of schizophrenia. This may explain the early view of OCD as a positive prognostic indicator in schizophrenia, protecting against "personality disintegration" and a "malignant schizophrenic course" (Jahrreis, 1926; Stengel 1945; Rosen, 1956), which was later refuted by Fenton and M.Glashan (1986) and Berman et al. (1995). Accordingly, more severe negative symptomatology has been observed in patients with chronic schizophrenia and OCD (Fenton and McGlashan, 1986; Hwang et al., 2000). Since negative, but not positive, schizophrenia symptoms are associated with a greater likelihood of cognitive impairment and poor clinical outcome, it is not surprising that schizo-obsessive patients generally have a poor prognosis (Fenton and McGlashan, 1986; Berman et al., 1995; Hwang et al., 2000). With the exception of one study showing a higher level of functioning in schizo-obsessive pattients (Tibbo et al., 2000), researchers report that compared to "pure" schizophrenia, schizophrenia associated with OCD is generally charatecrized by a lower level of social functioning (Fenton and McGlashan, 1986; Berman et al., 1995a; Hwang et al., 2000; Poyurovsky et al., 2001;), longer duration of hospitalizations (Fenton and McGlashan, 1986; Berman et al., 1995; Hwang et al., 2000), more suicide attempts, more neurocognitive deficits (Berman et al., 1998; Hwang et al., 2000), and treatment resistance (Poyurovsky et al., 1999; Zohar et al., 1993; Berman et al., 1995; Bermanzohn et al., 1997)

Course of OC Symptoms in Schizophrenia

In about half the reported cases, OC symptoms preceded the onset of schizophrenia; in the remainder, it occured as a prodromal phase or aggravated the progression of the schizophrenic process (Eisen et al., 1997; Kruger et al., 2000; Ohta et al., 2003; Poyurovsky et al., 2003). Hwang and Opler (2000) noted that when OC symptoms preceded schizophrenia, they were often long-standing, and the patients were initially diagnosed as having OCD. However, all these studies were limited by their cross-sectional design and retrospective evaluation of the interrelationship between OC and schizophrenia symptoms. In a prospective, short-term study, Fabish et al (2001) noted that OC symptoms remained stable during the period of acute exacerbation of schizophrenia. By contrast, Craig et al (2002) evaluated first-admission patients with schizophrenia and found a substantial rise in the occurrence of OC symptoms/OCD during the first 24 months, and suggested that the lifetime occurrence rate of OC phenomena in schizophrenia may be associated with age at onset or duration of illness. The high attrition rate in this study limited the interpretation of the longitudinal course of OC symptoms/OCD in schizophrenia. Interestingly, Poyurovsky et al. (2003) found that the severity of the OC symptoms seems to increase with a progression in the course of schizophrenia, as incidated by the significantly higher scores on the Yale-Brown Obsessive-Compulsive Scale (Y-BOCS) in patients with recurrent episodes of schizophrenia compared to those with first-episode schizophrenia.

A large-scale prospective evaluation of the temporal occurrence of the two disorders, the interaction between the severity of OCS/OCD and schizophrenia symptoms, as well as further delineation of specific schizo-obsessive subgroups is warranted.

Table 1: Symptomatic Dimensions in Schizophrenia with and without OC phenomena (adapted from Poyurovsky et al., 2004)

Disorders	Positive		Negative	Disorganized	OCS	
	Delusions	Hallucination			Obsession	Compulsion
Schizophrenia	Present	Present	Present	Present	Absent	Absent
Schizophrenia with OCS	Present	Present	Present	Present	Subsyndromal	Subsyndromal
Schizophrenia with OCD	Present	Present	Present	Present	Present	Present

Present | Subsyndromal | Absent

Diagnosis

Considering the diagnostic pitfalls in the discrimination between obsessions and delusions, until more studies on the nature and course of OCD symptoms in schizophrenia become available, we suggest that the diagnosis of OCD-schizophrenia be confined to those patients who meet full DSM-IV criteria of both disorders. Eisen et al (1997) proposed that the diagnosis of OCD comorbidity in schizophrenia should be based on the presence of compulsions that seem to be less delusion-dependent. Patients who fail to recognize their OC symptoms as senseless and unreasonable and do not meet DSM-IV criteria for schizophrenia can be diagnosed as having OCD with poor insight, OCD with psychotic features (Insel & Akiskal, 1986), obsessive psychosis (Solyom et al., 1985; Robinson, 1970), or atypical OCD (O'Dwyer & Marks, 2000). (Schematic representations of the major dimensions of OC and schizophrenic psychopathology in schizophrenia is shown in Table 1).

Genetic Predisposition in Schizo-Obsessive Disorder

Both schizophrenia and OCD strongly aggregate in families. First-degree relatives of patients with schizophrenia have higher rates of schizophrenia and schizophrenia-spectrum disorders, including schizoaffective disorder, other nonaffective psychoses, and schizotypal and paranoid personality, than the general population disorders (Kendler & Diehl 1993; Asarnow et al 2001). Similarly, first-degree relatives of OCD probands have a higher morbid risk for OCD compared to relatives of healthy controls (Pauls et al., 1995; Nestadt et al., 2000). Both OCD probands and their first-degree relatives had a higher prevalence of OC personality disorder (OCPD), indicating that OCPD may share a common familial etiology with OCD (Samuels et al., 2000).

The validity of a putative schizo-obsessive diagnostic entity may be supported by a comparison of differential familial aggregation of schizophrenia-spectrum disorders vs. OC-associated disorders in first-degree relatives of schizophrenia probands with and without OCD. If the OC component constitutes an independent dimension in schizophrenia, the rate of occurrence of OC –associated disorders in first-degree relatives of schizo-obsessive probands should be higher than in relatives of non-OCD schizophrenia probands.

In a study conducted by Poyurovsky et al. (2005), 182 first-degree relatives of 57 schizo-obsessive probands with, 210 relatives of 60 non-OCD schizophrenia probands, and 165 relatives of 50 community subjects were interviewed, either directly using the SCID for for Axis-I DSM-IV Disorders and Axis II DSM-III-R Personality Disorders [59.3% (108/182), 51.9% (109/210) and 54.5% (90/165), respectively], or indirectly, using the Family History Research Diagnostic Criteria. They found that compared to the relatives of the non-OCD schizophrenia probands, the relatives of the schizo-obsessive probands had significantly higher morbid risks for schizo-obsessive disorder (2.2% vs 0%; P=0.033) and OCPD (7.14% vs 1.90%; P=0.014), and a trend towards a higher morbid risk for OCD (4.41% vs 1.43%; P=0.08). When the morbid risks for OCD, OCPD, and OCD-schizophrenia were pooled, the significant between-group difference became robust (13.74% vs. 3.33%; P=0.0002). The validity of these findings was supported by the similarity between the morbid risk for schizophrenia in the two schizophrenia groups (9.4% and 7.5%), consistent with the average risk of schizophrenia in first-degree relatives established in contemporary family studies of schizophrenia (6% - 9%) (Gottesman 1991; Kendler 2000). The fact that the relatives of the two schizophrenia groups did not differ significantly in morbid risks for schizophrenia-spectrum disorders, mood disorders, or substance abuse disorders suggests that shizo-obsessive disorder is associated with a specific elevation in familial rates of OC-related disorders rather than an elevation in psychopathology in general. Thus, schizo-obsessive disorder is to some degree familial: if a patient suffers from this disorder, his/her first-degree relatives will also have an increased risk, and vice versa. Furthermore, the OCD-schizophrenia in probands is associated with a substantially increased risk for OC-associated disorders in their first-degree relatives. Overall, these findings further support the validity of the unique schizo-obsessive diagnostic entity.

PHARMACOLOGICAL TREATMENT

The data on the pharmacotherapy of schizo-obsessive disorder is sparse and based on case reports and small, mostly uncontrolled clinical trials. Nevertheless, there is a general consensus that compared to non-OCD schizophrenia, schizo-obsessive patients are difficult to treat and require distinct therapeutic approaches

Clomipramine

In view of the efficacy of clomipramine in the treatment of OCD, the initial reports on treatment of schizo-obsessive disorder dealt with its adjunctive administration with neuroleptics. Clomipramine has been reported to alleviate OCS, reduced the anxiety associated with compulsive rituals,, and improved the positive and negative symptoms of schizophrenia in some patients (Zohar et al, 1993; Kurokawa et al, 1997). However, lack of therapeutic effect, and an exacerbation of the psychosis were also noted (Bark and Lindenmayer 1992). In addition, the anticholinergic properties of clomipramine as well as its cardiovascular side effects and tendency to induce weight gain limit its utility in patients with schizophrenia, particularly those being treated with low-potency typical antipsychotics, anticholinergic agents, or atypical antipsychotics, primarily clozapine.

SSRIs

SSRIs are currently the first-line treatment of OCD due to their efficacy and safety. A series of case reports demonstrated a beneficial effect of adjunctive fluoxetine, paroxetine, and sertraline in neuroleptic-treated schizo-obsessive patients. However, negative results of fluoxetine addition were also reported (Sasson et al., 1997).

In one open-label study, fluvoxamine (up to 150mg/day for 12 weeks) was added to the ongoing regimen of typical antipsychotic agents in 10 inpatients with clinically stable DSM-IV schizophrenic disorder and accompanying OCD (Poyurovsky et al, 1996). Biweekly evaluation with the Y-BOCS (Goodman et al., 1989) and the Schedules for the Assessment of

Positive (SAPS) (Andreasen, 1983) and Negative Symptoms (SANS) (Andreasen, 1983) showed a significant improvement in obsessions ($P<0.02$), positive ($P<0.01$) and negative ($P<0.05$) schizophrenia symptoms, but not compulsions. By the end of the trial, 3 of the 10 patients (30%) showed a more than 50% reduction in the Y-BOCS score, with complete amelioration of OC symptoms in one of them. There were no exacerbations or new onset of extrapyramidal side effects. However, 3 patients dropped out of the study within 4 weeks because of increased aggressiveness (2 patients) or psychotic exacerbation (1 patient). Since impulsivity and aggressive behavior were also evident prior to fluvoxamine initiation in 2 of the participants, the authors suggested that patients with clinically significant aggressiveness may be at higher risk of psychotic exacerbation during adjunctive fluvoxamine treatment.

Atypical Antipsychotic Agents

Monotherapy with typical antipsychotic agents is of limited value in schizo-obsessive patients. The majority of studies with second-generation antipsychotics (clozapine, risperidone, olanzapine, quetiapine) reported that they may aggravate preexisting OC symptoms in schizophrenia patients or induce de novo OC symptoms [see next section]. However, a few preliminary clinical observations indicate that clozapine and olanzapine, either alone or in combination with SSRIs might alleviate both schizophrenia and OC symptoms in some cases (Strous et al, 1999). Thus, three schizo-obssessive patients who had been unsuccessfully treated with various conventional neuroleptics combined with anti-obsessive agents, followed by resistance or intolerance to clozapine showed significant improvement with olanzapine therapy (10-20 mg/day) in both schizophrenia and OC symptoms (Poyurovsky et al, 2000). However, the improvement in OC symptoms in 2 of the patients may have been partially attributable to the discontinuation of clozapine prior to the trial.

In another series, a beneficial effect of adjunctive olanzapine (6.5 ± 2.3mg/day for 8 weeks) was reported in 9 patients with comorbid schizophrenia and OCD who had unsuccessfully completed an adequate trial with at least one SSRI or clomipramine combined with either typical or atypical antipsychotics (Sasson et al, 2001). Four were categorized as responders (>40% decrease in Y-BOCS score) and 2 as partial responders. In one patient, the OC symptoms worsened.

Treatment Guidelines for OC Symptoms/OCD in Schizophrenia

In the absence of evidence-based data, our recommendations for the pharmacotherapy of patients with schizo-obsessive disorder are as follows. Careful evaluation of the potential risks and benefits of adjunctive pharmacotherapy in schizo-obsessive patients is required. Due to the risk of psychotic exacerbation or increased aggressive behavior, anti-obsessive agents (SSRIs or clomipramine) should be initiated for OC symptoms only in neuroleptic-stabilized patients.OC symptoms in schizophrenia should be considered a target for therapeutic intervention only when their severity is of clinical significance. The suggested guidelines for the treatment of schizophrenia patients with accompanying OC symptoms/OCD are:

1. Since preliminary uncontrolled data demonstrates olanzapine's beneficial effect on both schizophrenia and OCD in some schizo-obsessive patients (Poyurovsky et al, 2000; Sasson et al, 2001) it seems that this agent should be the first option when a second-generation antipsychotic is to be used as the first-line treatment. Data on the therapeutic efficacy of other atypical antipsychotics (risperidone, quetiapine, amisulpride, aripiprazole and ziprasidone) in schizo-obsessive patients are still missing. The risk/benefit ratio for each atypical antipsychotic should be considered.
2. If there is no response to atypical antipsychotic monotherapy, a SSRI may be added.
3. Lack of response to the first atypical/SSRI combination may justify switching to an alternative atypical/SSRI or clomipramine combination.
4. In case of failure, a ziprasidone typical antipsychotic/SSRI combination should be tried.

   For steps 2-4, pharmacokinetic interactions and potential side effects should be closely monitored. SSRIs with minimal drug-drug interactions, such as citalopram and sertraline, are preferable as adjunctive agents.
5. Clozapine monotherapy should be reserved for treatment-resistant schizo-obsessive patients. A good response was noted for a relatively low dose range (75mg - 300 mg) (Straus et al, 1999; Tibbo and Gendemann, 1999). Slow up-titration of clozapine and close monitoring of its potential OCS-improving vs OCS-provoking effect in schizophrenia patients is recommended.
6. If the patient does noe respond to clozapine monotherapy, a trial with clozapine/SSRI combination is recommended. SSRIs should be added to clozapine with caution. Those devoid of clinically significant drug-drug interactions (citalopram or sertraline) seem to be safer.
7. Electroconvulsive therapy is the last resort when pharmacotherapy fails.

References

Andreasen NC. Scale for the assessment of positive symptoms (SAPS). Iowa City; University of Iowa, 1984

Andreasen NC. Scale for the assessment of negative symptoms (SANS). Iowa City: University of Iowa, 1983

Appelbaum PS, Robbins PC, Roth LH. (1999) Dimensional approach to delusions: comparison across types and diagnoses. *Am J Psychiatry*, 156, 1938-1943.

Asarnow RF, Nuechterlein KH, Fogelson D, Subotnik KL, Payne DA., Russell AT, Asamen J, Kuppinger H., Kendler KS,. (2001) Schizophrenia and schizophrenia-spectrum personality disorders in the first-degree relatives of children with schizophrenia: the UCLA family study. *Arch Gen Psychiatry*, 58, 581-588.

Bark N, Lindenmayer JP. (1992) Ineffectiveness of clomipramine for obsessive-compulsive symptoms in a patient with schizophrenia. *Am J Psychiatry*, 149, 136-137.

Berman I, Kalinowski A, Berman S, Lengua J, Green AI. (1995) Obsessive-compulsive symptoms in chronic schizophrenia. *Compr Psychiatry*, 36, 6-10.

Berman I, Merson A, Viegner B, Losonczy MF, Pappas D, Green AI. (1998) Obsessions and compulsions as a distinct cluster of symptoms in schizophrenia: a neuropsychological study. *J Nerv Ment Dis*, 186, 150-156.

Bermanzohn PC, Porto L, Arlow PB, et al. (1997) Are some neuroleptic-refractory symptoms of schizophrenia really obsessions? *CNS Spectrums*, 2, 51-57.

Bermanzohn PC, Porto L, Arlow PB, Pollack S, Stronger R, Siris SG. (2000) Hierarchical diagnosis in chronic schizophrenia: a clinical study of co-occurring syndromes. *Schizophr Bull*, 26, 517-525.

Bland RC, Newman SC, Orn H. (1987) Schizophrenia: lifetime co-morbidity in a community sample. *Acta Psychiatr Scand*, 75, 383-391.

Catapano F, Sperandeo R, Perris F, Lanzaro M, Maj M. (2001) Insight and resistance in patients with obsessive-compulsive disorder. *Psychopathology*, 34, 62-68.

Craig T, Hwang MY, Bromet EJ. (2002) Obsessive-compulsive and panic symptoms in patients with first-admission psychosis. *Am J Psychiatry*, 159, 592-598.

Dominquez RA, Backman KE, Lugo SC. (1999) Demographics, prevalence and clinical features of the schizo-obsessive subtype of schizophrenia. *CNS Spectrums*, 12, 50-56.

Eisen JL, Rasmussen SA. (1993) Obsessive-compulsive disorder with psychotic features. *J Clin Psychiatry*, 54, 373-379.

Eisen JL, Beer DA, Pato MT, Venditto TA, Rasmussen SA. (1997) Obsessive-compulsive disorder in patients with schizophrenia and schizoaffective disorder. *Am J Psychiatry*, 154, 271-273.

Fabisch K, Fabisch H, Langs G, Huber HP, Zapotoczky HG. (2001) Incidence of obsessive-compulsive phenomena in the course of acute schizophrenia and schizoaffective disorder. *Eur Psychiatry*, 16, 336-341.

Fenton WS, McGlashan TH. (1986) The prognostic significance of obsessive-compulsive symptoms in schizophrenia. *Am J Psychiatry*, 143, 437-441.

Foa EB, Kozak MJ, Goodman WK. (1995) DSM-IV field trial: obsessive-compulsive disorder. *Am J Psychiatry*, 152, 90-96. Erratum in: *Am J Psychiatry*, 152, 654.

Goodman WK, Price LH, Rasmussen SA, Mazure C, Delgado P, Heninger GR, Charney DS. (1989) The Yale-Brown Obsessive-Compulsive Scale. I. Development, use, and reliability. *Arch Gen Psychiatry*, 46, 1006-1011.

Gordon A. (1950) Transition of obsessions into delusions: evaluation of obsessional phenomena from prognostic standpoint. *Am J Psychiatry*, 107, 455-458.

Gottesman II. (1991) Schizophrenia Genesis: The origins of Madness. Freeman: New York.

Gross-Isseroff R, Hermesh H, Zohar J Weizman A. (2003) Neuroimaging communality between schizophrenia and obsessive-compulsive disorder: a putative basis for schizo-obsessive disorder? *World J Biol Psychiatry*, 4, 129-134.

Hwang MY, Morgan JE, Losconzcy MF. (2000) Clinical and neuropsychological profiles of obsessive-compulsive schizophrenia: a pilot study. *J Neuropsychiatry Clin Neurosci*, 12, 91-94.

Hwang MY, Opler LA. (2000) Management of schizophrenia with obsessive-compulsive disorder. *Psychiatric Ann*, 30, 23-28.

Insel TR, Akiskal HS. (1986) OCD with psychotic features: a phenomenological analysis. *Am J Psychiatry*, 143, 1527-1533.

Jahrreis W. (1926) Obsessions during schizophrenia. *Archiv fur Psychiatrie und Nervenkrankheiten* (Berlin), 77, 740-788.

Karno M, Golding JM, Sorenson SB, Burnam MA. (1988) The epidemiology of obsessive-compulsive disorder in five US communities. *Arch Gen Psychiatry*, 45, 1094-1099.

Kendler K, Glazer WM, (1983) Morgenstern H. Dimensions of delusional experience. *Am J Psychiatry*, 140, 466-469.

Kendler, K.S., Diehl, S.R. (1993) The genetics of schizophrenia: a current, genetic-epidemiologic perspective. *Schizophr Bull.*, 19, 261-285.

Kendler, K.S. (2000) Schizophrenia genetics. In: B.J. Sadock and V.A. Sadock (Eds) Kaplan and Sadock's Comprehensive Textbook of Psychiatry, Vol.1, Philadelphia: Lippincott, Williams and Wilkins.

Kruger S, Braunig P, Hoffler J, Shugar G, Bommer I, Langkrar J. (2000) Prevalence of obsessive-compulsive disorder in schizophrenia and significance of motor symptoms. *J Neuropsychiatry Clin Neurosci*, 12, 16-24.

Kurokawa K, Tanino R. (1997) Effectiveness of clomipramine for obsessive-compulsive symptoms and chronic pain in two patients with schizophrenia. *J Clin Psychopharmacol*, 17, 329-330.

Lelliott PT, Noshirvani HF, Basoglu M, Marks IM, Monteiro WO. (1988) Obsessive-compulsive beliefs and treatment outcome. *Psychol Med*, 18, 697-702.

Lysaker PH, Marks KA, Picone JB, Rollins AL, Fastenau PS, Bond GR. (2000) Obsessive and compulsive symptoms in schizophrenia. Clinical and neurocognitive correlates. *J Nerv Ment Dis*, 188, 78-83.

Matsunaga H, Kiriike N, Matsui T, Oya K, Iwasaki Y, Koshimune K, Miyata A, Stein DJ. (2002) Obsessive-compulsive disorder with poor insight. *Compr Psychiatry*, 43, 150-157.

Nechmad A, Ratzoni G, Poyurovsky M, Meged S, Avidan G, Fuchs C, Bloch Y, Weizman R. (2003) Obsessive-compulsive disorder in adolescent schizophrenia patients. *Am J Psychiatry*, 160, 1002-1004.

Nestadt G, Samuels J, Riddle M, Bienvenu OJ 3rd, Liang KY, LaBuda M., Walkup J, Grados M, Hoehn-Saric R. (2000) A family study of obsessive-compulsive disorder. *Arch Gen Psychiatry*, 57, 358-363.

O'Dwyer AM, Marks I. (2000) Obsessive-compulsive disorder and delusions revisited. *Br J Psychiatry*, 176, 281-284.

Ohta M, Kokai M, Morita Y. (2003) Features of obsessive-compulsive disorder in patients primarily diagnosed with schizophrenia. *Psychiatry Clin Neurosci*, 57, 67-74.

Pauls DL, Alsobrook JP II, Goodman W, Rasmussen S, Leckman JF. (1995) A family study of obsessive-compulsive disorder. *Am J Psychiatry*, 152, 76-84.

Porto L, Bermanzohn PC, Pollack S. (1997) A profile of obsessive-compulsive symptoms in schizophrenia. *CNS Spectrums*, 2, 21-25.

Poyurovsky M, Hermesh H, Weizman A. (1996) Fluvoxamine treatment in clozapine-induced obsessive-compulsive symptoms in schizophrenic patients. *Clin Neuropharmacol*, 19, 305-313.

Poyurovsky M, Fuchs K, Weizman A. (1999) Obsessive-compulsive symptoms in patients with first episode schizophrenia. *Am J Psychiatry*, 156, 1998-2000.

Poyurovsky M, Dorfman-Etrog P, Hermesh H, Munitz H, Tollefson GD, Weizman A. (2000) Beneficial effect of olanzapine in schizophrenic patients with obsessive-compulsive symptoms. *Int Clin Psychopharmaco*, 15, 169-173.

Poyurovsky M, Hramenkov S, Isakov V, Rauchverger B, Modai I, Schneidman M, Fuchs C, Weizman A. (2001) Obsessive-compulsive disorder in chronic institutionalized schizophrenic patients. *Psychiatry Res*, 102, 49-57.

Poyurovsky M, Kriss V, Weisman G, Faragian S, Kurs R, Schneidman M, Fuchs C, Weizman A, Weizman R. (2003) Comparison of clinical characteristics and comorbidity in schizophrenia patients with and without obsessive-compulsive disorder. *J Clin Psychiatry*, 64, 1300-1307.

Poyurovsky M, Weizman A, Weizman R. (2004) Obsessive-compulsive disorder in schizophrenia. Clinical characteristics and treatment. *CNS Drugs*, 18, 989-1010.

Poyurovsky M, Kriss V, Weisman G, Faragian S, Schneidman M, Fuchs C, Weizman A, Weizman R. (2005) Familial aggregation of schizophrenia-spectrum disorders and obsessive-compulsive associated disorders in schizophrenia probands with and without OCD. *Am J Med Genet B Neuropsychiatr Genet*, 133, 31-36.

Robins E, Guze SB. (1970) Establishment of diagnostic validity in psychiatric illness: its application to schizophrenia. *Am J Psychiatry*, 126, 983-987.

Rosen I. (1956) The clinical significance of obsessions in schizophrenia. *J Mental Sci*, 103, 773-785.

Samuels J, Nestadt G, Bienvenu J, Costa PT, Riddl, MA, Liang K, Hoehn-Saric R, Grados MA, Cullen BAM. (2000) Personality disorders and normal personality dimension in obsessive-compulsive disorder. *Br J Psychiatry*, 177, 457-462.

Sasson Y, Bermanzohn PC, Zohar J. (1997) Treatment of obsessive-compulsive syndromes in schizophrenia. *CNS Spectrums*, 2, 34-37.

Solyom L, DiNicola VF, Phil M, Sookman D, Luchins D. (1985) Is there an obsessive psychosis? Aetiological and prognostic factors of an atypical form of obsessive-compulsive neurosis. *Can J Psychiatry*, 30, 372-380.

Spitzer M. (1990) On defining delusions. *Compr Psychiatry*, 31, 377-397.

Stengel EA. (1945) A study of some clinical aspects of the relationship between obsessional neurosis and psychotic reaction types. *J Mental Sci*, 91, 166-187.

Strous RD, Patel JK, Zimmet S, Green AI. (1999) Clozapine and paroxetine in the treatment of schizophrenia with obsessive-compulsive features. *Am J Psychiatry*, 156, 973-974.

Tibbo P, Warneke L. (1999) Obsessive-compulsive disorder in schizophrenia: epidemiologic and biologic overlap. *J Psychiatry Neurosci*, 24, 15-24.

Tibbo P, Kroetsch M, Chue P, Wameke L. (2000) Obsessive-compulsive disorder in schizophrenia. *J Psychiatric Res*, 34, 139-146.

Zohar J, Kaplan Z, Benjamin J. (1993) Clomipramine treatment of obsessive-compulsive symptomatology in schizophrenic patients. *J Clin Psychiatry,* 54, 385-388.

In: Obsessive-Compulsive Disorder and Comorbidity
Editors: R. Gross-Isseroff and A. Weizman, pp. 47-57 ISBN 1-59454-884-6

Chapter 5

OBSESSIVE-COMPULSIVE DISORDER AND ATTENTION DEFICIT DISORDER: A CHALLENGING COMORBIDITY

Tamar Steinberg and Alan Apter
Departments of Neurology and Psychiatry, Feinberg Child Study Center,
Schneider's Children's Medical Center of Israel

DEFINITIONS

Attention deficit is one of the most prevalent disorders in childhood. It is defined in the DSM- IV as an impairment of attention, or hyperactivity and impulsivity or both, beginning before the age of seven, and persisting for at least six months to a degree that is maladaptive or immature. It is a persistent disorder that influences psychological development and often persists into adolescence and adult life. Diagnosis requires that there should be clear evidence of clinically significant impairment, which implies not only to severity or frequency of symptoms but also to interference in major life domains of the child e.g. at home, at school, with friends or elsewhere. However, it is not clear whether the poor outcome is caused by the disorder itself or by the frequent co existing disorders.

OCD can be divided into adult and juvenile onset. Juvenile OCD differs from adult OCD in certain respects. Juvenile OCD shows positive association with chronic tics, major depressive disorder, body - dysmorphic disorder and with ADHD. It has been suggested that ADHD may be a developmental marker of juvenile OCD (Jaisoorya et al., 2003).

Although ADHD seems to be present in a substantial minority of children with OCD the concurrence of these conditions has not been the subject of much interest in the literature.

Epidemiology

ADHD is present in at least 4-7% of all school age children (Buitelaar 2002), As many as two thirds of all children with ADHD in the general population meet criteria for at least two additional DSM-III-R diagnoses meaning that young children with ADHD are usually handicapped by several different psychiatric developmental problems (Gilbert 2004).

Very few studies have examined the co-existence of OCD with ADHD. It has been reported that about 75% of children with OCD show associated psychiatric disorders mostly tic disorders and emotional problems while ADHD usually co-exists in 6-15% of the cases (Swedo et al, 1989).

In recent years there has been a suggestion that ADHD is common in pediatric OCD patients. This has been reported as being as high as 30% in both specialized and general clinical settings. Geller et al., (1996) reported that juvenile OCD was comorbid with ADHD in 25% of cases. Jaisoriya et al., (2003) reported an incidence of 18% co- morbidity. A prospective longitudinal study of an epidemiological cohort of almost 1000 children aged 1 to 10 years was followed up in adolescence and adulthood. ADHD in adolescence predicted OCD in adulthood and vica versa (Peterson 2001)

Clinical Manifestation

The question is whether or not these inattention and hyperactivity symptoms are a direct result of internal distraction and anxiety or represent true ADHD. These questions are especially important in the inattentive subtype of ADD. Most of the evidence for this co morbidity between OCD and ADHD comes from studies using structured clinical interviews. Since such studies are vulnerable to interpretation by assessors this association is not completely proven.

Geller et al., (2004) attempted to bypass this limitation by using objective assessment methods such as the Child Behavior Checklist. This empirical derived instrument is based on factor analytic studies of symptoms and thus uses a different classification structure than the DSM IV. The CBCL includes an attention scale that is highly associated with the diagnosis of ADHD. CBCL findings in ADHD children were similar to previous findings reported in ADHD youth irrespective of the presence or absence of comorbid OCD. Comorbid youth generally had additive scores on the CBCL scales reflecting the independent contribution of symptomatic and functional impairment from each disorder. The authors concluded that when ADHD –like symptoms are seen in OCD youth they reflect a true comorbid state of OCD plus ADHD. The comorbid youth also had significantly higher social and attention problems and delinquent and behavior scale symptoms than those with OCD alone. This study also suggests that the inattention in children with OCD is not simply an artifact of obsessional anxiety.

There is also evidence that children with ADHD showed more severe obsessive-compulsive traits compared to children with tic disorders, especially when contamination fears, repetition, over conscientiousness and hoarding were taken into consideration (Moll, 2000). It was also speculated that some of those children with ADHD developed obsessive-compulsive symptoms when treated with stimulants because of this tendency (Kotsopoulos 2001).

Children with both disorders concomitantly have lower overall psychosocial functioning and this has important implications for treatment and prognosis. Thus CBT for OCD is less successful when the child has ADHD since the child is unable to comply with the demands of the therapy

SYMPTOMATOLOGY

On occasion, children with OCD are mistakenly diagnosed with attention-deficit/hyperactivity disorder, since frequent intrusive obsessions can lead to inattentiveness, and ritualistic or avoidant behaviors can make the child appear overactive or impulsive. However, the purposeful nature of the OCD child's movements and their association with obsessive thoughts can be used to distinguish compulsions from motor hyperactivity. Other comorbid disorders that are often associated with attention problems that may be confused with OCD include those with perseverative and stereotypic behaviors that are characteristic of pervasive developmental disorders such as autistic and Asperger's disorders. These can usually be differentiated from compulsions, since the former behaviors are neither distressing to the child nor performed in response to an obsession. In some cases, the fixed nature of bizarre or unusual obsessional beliefs can have a delusional quality and thus resemble schizophrenic symptomology. Schizophrenia too is often associated with attention and learning difficulties. OCD can be distinguished from schizophrenia by the absence of other schizophrenic symptoms (e.g., hallucinations, formal thought disorder) and the ability to engage in reality testing. Several neurological disorders should be considered in the differential diagnosis of OCD, including temporal lobe epilepsy and complications secondary to CNS insults or tumors.

The differential diagnosis of ADHD versus other types of disruptive behavior disorders is generally straightforward by clinical history and examination of specific symptoms and behavior patterns. Descriptions of inattention, overactivity, and impulsivity should be evident across situations and to multiple observers. Other sources of inattention and frustration in school settings, such as learning disorders, can be discerned by differences in behavior across settings, school grades, and results of psycho- educational evaluations. At times, these problems may co-occur, making accurate diagnosis more complex.

Another diagnostic challenge lies in separating interference from other psychopathology such as mood or anxiety disorders on concentration, school adjustment, and performance. In general, ADHD is distinguished by its chronicity and early onset rather than an episodic pattern, although school impairment from ADHD may be progressive, with increasing academic demands over many years. The temporal relationship between the appearance of internalizing symptoms with greater school difficulty usually is evident in instances of mood or anxiety disorders uncomplicated by ADHD

The Special Case of Tourette Syndrome

The most dramatic and important comorbidity between ADHD and OCD is seen in children with Tourette syndrome (TS). The hallmark symptoms of this condition are chronic motor and vocal tics that wax and wane over time, behavior disorders, anxiety disorders, and especially OCD and ADHD.

About 85% of patients with Tourette syndrome show associated neuropsychiatric problems. These are often responsible for the most prominent psychosocial impairments. About half of the cases with chronic tics or TS also meet criteria for ADHD and there seems to be a correlation between tic severity and ADHD severity (Comings et al 2000).

Epidemiological studies suggest that a substantial number of TS patients develop OCD, it is suggested that there are inherent differences between adult OCD and OCD with TS which usually starts in an earlier age, OCD with TS is associated with more need to symmetry, touching, blinking or staring compulsions, and counting compulsions (Petter et al 1998). TS serves as an instructive model for the study of developmental psychopathology, since different comorbid disorders often appear at a characteristic age, with ADHD being the first disorder, followed by tic symptomatology, and later on TS related OCD. McMahon et –al (2003) have followed a cohort of TS offspring at risk for developing TS. They showed that these children have a higher risk than controls of developing TS, OCD and ADHD. Thus 29% developed a tic disorder, 17.6% OCD, and 41.2% met criteria for the diagnosis of ADHD. Interestingly the age of onset of these disorders was earlier than typically reported in the literature, partly due to the fact that it was a prospective study.

TS seems to result from an interaction of genetic and environmental factors, the general hypothesis is that it is caused by a combination of major genes modifying genes and environmental factors that can exacerbate or ameliorate the severity. The increased rate of tic, OCD, and ADHD disorders in children with two affected parents compared to children with one affected parent and controls may reflect a gene dosage effect (McMahon et –al 2003).

Since ADHD starts earlier than tics and OCD it can be argued that early ADHD can be seen as a risk factor for these psychiatric disorders.

Etiology

The association of attention-deficit/hyperactivity disorder and other disruptive behaviors such as aggression with Tourette's disorder is robust among clinic-referred children and adolescents, with 40 to 60 percent of children with Tourette's disorder meeting criteria for attention-deficit/hyperactivity disorder, possibly reflecting shared deficits in response inhibition affecting greater portions of corticostriatothalamocortical circuitry (Channon S, Robertson MM 2003). Curiously, epidemiological samples of individuals with Tourette's disorder do not display the extensive co morbidity with attention-deficit/hyperactivity disorder, perhaps reflecting ascertainment differences. In most instances, the burden of symptoms created by the child's attentional problems, academic underachievement, and impulsivity far outweigh that produced by tic severity. However, treatment of these associated comorbid conditions can be challenging because of the adverse effects of some treatments on tics, the temporal fluctuations in symptoms, and the frequent presence of other common associated problems such as learning disorders (The Tourette's Syndrome Study Group 2002).

One interesting recent area of interest in the communal expression of OCD and ADHD symptoms is the discovery that antineuronal antibodies can also arise following infection with group A b-hemolytic streptococcal infections, as exemplified by Sydenham's chorea. Considering that children with Sydenham's chorea frequently exhibit obsessive-compulsive symptoms, emotional lability, and hyperactivity, there may be a spectrum of pediatric autoimmune neuropsychiatric disorders associated with streptococcal infections (PANDAS). In particular, sudden onset of obsessive-compulsive disorder, tics, attention-deficit/hyperactivity disorder, and other psychiatric syndromes has been characterized in children following infection with group A b-hemolytic streptococcus. These findings in conjunction with the indication of a genetic vulnerability to this condition (high frequency of binding of a monoclonal antibody designated D8/17) represent an exciting new development in the etiology and possible treatment of these disorders(Singer HS 1997, Swedo SE et-al 1991, Allen aj 1995)

Genetics

Family and twin studies support a strong genetic factor in the etiology of OCD. Two family studies found a higher risk of OCD in family members of OCD probands compared to relatives of controls (Nestadt et-al 2000; Pauls et-al 1990).

So far most of the genetic studies in OCD have used the candidate gene approach, and some authors reported positive association between OCD and the gene encoding the enzyme catechol-o-methyltransferase, which is involved in the degradative pathways of catecholaminergic neurotransmitters (Alsobrook et-al 2002).

The exact etiological pathways of ADHD are also unknown, twin studies have found considerable heritability with genetic factors contributing 65-90% of the phenotypic variance in the population (Todd et al 2001). Molecular genetic studies have found associations with some of the dopamine receptor genes, which are also important in the understanding of the molecular basis for ADHD.

While the familiality of Tourette's disorder was recognized in the earliest descriptions of the condition, it has proved a difficult disorder to fully understand using current techniques and models of genetic disorders. The inability to confirm a clear genetic basis for the condition may reflect some genetic and etiologic heterogeneity among families with members afflicted with Tourette's disorder. Nevertheless, twin and family studies convincingly demonstrate patterns of inheritance in many families that are consistent with an autosomal dominant disorder with incomplete penetrance (Pauls 1991). Furthermore, careful screening of relatives with Tourette's disorder has consistently revealed a relation between Tourette's disorder, other tic disorders, and obsessive-compulsive disorder in some families, suggesting that obsessive-compulsive disorder and less severe forms of tic disorders may reflect alternative expressions of a common genetic vulnerability (Eapen et-al 1997). The high rate of comorbidity of tic disorders with disruptive behavior disorders such as attention-deficit/hyperactivity disorder provides some support for inclusion of attention-deficit/hyperactivity disorder as a possible alternative phenotype. Although some have suggested that tic disorders are part of a spectrum of psychiatric disorders that includes many other disorders with repetitive behaviors, preoccupations, and poor impulse control, evidence supporting a broader spectrum concept is lacking. The recognition that less than half of the offspring of individuals with Tourette's disorder will display Tourette's disorder or related phenotypes has led to the conclusion that epigenetic, or environmental, factors may also influence the expression, severity, and manifestations of tic disorders. These interacting epigenetic factors may include intrauterine experience, birth weight, and other pregnancy or delivery complications. Initial attempts at testing the possible association of candidate genes suspected of causal involvement with Tourette's disorder have had little success, although some positive findings have been reported including an association with the "seven-repeat" allele of the dopamine type 4 (D4) receptor subtype (DRD4.7). Additional progress in understanding the molecular genetics of Tourette's disorder is expected shortly from ongoing multisite genetic studies of affected sib pairs with Tourette's disorder (Alsbrook JP, Pauls DL 1997).

Comorbidity in children and adolescents with OCD is common, with up to 80 percent of affected youths meeting diagnostic criteria for an additional Axis I disorder and as many as 50 percent experiencing multiple comorbid conditions. The most common comorbid disorders include other anxiety disorders (26 to 75 percent, depending on the sample), depressive disorders (25 to 62 percent), and disruptive behavior disorders (18 to 33 percent). The fact that depressive symptoms commonly appear after the OCD suggests that concurrent mood disturbance may be reactive. Obsessive-compulsive personality disorder has been reported in 11 to 14 percent of pediatric OCD samples. Motor and vocal tics are common in children with OCD, and 20 to 30 percent also suffer from Tourette's disorder. Youngsters with tic-related OCD (i.e., OCD with comorbid Tourette's disorder) are less likely to report engaging in ordering, hoarding, and washing compulsions than youngsters with OCD only.

Treatment Implications

The most practical implication of the comorbidity between OCD and ADHD lies in the context of treatment. Most cases of juvenile onset OCD are associated with tics whether or not in conjunction with clear-cut TS. Since as pointed out above, the major impairments of TS and juvenile OCD subjects are in many ways related to the attention problems it follows that treatment of attention in the context of OCD/TS is of major importance.

However the pharmacological treatment of children with the combination of OCD/Tics and ADHD is problematic since it has been said that stimulant medications such as methylphenidate should be avoided since their use has been associated with the worsening of tics. In addition as juvenile OCD subjects are at high risk for developing tics it follows that treatment of such children with stimulants might result in the de-novo development of tics in these patients.

The use of stimulants with children with tics or at risk for tics has been controversial. Some authors have argued that the reported worsening of tics in response to stimulants may actually be a result of the natural waxing and waning of symptoms, others reported that many patients with TS did not experience a worsening of tics, or even showed evidence of tic reduction (Gadow et al 1999, Erenberg et al 1986).

One alternative medication, which does not aggravate tics and may actually improve them is the alpha 2 nor-adrenergic agonist clonidine. However this agent has unproven efficacy for ADHD.

To clarify the optimal treatment of ADHD in children with TS the Tourette Syndrome Study Group conducted a multi-center randomized placebo control study of MPH and clonidine alone and in combination in children with TS and ADHD.

The greatest cffect on ADHD severity was observed in the combination therapy, and MPH was not shown to be more effective than clonidine. Tic severity was decreased in all treatment groups after 16 weeks of treatment. This study concluded that ADHD in the context of TS is as responsive to stimulant treatment as is primary ADHD and that the effect of stimulants on tics is not a problem(Gadow et al 1990).

Nonetheless there may still be a need for a non-stimulant treatment of ADHD in children with the potential for developing tics such as those with OCD or TS. The following non-stimulant medications have been proposed as alternative therapies for ADHD: Atomoxetine, tricyclicantidepressants, buproprion, alpha-2-agonists and Serotnin and Noradrenalin reuptake inhibitors (SNARI). Monoamineoxidase inhibitors (MAOI), buspirone, neuroleptics, cholinergic drugs.

The agent, which seems to be most promising in this context, is atomoxetine. This compound is a highly selective inhibitor of the presynaptic nor-adrenalin transporter with relatively low affinity for the serotonin (5HT) and dopamine transporter. The efficacy and tolerability of atomoxetine in ADHD has been established in many trials both open and controlled. More than 4000 subjects have been investigated and followed up for 6 months. It appears to be efficacious and safe and is the first and only non-stimulant medication approved by the FDA for the treatment of ADHD in children, adolescents and adults. Its efficacy in ADHD is comparable to that of methylphenidate. Interestingly this agent may be effective in the treatment of ADHD with concurrent depression and anxiety, symptoms that commonly occur in children and adults with OCD. Unfortunately atomoxetine has no serotonin uptake inhibitory effects and at least theoretically should not benefit patients with OCD (Witcher et al 2003).

It has been suggested that atomoxetine may influence tics since it does not have any dopaminergic effects and indeed a double blind placebo controlled trial of 18 weeks found a decrease rather than an increase of tic severity. However it should be noted that King et al., (2004) have recently reported 4 cases of children whose tics were aggravated by atomoxetine and tic severity was improved greatly when the atomoxetine was stopped.

Of particular importance in the treatment of children with combined OCD and ADHD is the fact that dosage adjustments are necessary when atomoxetine is administered with CYP2D6 inhibitors such as paroxetine and fluoxetine. Inhibition of CYP2D6 blocks the CYP2D6 mediated biotransformation of atomoxetine to 4hydroxyatomoxetin and may substantially increase the plasma concentrations of atomoxetine and N-desmethylatomoxetine. In this situation atomoxetine should be iniated with standard doses but further dose increases should be made with caution. In addition atomoxetine should not be co administered with MAOI or within 2 weeks of administration of these agents because of the risks of precipitating a "cheese reaction" or a hypertensive crisis (Michelson et al 2002).

Tricyclic antidepressants (TCA) are also of interest in the context of OCD/tic/ADHD comorbidity since they are effective antidepressant and anti-anxiety agents and those that also block 5HT uptake may also be useful in the treatment of OCD itself. Robust response rates for ADHD symptoms have been consistently reported in patients with ADHD and comorbid depression or anxiety as well as with comorbid tic disorders(Biederman et al 2000). In patients with comorbid tics and ADHD desipramine was found more effective than clonidine and was effective in reducing both tics and ADHD. The relative efficacy of TCA vs. stimulant medication has been reviewed and found to be probably less effective than stimulants (Prince et al 2000). Clomipramine the TCA effective in the treatment of OCD because of its serotonin reuptake inhibitory effects is unfortunately not very successful in the treatment of children with ADHD because of low efficacy and a high rate of intolerable side effects. Desipramine and Imipramine the TCAs most effective in ADHD have no effect on OCD. The major problem with the TCAs is there possible cardio-toxic effects. It is important to note that the cardio-toxicity of the TCAs is enhanced by concomitant stimulant medications.

Bupropion is a second line ADHD agent that is less effective than stimulants (Casat et al 1989). Since Bupropion has indirect dopaminergic effects and no serotonergic effects theoretically it may increase tics and probably is not effective in the treatment of OCD.

The alpha 2 adrenergic agonists clonidine and guanfacine are used in the treatment of ADHD although their exact mechanism of action is unclear. Low levels of nor adrenalin (NA) release as well as high levels of NA release may disrupt cognitive functioning. Thus it has been hypothesized that alpha 2 agonists may be effective in treating ADHD symptoms by a) modulating the responsiveness of locus ceruleus to sensory signals by suppressing tonic noradrenergic activity and enhancing evoked responses of its neurons via a stimulation of presynaptic alpha 2 auto receptors. b) Directly stimulating alpha 2 receptors in the posterior parietal cortex and/or in the prefrontal cortex thereby increasing signal to noise ratio, priming the posterior parietal cortex to novel stimuli and suppressing the processing of task irrelevant stimuli. However presynaptic alpha 2 receptors are widely expressed on non nor adrenergic terminal throughout the brain and it still needs to be established that these substances do not exert their effect by sedation rather than by increased cognition (Willens et al 1999). A Meta analysis of 11 studies from 1980-1999 revealed a moderate effect size for clonidine of about 0.6 on symptoms of ADHD. Desipramine seems to be superior to clonidine for the treatment of ADHD in children with comorbid tic disorder. It should be noted that clonidine is contraindicated in cases with major depression a common comorbid disorder with OCD (Connors 1999).

Neuroleptics have a role in both OCD and ADHD. In OCD particularly in tic related OCD, the OCD most commonly associated with ADHD, Neuroleptics have an important role in the treatment resistant patient as augmentation. Although often used in the treatment of ADHD they seem to be less helpful than stimulants in thc treatment of ADHD and do not reliably produce cognitive improvement (Taylor et al 2004). Evidence suggests that low doses of Risperidon are effective in reducing aggressive and disruptive behavior in children with ADHD. Since such behaviors are also common in children with OCD neuroleptic may have an important role here too. Common adverse effects include weight gain and sedation. Prolactin levels are often raised and may cause symptoms such as amenorrhea, galactorrhea, gynecomastia and sexual dysfunction. Blood glucose and lipid metabolism are sometimes altered. Thus there use is somewhat limited.

Probably the best form of therapy for juvenile OCD vulnerable to tic disorder is cognitive behavior therapy (CBT), which has been shown to be highly effective in OCD and does not have any deleterious effects on tics. However tic related OCD responds less well to CBT (as well as to SSRI) probably because the concomitant ADHD impairs the child's ability to make use of the therapy. Similarly habit reversal therapy the psychological treatment most effective in tics is much less successful in children with ADHD for the same reason. Thus the combination of OCD and ADHD remains a challenge for clinicians, which is yet to be solved.

Conclusion

The combination of ADHD and OCD is a little studied topic. However the two conditions do seem to be related and may be confused with each other. When they occur together they present difficult problems for the treating clinician. There also seem to be interesting etiological and neuro-anatomical connections between the two disorders which make this combination a subject for further study.

References

Allen AJ, Leonard HL, Swedo SE. (1995) Case study: A new infection-triggered, autoimmune subtype of pediatric OCD and Tourette's syndrome. *J Am Acad Adolesc Psychiatry*, *34*, 307-311.

Alsobrook JP 2nd, Pauls DL. (1997) The genetics of Tourette syndrome. *Neurol Clin*, *15*, 381-393.

Alsobrook JP 2nd, Zohar AH, Leboyer M, Chabane N, Ebstein RP, Pauls DL. (2002) Association between the COMT locus and obsessive-compulsive disorder in females but not males. *Am J Med Genet*, *114*, 116-120.

Biederman J, Spencer T. (2000) Non-stimulant treatments for ADHD. *Eur Child Adolesc Psychiatry*, *9 Suppl 1*, I51.

Buitelaar JK. Epidemiology of Attention-deficit/Hyperactivity Disorder: what have we learned over the last decade? In: Sandberg S (ed) *Hyperactivity Disorders*. Cambridge, Cambridge University Press, pp 30-63.

Casat CD, Pleasants DZ, Schroeder DH, Parler DW. (1989) Bupropion in children with attention deficit disorder. *Psychopharmacol Bull*, *25*, 198-201.

Channon S, Pratt P, Robertson MM. (2003) Executive function, memory, and learning in Tourette's syndrome. *Neuropsychology*, *17*, 247-254.

Comings DE, Gade-Andavolu R, Gonzalez N, Wu S, Muhleman D, Blake H, Dietz G, Saucier G, MacMurray JP. (2000) Comparison of the role of dopamine, serotonin, and noradrenaline genes in ADHD, ODD and conduct disorder: multivariate regression analysis of 20 genes. *Clin Genet*, *57*, 178-196.

Connor DF, Fletcher KE, Swanson JM. (1999) A meta-analysis of clonidine for symptoms of attention-deficit hyperactivity disorder. *J Am Acad Child Adolesc Psychiatry*, *38*, 1551-1559.

Eapen V, Robertson MM, Alsobrook JP 2nd, Pauls DL. (1997) Obsessive-compulsive symptoms in Gilles de la Tourette syndrome and obsessive-compulsive disorder: differences by diagnosis and family history. *Am J Med Genet*, *74*, 432-438.

Erenberg G, Cruse RP, Rothner AD. (1986) Tourette syndrome: an analysis of 200 pediatric and adolescent cases. *Cleve Clin Q*, *53*, 127-131.

Gadow KD, Sverd J. (1990) Stimulants for ADHD in child patients with Tourette's syndrome: the issue of relative risk. *J Dev Behav Pediatr*, *11*, 269-271; discussion 272.

Gadow KD, Sverd J, Sprafkin J, Nolan EE, Grossman S. (1999) Long-term methylphenidate therapy in children with comorbid attention-deficit hyperactivity disorder and chronic multiple tic disorder. *Arch Gen Psychiatry*, *56*, 330-336.

Geller DA, Biederman J, Griffin S, Jones J, Lefkowitz TR. (1996) Comorbidity of juvenile obsessive-compulsive disorder with disruptive behavior disorders. *J Am Acad Child Adolesc Psychiatry*, *35*, 1637-1646.

Geller DA, Biederman J, Faraone S, Spencer T, Doyle R, Mullin B, Magovcevic M, Zaman N, Farrell C. (2004) Re-examining comorbidity of Obsessive-Compulsive and Attention-Deficit Hyperactivity Disorder using an empirically derived taxonomy. *Eur Child Adolesc Psychiatry*, *13*, 83-91.

Gillberg C, Gillberg IC, Rasmussen P, Kadesjo B, Soderstrom H, Rastam M, Johnson M, Rothenberger A, Niklasson L. (2004) Co-existing disorders in ADHD-implications for diagnosis and intervention. *Eur Child Adolesc Psychiatry*, *13*, 180-192.

Jaisoorya TS, Janardhan Reddy YC, Srinath S. (2003) Is juvenile obsessive-compulsive disorder a developmental subtype of the disorder? *European Child Adolesc Psychiatry*, *12*, 290-297.

Kotsopoulos S, Spivak M. (2001) Obsessive-compulsive symptoms secondary to methylphenidate treatment. *Can J Psychiatry*, *46*, 89.

Lee TS, Lee TD, Lombroso PJ, King RA. (2004) Atomoxetine and tics in ADHD. *J Am Acad Child Adolesc Psychiatry*, *43*, 1068-1069.

McMahon WM, Carter AS, Fredine N, Pauls DL. (2003) Children at familial risk for Tourette's disorder: Child and parent diagnoses. *Am J Med Genet*, *15*,105-111.

Michelson D, Allen AJ, Busner J, Casat C, Dunn D, Kratochvil C, Newcorn J, Sallee FR, Sangal RB, Saylor K, West S, Kelsey D, Wernicke J, Trapp NJ, Harder D. (2002) Once-daily atomoxetine treatment for children and adolescents with attention deficit hyperactivity disorder: a randomized, placebo-controlled study. *Am J Psychiatry*, *159*, 1896-1901.

Moll GH, Eysenbach K, Woerner W, Banaschewski T, Schmidt MH, Rothenberger A. (2000) Quantitative and qualitative aspects of obsessive-compulsive behaviour in children with attention-deficit hyperactivity disorder compared with tic disorder. *Acta Psychiatr Scand*, *101*, 389-394.

Nestadt G, Samuels J, Riddle M, Bienvenu OJ 3rd, Liang KY, LaBuda M, Walkup J, Grados M, Hoehn-Saric R. (2000) A family study of obsessive-compulsive disorder. *Arch Gen Psychiatry*, *57*, 358-363.

Pauls DL, Pakstis AJ, Kurlan R, Kidd KK, Leckman JF, Cohen DJ, Kidd JR, Como P, Sparkes R. (1990) Segregation and linkage analyses of Tourette's syndrome and related disorders. *J Am Acad Child Adolesc Psychiatry*, *29*, 195-203.

Pauls DL, Alsobrook JP 2nd, Almasy L, et al. (1991) Genetic and epidemiological analyses of the Yale Tourette's Syndrome Family Study data. *Psychiatr Genet*, *2*, 28.

Peterson BS, Pine DS, Cohen P, Brook JS. (2001) Prospective, longitudinal study of tic, obsessive-compulsive, and attention deficit/hyperactivity disorders in an epidemiological sample. *J Am Acad Child Adolesc Psychiatry*, *40*, 685-695.

Prince JB, Wilens TE, Biederman J, Spencer TJ, Millestein R, PolisnerDA, Bostic JQ, (2000) A controlled study of nortriptyline in children and adolescents with attention deficit hyperactivity disorder: a systematic chart reviewof 62 cases. *J Child Adolesc Psychopharmacol*, *10*, 193-204.

Singer HS, Giuliano JD, Hansen B. (1997) Antibodies to human basal ganglia and antistreptococcal antibodies in Tourette's syndrome [Abstract]. *Ann Neurol*, *42*, 53.

Swedo SE, Rapoport JL, Leonard H, Lenane M, Cheslow D. (1989) Obsessive-compulsive disorder in children and adolescents. Clinical phenomenology of 70 consecutive cases. *Arch Gen Psychiatry*, *46,* 335-341.

Swedo SE, Kilpatrick K, Shapiro MB, Mannheim G, Leonard HL. (1991) Antineuronal antibodies (AnA) in Sydenham's chorea (SC) and obsessive-compulsive disorder (OCD) [Abstract]. *Pediatric Res*, *29*, 364A.

Taylor E, Dopfner M, Sergeant J, Asherson P, Banaschewski T, Buitelaar J, Coghill D, Danckaerts M, Rothenberger A, Sonuga-Barke E, Steinhausen HC, Zuddas A. (2004) European clinical guidelines for hyperkinetic disorder - first upgrade. *Eur Child Adolesc Psychiatry*, *13 Suppl 1*, I7-I30.

The Tourette's Syndrome Study Group. (2002) Treatment of ADHD in children with tics: A randomized controlled trail. *Neurology*, *58*, 527-536

Todd RD, Rasmussen ER, Neuman RJ, Reich W, Hudziak JJ, Bucholz KK, Madden PA, Heath A. (2001) Familiality and heritability of subtypes of attention deficit hyperactivity disorder in a population sample of adolescent female twins. *Am J Psychiatry*, *158*, 1891-1898.

Wilens TE, Spencer TJ, Swanson JM, Connor DF, Cantwell D. (1999) Combining methylphenidate and clonidine: a clinically sound medication option. *J Am Acad Child Adolesc Psychiatry*, *38*, 614-619; discussion 619-22.

Witcher JW, Long A, Smith B, Sauer JM, Heilgenstein J, Wilens T, Spencer T, Biederman J. (2003) Atomoxetine pharmacokinetics in children and adolescents with attention deficit hyperactivity disorder. *J Child Adolesc Psychopharmacol*, *13*, 53.

In: Obsessive-Compulsive Disorder and Comorbidity ISBN 1-59454-884-6
Editors: R. Gross-Isseroff and A. Weizman, pp. 59-102

Chapter 6

AUTISM SPECTRUM DISORDERS, AUTISTIC TRAITS AND PERSONALITY DISORDERS IN OBSESSIVE-COMPULSIVE DISORDER

Susanne Bejerot
Karolinska Institutet, Department of Clinical Neuroscience, Psychiatry Section, Stockholm, Sweden

ABSTRACT

Approximately 20% of the clinical cases with obsessive-compulsive disorder (OCD) display autistic traits. These traits are often described as schizotypal personality disorder. Conversely, repetitive patterns of behaviours, sometimes difficult to separate from compulsions in OCD are included in diagnostic criteria for autism spectrum disorders (ASD, e.g. Childhood autism and Asperger syndrome). Moreover the "comorbidity" between OCD and tic disorders, and tics and ASD is significant. Frequently the OCD-autistic group are non-responders to medication and cognitive behaviour therapy (CBT). Since they are often excluded from pharmaceutical and CBT treatment trials due to "comorbid" schizotypal personality disorder, at present, treatment options are poorly studied.

Subjects with OCD and autistic traits are usually perceived as odd or aloof. They lack in emotional reciprocity and capacity to appeal. Instead they are considered as shy, inflexible or factual. Anxiety is rarely exposed by facial expressions, body language or tone of voice but often reported by the patient if he/she is actively asked about it. Although the OCD-autistic group may lack full insight into their OCD, they may well seek treatment due to distress caused by consequences of their obsessions and compulsions.

Significant differences in personality dimensions have been detected with a novel classification of OCD subtypes based on the presence of autistic traits or a history of tics. Those with autistic traits had often been clumsy as children and severely bullied at school. As adults they tend to live alone with little or no sexual experiences and are seldom parents. They are often hoarders, they may suffer from self-harming compulsions, and their global functioning is lower compared to other OCD patients. They usually fulfil the diagnostic criteria for a number of personality disorders but lack impulsive traits. Several patients will have family members diagnosed with autism or Asperger syndrome. The OCD-autistic group is proposed to be a form fruste of autism spectrum disorders and a valid endo-phenotype.

CASE REPORT: NOAH

Noah was an only child. His mother died when Noah was a young teenager. The father reported that the mother suffered from OCD with various cleaning rituals. Noah was an early learner; at the age of four he read and wrote fluently and he excelled all through school. When he finished at the age of 17 he had top grades in nearly all subjects and expected to have a bright future. He studied economics but dropped out after a year and never returned to studies due to severe OCD symptoms. Already at the age of 11, Noah experienced his first obsessions: Could a paper get stuck behind a radiator and cause fire? This obsession made him check behind the radiators repeatedly. With age he developed an extremely severe OCD, including most symptoms in the Y-BOCS checklist, in addition his obsessions had a considerable magical content. Certain combinations of numbers and words, related to death, frightened him. An uncle who lived in a Swedish suburb named Kista, which in Swedish spells (but is not pronounced) as the word coffin, died unexpectedly. Thereafter Noah refused to visit the suburb, as the word similarities in combination with the sudden death of his uncle made him feel uneasy. He felt that new deaths might follow visits to the suburb. Apart from this he did not appear particularly superstitious. However, he only wore certain clothes that made him feel safe, and only cut his hair at a certain day once a year, which also felt "safe" or just right for him.

Noah was religious but did not attend church. However, he had a strong fear that he might get absorbed in a religious, strict life and consequently be forced to refrain from the "good in life". On the other hand, Noah already avoided what many would refer to as "good in life"; he never drank alcohol and he avoided sexual relations from fear of contracting sexually transmitted diseases. This fear also led him to refrain from brushing his teeth, which he explained logically as follows "Several men at the restaurant where I have my luncheon appear homosexual, thus they are at risk of contracting aids. I can't trust the quality of the restaurant's dish washing, and can't exclude the possibility that HIV virus might spread through the use of forks and knives. I therefore have come to the conclusion that if I brush my teeth, my gum might bleed, and turn into a gateway for catching aids." His reasoning was logic, but did not make sense. Noah lacked insight and subsequently did not resist his intrusive thoughts.

Noah had problems passing doors, he could get stuck and it could take him hours to pass the main entrance to the hospital or to get on the train. At times he could not even get home but would remain at his work place all night standing outside the door. His personal hygiene represented another great problem; Noah was dirty at times even smelly. Previously, however, he had been a compulsive washer. Gradually, taking a bath had become exceedingly complicated and a bath lasted for at least three hours. Accordingly showers were avoided altogether. The morning rituals took him hours to complete, which in turn made him late for work. Although Noah often was irritated at home with his father and shouted at him, he was friendly with his co-workers. His insufficiency however resulted in conflicts. Eventually Noah at the age of 32 was referred to a psychiatric hospital and was diagnosed as schizophrenic, although he had never experienced any psychotic symptoms. Noah refused drug treatments; he believed that medication might cause him harm, at least in a distant future. In addition, he did not agree to participate in cognitive behaviour therapy when this was offered to him. His OCD has deteriorated and after living more or less independently he now, at the age of 45 lives in a home for chronic schizophrenic patients. Fixed ideas and rituals fill his day.

High-functioning autism or Asperger syndrome has not been discussed as possible differential diagnoses until recently although he in fact fits the diagnostic criteria. In line with this diagnoses, Noah has only two friends, and has never experienced a romantic or sexual relationship. He is extremely interested in various intellectual topics, and he was already as a child referred to as the "little professor". He stands out by an impressive memory for facts and is talkative and hard to interrupt. In addition he has a formal, pedantic language and does not hesitate to correct other people's grammar in a conversation. He is not a good listener, and can only talk of things he has interest in. He resists any changes in his life, and refuses to leave the institution even for a short trip into town. Is Noah a case of a gifted boy turning into a chronic OCD patient, or the case of a boy with Asperger syndrome who developed catatonia and repetitive behaviours? I would suggest the latter.

Case Report: Tom

Tom, today age 60, had his first contact with the child psychiatric unit at the age of 4, due to anxiety. He always clinged to his parents, he feared leaving home, and doing anything on his own. Since the age of two, he was uninterested in food and could go without for days. Already in early childhood his social interaction was poor, and other children beat him. Tom's parents explained that Tom lacked ability to respond; he never showed signs of sadness, anger or fear when hit by others, and was extremely capable of tolerating physical pain. Additionally Tom was unable to organize his own things and left everything in complete disorder.

Tom's teacher reported that the boy was not concentrating, living in his own world, and hard to understand. Therefore it was often impossible to establish contact with him. Tom could sit and sing or speak to himself during the lessons, but when reminded of his behaviour he would stop and follow the lesson for a while. He was a late reader, he also found writing and mathematics difficult, but was able to attend a normal class. At home he became irritable and demanding and he regressed in his speech. He refused to speak properly and to dress himself without assistance. The child psychologist described Tom as a stiff, inhibited and passive boy. In a play observation situation, Tom didn't play with the toys, but just placed them out on the floor. Repeatedly he rubbed his hand against each other, and flexed his elbows as he walked.

At the age of 18 he was described as a quiet young man with learning problems and he had few, if any, friends. He left school and worked as a newspaper distributor for a while, but soon received sick pension. At 30 he lacked ability to form acquaintances, relate to others, he was passive and unable to hold a job. His favourite topics, which he spoke of in lengths, were clean-living, healthy lifestyle, ecology and jazz music. He followed a strict unbalanced diet and was under-weight. He was described by a psychiatrist as a man with severe problems with social interaction. Tom had lost his front teeth in an accident and had a permanent gold bridge installed which he later wanted removed, in his mind the bridge contained cadmium causing an allergy of a facial rash. Tom explained that the cadmium was placed in the bridge by "multinational companies". When the dentist refused to remove the bridge, Tom saw it off by himself. He was also afraid of being contaminated by others with gold bridges, and avoided close contact with such people. The psychiatrist described him as an odd man who lacked face movement and didn't smile. His emotional contact was poor. During the consultation Tom screw up his eyes, put his hands over the face in a strange way, and responded in detail to every question, anxious about being misunderstood. Tom developed more obsessions in 1986, as a result of the nuclear plant accident in Chernobyl. He was convinced that his apartment was contaminated by radioactive dust. He moved back into his parents' home. Since then he has been obsessed by fear from electromagnetic radiation and power cables, and distressed by the risk of having a burglary. In addition he was terrified of the risk of how stress and anxiety could affect his brain and also he was afraid of the risk of vitamin deficiency. He suffered from tinnitus but refused all medications as he wanted to live without artificial influence. However, in 2002 haloperidol was prescribed as Tom was viewed as paranoid. One of his obsessions was the distressing thought that a bookshelf was liable to fall on him in his home. Another symptom was a great fear of dust which in his opinion would cause obstructive pulmonary disease. As he was unable to keep his home clean and orderly and refused outside help he finally moved back into his parent's home. There he spent his day checking the stove and faucets for at least thirty minutes a day. He eventually refused leaving the house at all as he obsessed that he might become stuck during checking the out side door and instead avoided it all together. He became more desperate and finally accepted haloperidol but it proved ineffective and eventually he developed suicidal thoughts. Finally he was therefore admitted to a psychiatric hospital for a week where the treatment was changed into sertraline 150 mg per day, this soon resulted in great improvement. Tom suffered from fewer obsessions and compulsions and he could return to his own home, participate in daily activities and generally felt much better.

Tom's showed all the hallmarks of autism spectrum disorder (high functioning autism or Asperger syndrome) with social and communicative impairment, lack of imagination and distorted perceptions. These impairments could explain his obsessions and delusions. Consequently his OCD was misdiagnosed as a psychotic disorder, but his condition did not improve from neuroleptics, but as a result of treatment with a serotonin reuptake inhibitor. Tom clearly suffered from both autism spectrum disorder and OCD.

Autism Spectrum Disorders (ASD)

Lorna Wing (1997) suggested the use of the term autistic spectrum for a group of disorders of development, with life-long effects. They share a triad of impairment in social interaction, communication, imagination but also behaviour is affected and is typically described as restricted and repetitive pattern of behaviour. Wing points out that the variations within the triad of symptoms depend on the person's ability. Autism spectrum disorders

(ASD) include "autistic disorder", "Asperger disorder" and "pervasive developmental disorders not otherwise specified" (PDD-NOS) according to the diagnostic criteria for DSM-IV and "Childhood autism", "Atypical autism" and "Asperger syndrome" according to International Classification of diseases (ICD-10). They are all classified as Pervasive developmental disorders.

Table 1. The diagnostic criteria for Autistic Disorder according to DSM-IV (American Psychiatric Association, 1994) are as follows.

A. A total of six (or more) items from (1), (2), and (3), with at least two from (1), and one of each from (2) and (3):
   (1) qualitative impairment in social interaction, as manifested by at least two of the following:
      (a) marked impairment in the use of multiple non-verbal behaviours such as eye-to-eye gaze, facial expression, body postures, and gestures to regulate social interaction
      (b) failure to develop peer relationships appropriate to developmental level
      (c) a lack of spontaneous seeking to share enjoyment, interests, or achievements with other people (e.g., by a lack of showing, bringing, or pointing out objects of interest)
      (d) lack of social or emotional reciprocity
   (2) qualitative impairment in communication as manifested by at least one of the following:
      (a) delay in, or lack of, the development of spoken language (not accompanied by an attempt to compensate through alternative modes of communication such as gesture or mime)
      (b) in individuals with adequate speech, marked impairment in the ability to initiate or sustain a conversation with others
      (c) stereotyped and repetitive use of language or idiosyncratic language
      (d) lack of varied, spontaneous make-believe play or social imitative play appropriated to developmental level
   (3) restricted repetitive and stereotyped patterns of behaviour, interests and activities as manifested by at least one of the following:
      (a) encompassing preoccupation with one or more stereotyped and restricted patterns of interest that is abnormal either in intensity or focus
      (b) apparently inflexible adherence to specific, non-functional routines or rituals
      (c) stereotyped and repetitive motor mannerism (e.g., hand or finger flapping or twisting, or complex whole-body movements)
      (d) persistent preoccupation of parts of objects

B. Delays or abnormal functioning in at least one of the following areas, with onset prior to age 3 years: (1) social interaction, (2) language as used in social communication, or (3) symbolic or imaginative play.

C. The disturbance is not better accounted for by Rett's Disorder or Childhood Disintegrative Disorder.

The spectrum includes but is wider than the syndromes originally described by Leo Kanner and Hans Asperger. ASD can be viewed as inborn personality and cognitive disorders with a life-long duration. However the understanding of ASD as an unchanging personality trait fails to fully appreciate the developmental aspects of the disorders (Klim & Volkmar, 2004). ASD affects at least half a percent of the general population (Gillberg & Billstedt, 2000). Amazingly, a 556% increase in paediatric prevalence has been reported between 1991 and1997, but this jump is probably attributable to heightened awareness and changing diagnostic criteria rather than to new environmental influences. ASD is a syndrome with multiple nongenetic and genetic causes. Data from whole-genome screens in multiplex families suggest interactions of at least 10 genes in the causation of autism (Muhle et al, 2004). Males are affected with ASD three-four times more often than females, but among those with profound disabilities the male excess is less pronounced than for those with higher ability (Wing, 1997). This may be explained by the differences in social cognition skills between normal girls and boys (Scourfield et al,1999); girls are significantly superior to boys. Subsequently females with ASD may go unrecognized, which can explain the male preponderance among the high functioning ASD group.

Childhood Autism - Autistic Disorder

Leo Kanner published his original paper on autism in 1943 where he described extremely aloof children with an anxiously obsessive desire for the preservation of sameness. He referred to their pattern of behaviour as "early infantile autism". Kanner and Eisenberg revised this description of autism in 1956 by adding the extreme self-isolation and an anxiously obsessive desire for the preservation of sameness manifested as preoccupation with “elaborately conceived rituals” (Kanner & Eisenberg, 1956). Persons, who fulfil the criteria for autism, are perceived to have at least normal cognitive ability or even within the superior range, are often referred to as "high-functioning autism".

Pervasive Developmental Disorder not Otherwise Specified (Including Atypical Autism)

Pervasive developmental disorder not otherwise specified (PDD-NOS) is a definition that can be used when the person has symptom in the autistic field without quite meeting the diagnostic criteria for Asperger disorder or autistic disorder. It is often referred to as “atypical autism”. Atypical autism/ PDD-NOS can be atypical in regard to age onset, symptomatology or both according to ICD-10 and DSM-IV.

Subgrouping Autism Spectrum Disorders

The autistic spectrum (ASD) includes persons with varied levels of impairments in social interaction, communication, imagination and behaviour (narrow and repetitive pattern of behaviour) (Wing, 1997). *Social impairment* can vary from aloofness and indifference to active but inappropriate social approaches; *Communication impairment* can vary between complete absence of any form of communication, apart from disturbed behaviour, up to fluent speech with excellent grammar and vocabulary used only to talk about things of interests to the person concerned; *Imagination impairment* can vary from handling objects for simple sensation up to the invention of a complete idiosyncratic, imaginary world based on set rules that are complex but rigid; *Repetitive activities and routines* can vary from simple bodily movements to complex intellectual rituals.

Table 2. The DSM-IV definition of Asperger disorder (APA, 1994).

A. Qualitative impairment in social interaction, as manifested by at least two of the following:
   (1) marked impairment in the use of multiple nonverbal behaviours such as eye-to eye gaze, facial expressin, body postures, and gestures to regulate social interaction
   (2) failure to develop peer relationships appropriate to developmental level
   (3) a lack of spontaneous seeking to share enjoyment, interests, or achievements with other people
   (4) lack of social or emotional reciprocity
B. Restricted repetitive and stereotyped patterns of behaviour, interests and activities as manifested by at least one of the following:
   (1) encompassing preoccupation with one or more stereotyped and restricted patterns of interest that is abnormal either in intensity or focus
   (2) apparently inflexible adherence to specific, non-functional routines or rituals
   (3) stereotyped and repetitive motor mannerism
   (4) persistent preoccupation of parts of objects.
C. The disturbance causes clinically significant impairment in social occupational, or other important areas of functioning
D. There is no clinically significant delay in language (e.g. single words used by the age of 2 years, communicative phrases used by age of 3 years)
E. There is no clinically or delay significant delay in cognitive development or in the development of age-appropriate self-help skills, adaptive behaviour (other than social interaction), and curiosity about the environment in childhood
F. Criteria are not met for other specific Pervasive Developmental Disorder or Schizophrenia.

Accordingly there is no clear distinction between Asperger syndrome and Kanner's syndrome, rather it is a continuum that "ranges from the most profoundly physically and mentally retarded person, who has social impairment as one item among a multitude of problems, to the most able, highly intelligent person with social impairment in its subtlest form as his only disability" (Wing, 1991). Wing states that some children's autism may develop into Asperger syndrome or blend into normality with age, albeit in the eccentric span in adulthood, which highlights the plasticity of the symptomatology. The clinical picture of Asperger syndrome is strikingly similar to obsessive-compulsive personality disorder according to DSM-IV (Gillberg & Billstedt, 2000).

Wing has suggested a subgrouping of the autistic spectrum for clinical practice based solely on a description of the type of social impairment (1997): The Aloof group, Passive group, Active but odd group and the Loners:

The Aloof Group - The aloof group is the traditional definition of childhood autism with higher levels of skills in visuospatial tasks or rote memory. Most of them have cognitive ability below the normal range. The patterns of activities is dominated by repetitive routines such as putting objects in straight lines or insisting on lengthy routines that can dominate family life as the persons may have tantrums if any changes is introduced.

Passive Group - The group of children who are defined as "passive" do not spontaneously interact with other children but accept approaches from others. They are less likely to get upset if interrupted in their repetitive routines. Their problems are less obvious than in the aloof group.

Active but Odd Group - This group tend to fit into the Asperger group; they make social approaches in a one-sided, naïve and odd way. The repetitive routines are within the special interest field, as time tables, or for instance species of birds, and the interests may change from time to time. They have an inquiring mind for facts. Stubbornness is common, some may have behaviour difficulties with verbal and physical aggression, especially as young.

Loners - This group is the most subtle form of the triad according to Wing. This group may have normal to outstanding abilities including fluent speech. They tend to find the world confusing and stressful but as adults they might have successful academic careers. They may learn how to manage social interaction by rote, or live alone.

Additional Clinical Features

Other very common symptoms in ASD, but not included in the diagnostic criteria for autism or Asperger syndrome are *abnormal response to sensory stimuli*; a background sound, dazzling light, shades, a light touch, a slight smell, warmth, chilliness, sticky fingers, prickly clothes, a pair of tight trousers or a piece of jewellery might be perceived by the person as unbearable and agonizing to see, hear, smell, feel, watch or just sense. The *activity level* is often high, at least in children and *attention span* low, which may lead the clinician to diagnose an ADHD, if not aware of the underlying ASD. Some of the children may have symptoms seen in the inattentive type of ADHD, with passivity and a blank stare. Many persons with ASD *stares blankly* into the blue for lengths of time (Kobayashi & Murata, 1998) *Aggressive behaviours*, and *self-injury* are often reported (Gillberg & Coleman, 2000). Sometimes self-injury is though to be a kind of *self-stimulation* as rocking, due to abnormal response to sensory stimuli. Commonly seen *personality traits* in the high functioning group are stubbornness, inability to take advice and a tendency to take offence. *Food fads* are common; many refuse to eat anything but certain things, with acceptable consistence, ingredients or colour. Veganism and vegetarianism appear to be much more common than in the normal population according to our observations. Difficulties with sleep and *abnormal sleep patterns* with early awakening can be expected. Persons with ASD often have an *awkward gait pattern* and have deficits in visual-motor coordination. *Clumsiness* should be expected, especially in those with Asperger syndrome (Gillberg, 1991). Their way of *clothing* may contribute to certain strangeness, as they don't spontaneously know what clothes are suitable for the situation and they usually prefer "loose-fit". Although a person has fluent speech and normal prosody there may be *semantic-pragmatic problems* which can be observed during a conversion, i.e. the person might start to speak abruptly without a warning, suddenly and unexpectedly shift topics or misunderstands irony and jokes. Presence of pragmatic difficulties in a person with communication problems should prompt the clinician to evaluate autistic symptomatology, but it is dangerous to assume that all children with pragmatic difficulties have autism or ASD (Bishop & Norbury, 2002).

Physical anomalies, epilepsy, and problems with vision and hearing along with other specific syndromes are common in ASD (Wing, 1997), especially among those with low intelligence. Minor physical anomalies as large head circumference, but also flatfoot and low muscular tonus are frequently observed in the whole group.

Many adults with Asperger syndrome look strikingly young for their age (Gillberg, 1995), which also holds true for the whole group with ASD. Moreover males often lack in masculinity and virility and the opposite is often noted among the females. A lack of sex drive or *homosexuality* are often reported and occasionally also *gender identity disorder*. Interestingly one of Hans Asperger´s few original cases "Harro L", a bright eight year boy with conduct problems, involved himself in homosexual acts.

In conclusion there are no neat cut-off points between autism, Asperger syndrome and PDD-NOS. The triad of autistic symptoms can occur on its own but is very often found in association with other problems, summarized in Table 3 (Wing, 2002).

Table 3. Symptoms that can occur along with Autism spectrum disorders Published with kind permission from L Wing, 2004

- Impairment of cognitive ability
- Impairment of language comprehension and use
- Unusual responses to sensory stimuli
- Unusual patterns of posture and movement
- Abnormalities of attention and activity level
- Disturbance of behaviour
- Abnormalities of eating, drinking and sleeping
- Any kind of developmental, physical or psychiatric condition

Psychiatric Symptoms and Disorders, Commonly Seen in ASD

Depression is common both among children (Ghaziuddin & Greden, 1998), adolescents (Green et al, 2000) and adults with ASD, even suicide attempts are reported as relatively common (Wing, 1981). Among adults with Asperger syndrome, depressions are frequently their primary reason to seek professional help. In a follow up of 187 young adults with autism (Kobayashi & Murata, 1998) of whom a quarter were of normal intelligence, 47% were reported to be moody at least to some degree, *nervousness* was reported in 66% of the cases and 35% were described as fearful and anxious. *Social and separation anxiety* were reported in high functioning children with autism more often compared to children with specific language impairment or normally developing children (Gillottet al, 2001). Also ASD may cause *social anxiety* due to low communicative and social abilities and could be misdiagnosed as social phobia (Schneier et al, 2002). Contrary to "real" social phobia, the patient with ASD will be socially impaired not only in groups or with peers but also in a one-to-one setting. In addition, according to my experience tremor and blushing are less common in the ASD group contrary to the social phobia group, see social anxiety spectrum *p. x* in this chapter. Many persons with ASD will be perceived to suffer from *generalized anxiety disorder* as these unspecific symptoms are common in ASD. About every patient will complain of being easily fatigued, irritability, muscle tension, sleep disturbances, concentration difficulties along with a certain amount of anxiety, complains and worry. Additionally many will suffer from gastrointestinal symptoms.

Several adults with ASD have reported severe *anxiety* in their biographies (Brattberg 1999; Williams, 1993; Grandin 1996; Gerland,1997), perhaps secondary to the lack of ability to process information from the surrounding world. However, as persons with ASD lack ability to communicate her feelings by words and physical clues i.e. facial expression, body language or tone of voice, their high anxiety level is far from obvious. Rather the contrary is true; the patient may appear to be overly controlled with an indifferent stone-face look. Through the glasses of the clinician, the patient may be perceived as suffering from *alexitymia* or intellectualizing the problems. Panic disorder is a "communicative" disorder: the patient sends a strong appeal to the care-giver, and refrains from being alone. Not surprisingly, panic disorder seems, according to my observations, less common in ASD.

In a controlled follow up of patients with *anorexia nervosa* 18% had ASD (Nilsson et al, 1999). Anorexia nervosa in males is rare, but we have had a case of ASD and OCD, who had starved himself as he believed this "cleaning process" would cure his OCD (it didn't). Obsessive-compulsive personality disorder is much more common in persons with eating disorder than would be expected. Two-thirds of the patients with anorexia nervosa and approximately one-third of the patients with bulimia nervosa reported perfectionism and traits reflecting rigidity in childhood (Anderluh et al, 2003). Over-eating is less common than anorexia but has also been reported among persons with ASD (Gillberg & Billstedt, 2000).

Several researchers have reported a high incidence of attention deficit and hyperactivity in ASD (Ghaziuddin et al, 1998; Eaves et al,1994; Noterdaeme et al, 2001; Ståhlberg et al, 2004). In addition autistic traits and ASD are common in *ADHD* (Clark et al., 1999). However impulsivity is not common in ASD at least among those without tics, which probably is the reason for low prevalence of smoking in this group (Bejerot & Nylander, 2003).

Patients with ASD frequently exhibit repetitive movements (stereotypies) (Turner, 1999), but also motor and phonic *tics* are common (Ringman & Jankovic, 2000; Kadesjö & Gillberg, 2000). In conclusion many of the non-psychotic psychiatric symptoms and disorders overlap with ASD, see *Figure 1*.

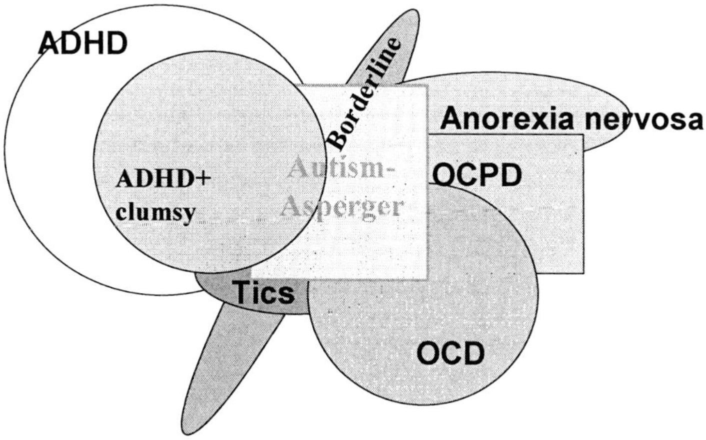

Figure 1. Psychiatric disorders that frequently overlap with Autism and Asperger syndrome. Based on C Gillberg: Differential diagnosis in autism. Overlap with other clinical syndromes (Gillberg, 1992). ADHD=attention deficit hyperactivity disorder, OCPD=obsessive-compulsive personality disorder, OCD=Obsessive-compulsive disorder. Printed with kind permission from C Gillberg, 2004.

Also symptoms that commonly are associated with schizophrenia may overlap with ASD. For instance Catatonia, in its various shapes, appears to be a late complication of ASD (Wing & Shah, 2000) and is rarely reported in children below the age of 15, see p. x in this chapter. Auditory hallucinations are rare in ASD but hypersensitivity to sound or an extremely good hearing may be misdiagnosed as schizophrenic symptoms. Some will be treated as suffering from schizophrenia as well, and may respond well to antipsychotic medication as they may function as a "filter" for overwhelming perceptions. Probably many are being diagnosed as suffering from personality disorders (Wing, 1981). Schizoid personality disorder lacks a link to schizophrenia (Fulton & Winokur, 1993) and in children it is regarded as similar to Asperger syndrome (Wolff, 1991). The patients with ASD may develop a picture identical to schizotypal personality disorder (Wolff & McGuir, 1995) and/or obsessive-compulsive personality disorder (Gillberg & Billstedt, 2000). Others will be avoidant to the extent of matching the diagnosis of selective mutism (Gillberg & Billstedt, 2000). Female ASD patients with a combination of self-harm, anxiety, depression, feeling of emptiness and perhaps eating disorder are probably diagnosed as borderline personality disorder. Some persons with ASD will mimic others or try to take on "a personality" and show signs of identity confusion which at least in the US may lead to the diagnoses dissociative identity disorder, previously referred to as multiple personality disorder. Abuse is often reported in both dissociative identity disorder and in ASD. Moreover, delusional disorder, and overvalued ideas can be expected to be common (Wing, 1981) due to the disability in ASD to comprehend the codes in the surrounding world. Erroneously some persons with ASD will be diagnosed as suffering from paranoid psychosis, partly due to their sensitivity and partly due to over- suspiciousness based on a long history of being bullied, criticized and made fun of (Wing, 1981). Women with erotomania are characterized by avoidant and/or paranoid premorbid personality traits with difficulties in establishing relationships, and life-long social isolation (Retterstøl & Opjordsmoen, 1991). This clinical picture links nicely to Wing's description of "the loners" with ASD. Furthermore, stalking has been identified in persons diagnosed with ASD (Heden & Kristiansson, 2003). In addition, dogmatism and opinionatedness, i.e. a proneness to legal complaints and lawsuits, are common features in persons with Asperger syndrome. Several of my patients run various legal processes, due to meticulous interpretations of laws and rules, stubbornness, high verbal ability and lack of common sense. They may present a number of neat files with extensive correspondences with authorities over small matters. Although crime can be expected to be rare among persons with ASD, this group is in fact over-represented in a forensic setting: Four percent (N= 4, two men and two women) fulfilled the DSM-IV criteria for autistic disorder or Asperger disorder in a study of 100 inmates. They were convicted of arson, drug trafficking, robbery and murder (Söderström & Nilsson, 2003). Rituals or compulsions can be expected in ASD which is the obvious reason that many will be diagnosed with obsessive-compulsive disorder.

Stereotypies – Tics – Obsessions – Repetitive Interests – Repetitive Pattern of Activities – Rituals – Compulsions

Stereotypies refer to the excessive production of one type of motor act, or mental state, which necessarily results in repetition, is suggested to be related to the excess dopaminergic activity in the basal ganglia (Ridley, 1994). Stereotypies may represent a degree of detachment from the environment due to a disturbed interaction. In congenitally blind persons stereotyped behaviours is common (Fazzi et al, 1999), due to sensory deprivation since infancy, i.e. they are not able to make sense of incoming information at a critical period of development (Ridley, 1994). Analogues processes may very well be the cause for stereotypies or elaborate motor routines, in autism as well. There are no set rules for what behaviours are defined as stereotypies. Some less complex sterotypies such as tiptoe-walking and hand-flapping, are by some authors included among the elaborated repetitive routines (Gillberg & Coleman, 2000). In addition stereotypies are not always easy to distinguish from simple or complex motor tics (Comings, 1990). Moreover, complex motor tics are not easily distinguished from compulsions, and whether spitting, smelling, touching, tapping and rubbing are tics, compulsions, self-stimulation or just "odd behaviours" is not always easy to sort out. Persons with Gilles de la Tourettes reported significantly more 'impulsions' which are specific and non-anxiety-related phenomena. These impulsions possibly reflect differences in underlying mechanisms between Gilles de la Tourettes and OCD with tics (Cath et al, 2001). Impulsions and stereotypies may also be difficult to distinguish.

Gillberg and Coleman (2000) points out the bizarre attachment, sometimes referred to as "obsessions", to certain objects or parts of objects that is frequently seen in children with autism (such as stones, curls of hair, pins), parts of metal or plastic toys or objects that glitters (glasses, ear-rings etc.). These objects are usually selected because of some particular quality (e.g. colour, surface texture) and the child become distressed if someone tries to remove them. Other children with autism have repetitive patterns of activities as to line up toys or household equipment for hours, perhaps in order to reach a certain "just-right feeling". Others will be extremely fascinated or obsessed by round and spinning objects as coins or wheels of toy-cars, perhaps a form of self-stimulation. Need for certain rigid routines that need to be followed in detail are commonly seen in persons with autism. "Insistence of sameness" is mostly seen in relation to things or how activities are carried out, but can also be expressed as a demand that only certain words or phrases are used, or restriction of topics to be talked about, as for instance special interests. If things are not said in the "correct order" according to the patient, or if "bad words" are used the patient may get upset. But also normal activities, as taking a shower or having a collection of some items, may well turn into exaggerated and complex routines in more able persons with ASD. These tendencies probably reflect different types of perseverative behaviour i.e. restriction of behavioural possibilities without excessive motor activity, indicating frontal lobe dysfunction (Ridley, 1994).

Francesca Happé suggests that it is the odd focus and subject of the autistic person's anxiety and attention, i.e. the peculiar attachment of importance to apparently irrelevant things, that makes the person seem obsessive (Happé, 1991).

Obsessions and Rituals in ASD

There is an ongoing discussion on whether rituals and obsessions in persons with autism could be regarded as OCD or not. Many of the behaviours seen in ASD appear to the observer as identical to those in OCD, others are quite different. Several behaviours considered as typical for OCD are more common in ASD than expected. In a group of children with high-functioning autism, normally developed children and children with language impairment, the ASD children were more likely to score high on a subscale for measuring obsessive-compulsive disorder, than the other two groups (Gillott et al, 2001). Moreover, rituals and repetitive routines in autism are not only common in autism; they are also persistent over time (Kobayashi & Murata, 1998) as in the case of OCD. McDougle and co-workers (1995), reported that certain compulsions as repetitive ordering, hoarding, touching, tapping or rubbing, and self-damaging or self-mutilating behaviours occurred significantly more frequently among persons with autism than among persons with OCD without tics, however a substantial proportion of the patients in this study were mentally retarded. Recently, a controlled study was conducted on 40 subjects with ASD, 12 fulfilled the diagnostic criteria for OCD, moreover 16 subjects reported moderate or above levels of interference from the compulsions (Russell et al, in press). In an American study the Structured clinical interview for DSM (SCID) was applied on subjects with OCD in order to assess comorbidity (LaSalle et al, 2004). Asperger disorder was noted only in 3% of the cases, however these subjects were diagnosed with Asperger prior to the study, as the SCID does not identify pervasive developmental disorders.

Several researchers in autism have tried to explain obsessions and rituals in ASD. According to Baron-Cohen people with autism can't be said to have proper obsessions or compulsions since they cannot report the diagnostically crucial subjective experiences of distress, ego-dystonia and resistance; on the contrary they do not seem to resist their rituals but greatly enjoys acting on them (Rumsey et al,1986; Baron-Cohen, 1989). The strong, repetitive interests among children with autism cluster in the domain of "folk physics", which means an interest in how things work, for instance mechanical systems such as light switches or water taps, may reflect cognitive strengths (Baron-Cohen & Wheelwright, 1999). Baron-Cohen and Wheelwright suggest that the "need for sameness" or attempt to hold the environment constant might be a sign of superior "folk physics"; conducting mini-experiments in an attempt to identify laws governing events. This could explain why many highly able persons with ASD are successful with computers, engineering etc. These "obsessions" in persons with ASD typically follow their interests or hobbies and they experience their "obsessions" in a positive manner as oppose to obsessions in OCD, which include a distressing inability to trust ones senses, fears of harm and frustrated need for "just right feeling". It has nothing to do with "special interest or abilities".

Digby Tantam (1991) states that persons with Asperger syndrome "usually lack the marked stereotypies and unusual sensory preoccupations of more handicapped autistic people and, also unlike them, are generally not overly concerned with mere repetition although change usually upsets them and they often cleave to routine". Unusual restricted or asocial "special" interests were found in the vast majority of persons with Asperger syndrome.

Lorna Wing (1991) has an interesting approach to the problem. She suggests a dimensional relation in repetitive pattern of self-chosen activities depending on how capable the person is. Wing's definitions of these self-chosen activities are similar to what Baron-Cohen would call "obsessions". In the most severely handicapped/retarded group repetitive pattern of self-chosen activities are, according to Wing, simple bodily directed activities (e.g. face-tapping, self-injury), among those that are a bit more capable the activities are simple object-directed (e.g. spins, taps, switches lights), in the even less handicapped/retarded group the activities are complex routines or manipulation of objects (e.g. bedtime rituals, lining up objects, attachment to objects, whole-body movements) while persons with high functioning rather perform verbal, abstract activities (e.g. time-tables, movements of planets, repetitive questioning). Analogously movements, as flaps, jumps, rocks, tiptoe-walking, odd hand posture etc. which are usually defined as stereotypies, are marked in the severely handicapped group but minimal or absent in the least handicapped/retarded group.

Emotions and Feelings as the Origin of Behaviours

In OCD the person performs a compulsion as a response to a distressing thought or inner feeling. The compulsions doesn't provide the person with a sense of satisfaction or a "kick", rather it makes the patient's present inner state bearable for the moment. A tic on the other hand is a non-anxiety-related behaviour, sometimes referred to as an "impulsion" (Cath et al, 2001). It is rather like an urge that release the tic which provides the person with a sense of gratification similar to the one of a sneeze. However, in real life, there is not always a clear-cut line between tics and compulsions. Children and adolescents with OCD are often unable to explain what cognitions precede the compulsion. They may explain the reason for acting out a compulsion as an overwhelming inner feeling or emotion, rather than a proper thought. Especially common is this explanation among those with ordering or touching compulsions. According to Damasio (2003) feelings precede thoughts and accordingly feelings should be viewed as the origin of both tics and compulsions.

The lack of reward or "kicks" as a response to a compulsion may correlate to differences in the dopamine system between persons with ASD, OCD and chronic tic disorders (including Tourette's disorder). Persons with ASD are easily distressed, have difficulties to feel at ease, and reach flow in life. This experience is shared by many OCD patients which was observed already by Emil Kraepelin who reported in 1915: ... "their anxiety makes them believe that unimportant matters are important, which in turn drains their energy. The patient ends up in fruitless struggles regarding inessentials. They never become connoisseurs of the art of living, as every note in their life melody is emphasised in the same way" (translated by SB).

The chronic tic group, on the other hand, are often novelty-seekers, have a good capacity to associate and are often curious and out-going. Impulsivity is common and they run elevated risks for all kinds of addiction. Affective disorders are commonly seen among persons with tics. Smoking, which is rare among persons with ASD (Bejerot & Nylander, 2003) and OCD patients (Bejerot & Humble, 1999), especially in the group with a combined obsessive-compulsive personality disorder (Bejerot et al.2000, is reported as common among persons with tics and impulsivity (Comings & Blum, 2000).

In the autism literature, it is generally supposed that rituals in Asperger syndrome are ego-syntonic (Wing, 1981), and, hence, differ in nature from those of bona fide OCD. According to Lorna Wing (personal communication 2003): "rituals have a positive function for people with autism in many cases, however, the most able may try to stop them or confine them to times when they are alone, because they have become aware that their rituals are not socially acceptable, but the rituals themselves do not distress them." For other individuals however, this argument may not hold. The attitude towards the rituals varies considerably among capable persons with ASD. In several of my patients with ASD, the rituals are rather distressing compulsions that lead to severe anxiety and they seek professional help. Happé argued already in 1991 that autistic people's obsessions have been neglected in the research literature.

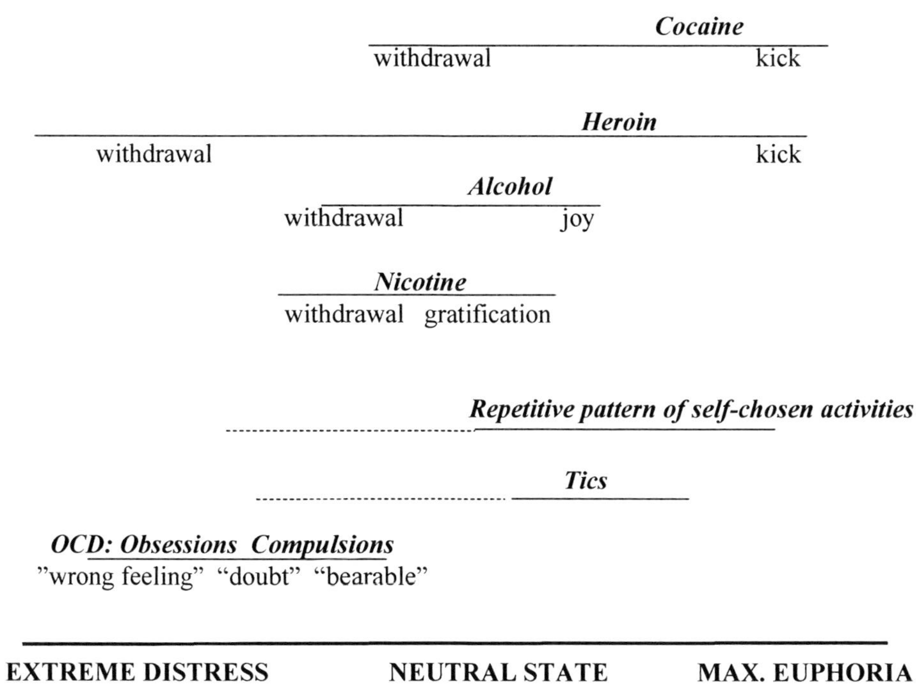

Figure 2. A hypothetic model over the span between maximal distress and maximal euphoria as (i) result of drugs, (ii) gratification from stereotyped self-chosen activities (from bodily directed activities, simple object-directed, complex routines, manipulation of objects, or abstract activities including special interests), (iii) tics and (iiii) span between the maximal distress of obsessions in OCD and the relative harmony that can be achieved by acting out compulsions. The dotted lines represent the expected distress when refrained from carrying out tics or stereotyped self-chosen activities.

In summary, stereotypies, tics, complex routines, repetitive interests, repetitive pattern of activities, rituals, obsessions and compulsions may differ in what feeling they induce in the patient and what feeling they cause if the person is prohibited to perform them. This craving for acting out certain behaviour due to an inner feeling has similarities to addiction. Addiction and OCD have in fact several resemblances: (1) the person may defend the compulsions/addiction and manipulate her relatives in order to be able to carry them out without interruptions; (2) the compulsion/addictive substance will bring on some level of gratification, which in turn will result in a craving for the compulsion/ addictive substance. (3) The person may carry on with compulsion/addiction at high social costs and compulsions/ addiction hold priority before elementary tasks such as keeping up relationships, hygiene or holding a job. Even elementary needs such as sex and sleep can be neglected. (4) If the person stops the compulsions/use the addictive substance for a period of time, relapses can be expected. However it is of crucial importance to understand that compulsions in OCD will never create a "high" as opposed to the ability of addictive substances.

Figure 2 illustrate a hypothetic model of the span between maximal distress and maximal euphoria in addiction, autism spectrum disorders, chronic tic disorder, and obsessive-compulsive disorder.

Evidence for a Close Relationship between ASD and OCD

Possibly, the most conspicuous finding linking ASD and OCD is the distress that many persons with a diagnosed ASD express as a result of their compulsions, and the obvious "schizoid" and "schizotypal" personality traits seen in many persons diagnosed with OCD However there is a large amount of research from other fields that points towards a close connection between OCD and ASD, that ought to be acknowledged, which is presented below.

Genetic Studies

A great deal of evidence indicates that autism is a complex genetic disorder resulting form oligogenic inheritance of an unknown number of susceptibility alleles (Folstein & Rosen-Sheidley, 2001). In search for a link between OCD and autism McDougle and co-workers (1998) have identified a polymorphism in the promoter region of the gene encoding the serotonin transporter protein (SLC6A4) in OCD patients, a finding that has previously been reported in autism. McCauley and co-workers (2004) have selected persons with autism characterized by compulsions and rigidity in order to find a link with OCD. There was significant sibling correlation in these families, suggesting that this phenotype is genetically relevant with an increased linkage to chromosome 17. However, they could not find evidence for an association with autism in the SLC6A4 locus. On the other hand, another molecular study (Ozaki etal, 2003) provides a possible genetic explanation of the link between treatment resistant OCD and Asperger syndrome/autism: An uncommon mutation in the coding region for the serotonin transporter, Ile425Val, was found in two unrelated families with OCD and other serotonin-related disorders. Six of the seven family members with this mutation had

OCD or obsessive-compulsive personality disorder and some also met diagnostic criteria for multiple other disorders (Asperger syndrome, social phobia, anorexia nervosa, tic disorder and alcohol and other substance abuse/dependence). Interestingly obsessive-compulsive personality disorder, severe social phobia, anorexia nervosa and tic disorders all seem related to ASD. Moreover, the similarity in the clinical picture between Asperger syndrome and severe form of obsessive-compulsive personality disorder, which in turn is over-representative in OCD, is striking.

Family Studies

Several family studies have shown that relatives of persons with either OCD or ASD are at risk for development of similar symptoms (Piven et al, 1997). In OCD obsessions are more inheritable than compulsions. In addition, obsessive-compulsive personality disorder and tics were markers for a greater risk of having relatives with OCD, as compared to OCD probands without these features (Nestadtet al, 2000). Both obsessive-compulsive personality disorder and tics are common in ASD.

In a study of 21 adults with OCD their off springs were compared to off springs of healthy controls (Black et al, 2003) Several psychiatric disorders as well as other symptoms and traits as nervousness, tenseness, stubbornness, a tendency to store un-needed items, repeating certain acts, confusion, fearfulness, picking nose or skin and easily jealous, were all more often observed among the OCD off-springs than among the control children. ASD were not assessed in this study however lower scores on the social subscales were identified among the OCD off-springs. ADHD on the other hand was not more common among OCD off-springs than among off-spring controls. The authors concluded that having a parent with OCD made it more likely that the children would have certain social, emotional, and behavioural disorders.

From the autism perspective Smalley and co-workers (1995) reported that the risk for social phobia was tenfold, major depression three-fold, and substance abuse twenty-fold in first degree relatives of 36 autistic probands as compared to 21 families to probands with tuberoses sclerosis or an unspecified seizure disorder. Interestingly they found that social phobia is significantly more common among the first degree relatives of non-retarded autistic probands than among relatives of individuals with autism and comorbid mental retardation, suggesting a relationship between high functioning autism/Asperger syndrome and social phobia. Piven and co-workers (1991) detected a ten-fold increased life time rate for anxiety disorders in parents to persons with autism as compared to parents to children with Down's syndrome. Bolton and co-workers (1998) reported an elevated risk for OCD, affective disorders and motor tics in first and second degree relatives to autistic probands as compared to relatives of probands with Down's syndrome (in all 1391 relatives to persons with autism and 625 relatives to persons with Down's syndrome). In 105 of the relatives a broader spectrum of the autism phenotype with either communication or social impairment was observed. Five of these had OCD, which was highly significantly more common compared to the remaining relatives (P=0.00001). In summary, OCD in these cases was strongly associated with the presence of communication or social impairments, suggesting that in these relatives OCD was also a manifestation of the genetic link to autism. The authors concluded that OCD may index an underlying liability to autism. In Bolton's study only 1.4% of first degree relatives of autistic probands had OCD compared to 0% among the probands of persons with Down's syndrome. This finding suggest that OCD is more rare than in the normal population among relatives to those of Down's syndrome rather than being elevated among autism relatives, else wise and more probable, OCD was under-reported in this study. But also other researchers have noted that clear cut obsessional and repetitive behaviours seem to occur only in a small minority of the relatives of autistic probands (Bailey et al, 1998), but still more common than expected in relatives with autism (Micali et al, 2004).

Hollander and co-workers (2003) investigated if children with autism with high scores on the Autism Diagnostic Interview (ADI-R) on the repetitive behaviours and stereotyped patterns domain, differed from those with low scores, in regard to OCD family morbidity. Thirty-nine of 233 (17%) children with autism had high total repetitive behaviours and 46% of these had at least one parents with obsessive-compulsive traits (mainly fathers) as compared to 25% of those with low scores. Relatives to subjects with narrow interests and compulsive rituals were nine times more likely to have parents with OCD, compared to those with low scores. In contrast to Bolton and co-worker's findings, OCD was present in 4% of the parents of probands with low scores, as compared to 34% with high scores, which suggest that the risk for OCD is elevated among all parents to autistic probands. On the other hand, other typical autistic symptoms as stereotyped and repetitive motor mannerisms such as hand, finger and complex body mannerism, preoccupation with parts of objects and unusual sensory interests, were *not* associated with OCD among the parents. This study suggests that there is heterogeneity in autism and those repetitive behaviours and narrow interests are related to OCD. Both Bolton's and Hollander's studies included persons with autism and low intelligence, which may represent those with a weaker link to OCD than the more able with autism or Asperger syndrome.

Biological Markers

Morphological and Functional Imaging Studies

Several studies of OCD have shown abnormal findings in the fronto-striatal pathways (Rauch et al, 1998) and reduced size of the orbital frontal region and amygdala (Szeszko et al, 1999). In addition increased regional grey matter density was found in multiple cortical areas, including the left orbitofrontal cortex, and in subcortical areas, including the thalamus. On the other hand, regions of reduction were confined to posterior parts of the brain, such as the left cuneus and the left cerebellum (Kimet al, 2001). Patients with OCD have been reported to have less total white matter but also significantly greater total cortex volumes (Jenike et al, 1996).

In an interesting f-MRI study by Mataix-Cols and coworkers (2004) symptom provocation was used on a sample of OCD patients and healthy controls. All patients watched the same pictures which would provoke disgust among those with washing compulsions, anxiety of forgetting something important among checkers, and anxiety among hoarders due to threat of being forced to throw away one's belongings. Patients demonstrated greater activity than controls in bilateral ventromedial prefrontal regions and right caudate nucleus (washing); putamen/globus pallidus, thalamus, and dorsal cortical areas (checking); left precentral gyrus and right orbitofrontal cortex (hoarding); and left occipitotemporal regions (aversive, symptom-unrelated). Moreover, the findings were associated to the patients' subjective feeling of anxiety.

Biological findings in ASD has been elegantly summarised by Murphy in 2002 "Neuropathological studies of patients with autism reported neuronal abnormalities in the cerebral cortex, cerebellum, and limbic system (Bauman & Kemper, 1985; Bailey et al, 1998). In vivo studies of brain anatomy described widespread abnormalities in brain morphometry and cerebral gyrification (Piven et al, 1990; Courchesne et al, 1993) but increasingly point to the pathoaeotiogical importance of mesolimbic and subcortical structures (Piven et al, 1995; Hazneder et al, 1997; Abell et al, 1999; Sears et al, 1999). Studies of brain metabolism and blood flow in autism using positron emission tomography reported delayed metabolic maturation of the prefrontal cortex (Zilbovicius et al,1995) and reduced functional associations between the frontal and parietal regions at rest (Horwitz et al, 1988) reduced prefrontal and anterior cingulate metabolism during attentional and verbal learning tasks (Seigel et al, 1995) and reduced medial prefrontal blood flow during theory-of-mind tasks (Happé et al, 1996). Recent functional magnetic resonance imaging studies of patients with autism reported reduced activation in the amygdala when making emotional judgments of eyes (Baron-Cohen et al, 1999); in the amygdala and cerebellar, mesolimbic, and temporal lobe cortical brain regions when processing facial emotion (Critchley et al, 2000); and in the temporal lobe during facial recognition tasks (Schultz et al, 2000)".

Although amygdala volume reduction in ASD has not been reported (Haznedar et al, 2000) amygdala dysfunction is repeatedly reported in ASD (Sears et al, 1999). Several other deviances similar to OCD, have been found in ASD. In a recent study cerebral grey matter volume was enlarged in both persons with high functioning autism and autism with low intelligence as compared with controls (Lotspeich et al, 2004). Also, people with Asperger syndrome had significantly less grey matter in cerebellar regions than controls, and widespread differences in white matter (McAlonan et al, 2002). In the study by Murphy and coworkers (2002) of 14 subjects with Asperger syndrome a correlation between abnormalities in the neuronal integrity of the prefrontal lobe and obsessive behaviour was found. Moreover, subjects with Asperger syndrome had a significantly higher prefrontal lobe concentration of N-acetylaspartate, creatine and phosphocreatine, and choline. N-acetylaspartate is closely correlated with mitochondrial energy metabolism and synthesis, and present in high concentration in grey matter and neurons. Therefore, N-acetylaspartat is often used as a measure of neuronal density and/or mitochondrial function, while creatine and phosphocreatine, and choline concentrations are used as measures of phosphate metabolism and membrane turnover, respectively. Frontal lobe concentration of N-acetylaspartate was significantly positively correlated with more severe obsessional/repetitive behaviour. As no differences were observed in parietal regions this implies that the frontal lobe may be more affected than the parietal lobe in Asperger syndrome. The authors concluded that it is unclear whether the neurobiological basis of obsessional behaviour in subjects with Asperger syndrome differs from that in OCD, and further studies are required.

Autoimmune Findings

Autoimmune findings have repeatedly been demonstrated in OCD. A relationship between group A β-hemolytic streptococcal infections, positive anti-neuronal titers and psychiatric dysfunction in a subgroup of children with a sudden onset of OCD and chronic tic disorder seems clear (Swedo et al, 2004). Since an increased rate of D8/17 an alloantigen found on B lymphocytes, was found in this group, this is suggested to be a marker of this variant of OCD and tic disorder. This etiologic hypothesis involves a series of factors including pathogenic strains of group A streptococci, host susceptibility, and abnormal immune response.

In a study of 18 patients with autism the frequency with elevated levels of D8/17 was significantly higher than among controls, moreover the elevation was related to severity of the repetitive behaviours (Hollander et al, 1999). According to this finding an autoimmune origin for compulsions is plausible in both OCD and autism.

An elevation of antibodies directed against caudate has been showed in both children with OCD symptoms (Kiessling et al, 1994) and in persons with autism (Singh & Rivas, 2004).

Neurochemistry

In a review of biological connections between OCD and autism several similarities were proposed (Gross-Isseroff et al., 2001). Oxytocin seems to be of interest in both OCD and ASD. It has been reported to be elevated in non-tic related OCD according to some earlier studies (Leckman et al, 1994), although this has been contradicted in a later study (Altemus et al, 1999). Treatment with oxytocin was not successful in a controlled trial on OCD patients (den Boer & Westenberg, 1992) however patients with ASD showed a significant reduction in repetitive behaviours following oxytocin infusion in comparison to placebo infusion (Hollander et al, 2003).

In OCD an early study showed elevated levels of 5- hydroxy-indol acetic acid (5-HIAA) in the spinal fluid (Thorén et al, 1980). A correlation between lower whole blood-5HT and platelet 5-HT with more severe OCD symptomatology is plausible (Flament et al, 1987; Humble et al, 2001).

5-HIAA and whole blood 5-HT has repeatedly been reported to be elevated in subjects with autism. A number of studies on autism have indicated dysregulation in the serotonin function, as worsening of symptoms such as whirling, flapping, and self-harming behaviours after depletion of tryptophan (McDougle et al, 1993) and, in contrast to OCD, hyperserotoninemia (Yuwiler et al, 1992). This indicates that the hyperserotoninemia in autism may not reflect the serotonin activity in the brain. However a connection between hyperserotoninemia in autism and OCD can not be ruled out as hyperserotonemic parents to children with autism display more OCD traits as compared to the parents with normal whole blood serotonine levels (Cook et al, 1994).

Pharmacotherapy

The golden standard for pharmacotherapy in OCD is clomipramine, a combined serotonin and norepinephrine reuptake inhibitor, but all selective serotonergic re-uptake inhibitors (SSRIs) are effective for the treatment of obsessions and compulsions. Several studies show that also autistic persons with rituals may respond favourable to serotonin reuptake inhibitors, but not to noradrenergic reuptake inhibitors or placebo (Gordon et al, 1993; McDougle et al, 1996; Harvey & Cooray, 1995).

In OCD anti-dopaminergic medication as risperidone may be an effective and well-tolerated augmentation strategy added to serotonin reuptake inhibitor in treatment-resistant OCD (Hollander et al, 2003), but are ineffective as mono-therapy. The treatment resistant OCD cases often have elevated scores in the positive schizotypal scales and especially perceptual aberrations are highly predictive for treatment failure (Moritz et al, 2004). Therefore it is not surprising that anti-dopaminergic drugs, filtering overwhelming perceptions, have been proven useful in ASD (McClellan & Werry, 2003). In conclusion, a combination of clomipramine and risperidone is the treatment of choice in both treatment resistant OCD and ASD with problematic ritualistic behaviours.

Neurological Soft Signs and Clumsiness

Persons with OCD often display neurological soft signs and are frequently clumsy. In a study of 64 adults with chronic OCD, 20% of males, and 50% of females reported difficulty to learn to ride a bike as a child and other signs of clumsiness (Bejerot, 2000). Patients with OCD present significantly more neurological soft signs on both sides of the body with slight predominance on the left-sided signs, as compared to controls measured with the Cambridge Neurological Inventory (Mataix-Cols et al, 2003). The patients had higher scores on total, motor coordination and sensory integration categories. In an earlier study (Hollander et al, 1990) OCD patients showed significantly more abnormalities in fine motor coordination, involuntary and mirror movements, and lower visuo-spatial skills, than expected. A correlation was found between neurological soft signs and severity of obsessive-compulsive symptomatology, measured with Y-BOCS total score (Bolton et al, 2000).

Neurological soft signs and clumsiness are also frequently found in persons with ASD (Weimer et al, 2001; Gillberg & Kadesjö, 2003). Clumsiness was noted already by Hans Asperger in his index series of boys who were later referred to as having Asperger syndrome (Asperger, 1944). Clumsiness and ill-coordinated movements have been proposed to be more common in Asperger syndrome than in autism, but this has not been confirmed in later trials (Ghaziuddin & Butler, 1998). Clumsiness in ASD correlates with lower intelligence, although the entire ASD group is conspicuously clumsy. Whether clumsiness is more prevalent among persons with ASD and compulsions, than among those without compulsions, remains to be studied. But it is clear that complex motor coordination is impaired in both OCD and ASD, and both groups can be described as clumsy.

Perceptions

OCD patients have a distorted feedback from their perceptions and sometimes it is perceptions rather than obsessions that cause compulsions. For instance, some OCD patients sense a distressing perception that something sticks to their fingers which cause repetitive washing, rather than obsessions about dirt or germs.

The ability to trust senses of seeing and feeling is regularly impaired in OCD. An OCD patient can therefore turn off the iron, stare at the lamp of the iron to be sure it is properly turned off, sense that it is cold, wrap the cord around the iron and yet have the urge to sense with the fingers that the plug is removed from its socket. The patient can thereafter hit her hand against the wall to feel the pain which will last for a while and remind her that she has in fact checked the iron properly when the doubts eventually returns. Still she may feel unsure. Others need a "just right" feeling in order to go on, and will repeat actions until this feeling is reached, which may take hours.

The "just right" phenomena but also symptoms of psychasthenia, are both found to be associated with the current severity of obsessive-compulsive symptoms in children and adolescents with OCD (Leckman et al, 1994).

In ASD distorted perceptions are the rule. The response to a certain touch, taste, vibration, pain, and temperature is idiosyncratic. Many refuse to eat food with certain colour or consistence. Cloths could be sensed as itchy or even as painful as bob wire (Wing, 1996) and jewellery may give raise to disgust and feeling of sickness (Gerland, 1997). Some refrain from showering as they sense pain from the streaming water of the shower, or the sense of chill afterwards. Sticky fingers may be intolerable to a person with ASD. Things must be performed in the "just right" way in order to be accepted and a small change of routines may cause temper tantrums. In summary, distorted perceptions, inability to filter information and the need for the "just right" feeling are common features in both ASD and OCD and may result in distress, disgust, compulsive behaviours and avoidance.

Cognitive Function

Cognitive deficits documented in OCD are impairments on measures of spatial working memory, spatial recognition, and motor initiation and execution (Purcell et al, 1998). When patients with OCD had to rely on internal representations to guide their selections, performance was compromised. An excess of findings on the left side of the body and abnormalities of cube drawing may suggest right hemispheric dysfunction in a subgroup of patients with OCD. There was also a correlation between abnormalities in visual memory and recognition on neuropsychological testing and total neurological soft signs (Hollander et al, 1990).

Right hemisphere cognitive deficits have also been suggested in Asperger syndrome (Ellis et al, 1994). Moreover, in autism and Asperger syndrome executive functions are also substantially impaired, which suggest a frontal lobe dysfunction. Executive function is an umbrella term covering a wide array of higher cognitive processes; the ability to disengage from context, inhibition of inappropriate responses, planning sequences of willed actions, staying on the task, monitoring performance and using feedback, and shifting attentional set (Duncan, 1995). Deficits in planning, organization switching set and preservation have been reported (Rumsey & Hamburger, 1990; Ozonoff et al, 1991; Pennington & Ozonoff, 1996). Both persons with OCD and those with ASD are impaired in tests for assessing executive functions as the Wisconsin card sorting test, word fluency test and working memory test (Head et al, 1989; Lucey et al, 1997).

Special Abilities

A proportion of individuals with Asperger syndrome diagnosed as such or not, has superior cognitive functions in an array of tests. They may achieve high academic positions as scientists, mathematicians (Baron-Cohen et al, 2001), computer experts or physicians. Others may also find a successful career as musicians (Brown et al, 2003), philosophers or artists (Fitzgerald, 2004). Geniuses with severe OCD should neither be forgotten: Samuel Johnson (1709-1784) the English author, poet, essayist, critic, journalist, lexicographer, conversationalist, regarded as one of the outstanding figures of 18th-century life. He wrote the first dictionary of the English language including definitions of over 40 000 words, illustrating them with about 114 000 quotations drawn from every field of learning. Johnson was a very eccentric man and is believed to suffer from both Tourette disorder and OCD, but his eccentricity and verbal skills may also suggest Asperger syndrome. Howard Hughes (1905-1976) was at times a pilot, a movie producer, a playboy, an eccentric, a recluse, and one of the wealthiest people in the world, a fortune that hc had inherited from his father. As a teenager, he declared that his goals in life were to become the world's best golfer, the world's best pilot, and the world's best movie producer. He was successful but later developed an incapacitating OCD, became extremely frail, wore Kleenex boxes as shoes, and stored his urine in jars. A long memo from Howard Hughes on how to open a can of fruit without contaminating began as follows: "The equipment used in connection with this operation will consist of the following items: 1 unopened newspaper; 1 sterile can opener; 1 large sterile plate; 1 sterile fork; 1 sterile spoon; 2 sterile brushes; 2 bars of soap; sterile paper towels" (Hack, 2001). Hughes' bizarre health rituals provide associations to the extreme interest in healthy living and fear that the slightest misstep could result in illness that we have noted in several persons with high intelligence and ASD. Another example is the Polish borne actor Klaus Kinski (1926-1991) who was, according to the director Werner Herzog, a person that washed his knives and fork with alcohol before he could use them, he resented to be touched by others and he washed himself excessively. He is described as one of the most eccentric and colourful personalities in the entire film history; he lived his life as strange as his films. Kinski was a fanatic in everything he did. His fevered and emotional portrayals on the stage are overwhelming, however, his lack of understanding to authority created great tension with his superiors and he constantly found himself without a job and homeless. His huge ego (he compare himself to Jesus Christ), resentment towards authorities, inability to compromise, wide reputation as an enfant terrible and inability to form stable relations could be signs of ASD. His life was a never-ending ride from one film to another and one woman to another, which can be described as a pattern of repetitive stereotyped behaviour. His autobiography is described as a book that "unravels the pitch-dark inner life of an actor who specialized in playing insane people, a man who well understood the psychology of the characters he portrayed."

Alexithymia

In a comparative evaluation of somatoform disorder, panic disorder, OCD, and depression, alexithymia was found to be related to OCD as opposed to panic disorder (Bankier et al, 2001). In a study of subjects with Asperger syndrome, and controls, persons with Asperger syndrome were significantly more alexithymic as compared to controls (Tani et al, 2004). Consequently alexithymia could be expected in both OCD and Asperger syndrome.

Personality and Personality Disorders

The reported comorbidity between categorical personality disorders and OCD ranges between 33 and 87 percent (Bejerot et al, 1998). Avoidant, dependent and obsessive-compulsive personality disorders are the most prevalent (Baer et al, 1992). Moreover, relatives to OCD probands had a higher prevalence of obsessive-compulsive personality disorder and higher neuroticism scores than relatives to control probands (Samuels et al, 2000). Interestingly OCD patients are also more likely to receive a diagnosis from cluster A (the odd and eccentric cluster), compared to other patients with anxiety disorders, in fact compared to all other non-psychotic patients (Rossi & Daneluzzo, 2002). The OCD patients do not appeal to the clinician in contrast to other anxiety patients. In accordance with this, Stanley (1990) reported schizotypal features in 28% of his OCD cases. Interestingly, schizotypal personality disorder, as defined by Westen & Shedler (1999), is an exact description of autistic traits, which further supports the link between OCD and ASD.

The resemblances between the diagnostic criteria for obsessive-compulsive personality disorder and Asperger syndrome have previously been pointed out (Gillberg & Billstedt, 2000) In addition it has been suggested that the schizoid personality pattern in childhood is really Asperger syndrome (Rutter, 1987). In a study of 38 patients with ASD, more than half fulfilled diagnostic criteria for avoidant, obsessive-compulsive and/or paranoid personality disorder in a self-report questionnaire for Axis II (personal communication, Lena Nylander & Maria Holmqvist, 2003).

Accordingly, autistic traits in OCD patients can be identified through an odd personality with paranoid, schizoid, schizotypal, avoidant and obsessive-compulsive traits combined with a conspicuous absence of histrionic traits.

Previous studies have shown that subjects with OCD and Asperger syndrome deviated similarly in regard to personality dimensions on the TCI, with higher harm avoidance and lower self-directedness and cooperativeness (Kusunoki et al, 2000; Söderström et al, 2002). This specific pattern was even more marked in subjects with OCD with autistic traits as compared to other OCD subjects; see *p xx* in this chapter.

A social anxiety spectrum has also been suggested to exist (Bailey et al, 1998; Schneier et al, 2002), which is of relevance for both OCD and ASD. It includes at least some forms of shyness, avoidant personality disorder, and selective mutism. Social anxiety spectrum is believed to be associated with other anxiety disorders in general and other phobias in particular. Moreover it also overlaps with several other disorders marked by social dysfunction or inhibition, paranoid disorder, autism, and Asperger syndrome.

Hoarding

Hoarding is regarded as a form of compulsion in OCD and it has repeatedly been shown to be associated with non-response to treatment and schizotypal personality or odd features (Frost et al, 2000). Samuels and co-workers reported that hoarders had an earlier age at onset, more severe obsessive-compulsive symptoms and also more severe comorbidity and family loading than non-hoarders (Samuels et al, 2002). Hoarders had greater prevalence of symmetry obsessions, counting compulsions, and ordering compulsions. Hoarders also had greater prevalence of social phobia, personality disorders, and pathological grooming behaviours. Hoarding and tics were more frequent in first-degree relatives of hoarding than non-hoarding probands.

Mataix-Cols and co-workers (2000) reported that high scores on the 'Hoarding' dimension were strongly related to the presence of any Axis II diagnosis, and to the number of personality disorders. Personality disorders within Cluster C, especially obsessive-compulsive and avoidant personality disorder had the highest partial correlations with 'Hoarding', independent of OCD symptom severity.

It is apparent that hoarding is the final common pathway for a variety of processes: compulsive hoarding in obsessive-compulsive disorder, fears of theft and poisoning in paranoid delusions, and the deterioration of habits in organic mental disorder (Greenberg et al, 1990). But hoarding is also commonly reported in ASD (McDougle et al, 1995) and is stated to be a severe problem among 6% of young adults with autism (Kobayashi & Murata, 1998). Hoarding is however typically ego-syntonic, as opposed to other compulsions. According to my experience, hoarding has even a closer link to ASD, than to OCD.

Obsessive Slowness and Catatonia

Obsessive slowness is regarded as rare in OCD, only prevalent in about three percent of OCD cases, according to a study of 665 patients with OCD (Ratnasuriya et al, 1991). Over 90% of the slowness cases were male. This group have more neurological deviances than healthy controls, including loss of motor fluency, hesitancy of initiation of limb movements, speech and gait abnormalities, cogwheel rigidity, complex repetitive movements and tics. Difficulties in cognitive set-shifting and complex spatial-and-shifting abilities were also found on neuropsychological testing (Hymas et al, 1991). Long time findings suggest that the slowness remains after other OCD symptoms accompanying had been successfully treated which suggests that the slowness was not secondary to the OCD (Takeuchi et al, 1997).

Obsessive slowness is a form of catatonia which is common in ASD. Catatonia was diagnosed by Wing and Shah (2000) in 17% of adolescents and adult referrals with ASD. Essential catatonic features include a wide range of behaviours: increased slowness affecting movements and verbal responses, difficulty in initiating and completing actions, increased reliance on physical or verbal prompting by others, and increased passivity and apparent lack of motivation. Other associated characteristics were: reversal of day and night, Parkinsonian features (tremor, eye-rolling, dystonia, odd stiff posture, freezing in postures), excitement and agitation, and increase in repetitive, ritualistic behaviour. Most subjects with ASD have some catatonic features although full-blown catatonia was found to be rare. Recently autism has been suggested to represent the infantile form of periodic catatonia (Dhossche, 2004).

Case report: Jack

Jack had problems of obsessive-compulsive nature since the age of three. At the age of 14 his parents took him to a child psychiatrist. There were no psychiatric disorders in his family, most of them were academics, but his own intelligence was a bit low, he scored around 80 on the WISC scale. However he attended a normal school. For a period he played the drum in a band but he did not have any friends. He developed a severe form of OCD in his early teens. At the age of 16, he needed assistance in nearly every aspect of daily living including to get dressed or to clean himself after he had been on the toilet. For instance at the first visit it took him several minutes to cross the room, suggesting obsessional slowness. Every so often he needed force or prompting to get him to move at all. When he was away with his family to a new environment as to their summer cottage or went skiing, his problems with getting stuck were reduced markedly.

Jack had multiple motor tics, blinking and finger movements. Another behavioral symptom was compulsory touching which he expressed by touching the door frame before he could enter the room. He was attacked quiet suddenly by impulses that he could not resist-like for instance once opening the door of the car in the middle of the highway. Neither could he resist touching others, also on their private parts. He felt distressed by these symptoms and had full insight into their senselessness, but lacked the ability to resist any of them. Other symptoms he had less insight in, he hoarded everything, and refused to discard anything. Eventually, he had to move into a home for mentally ill persons. He gradually developed paranoid ideas, and felt sure that things were stolen from his room. He called his parents several times a day to complain about the staff's behaviours, and even suspected them for doing things behind his back as for instance changing the tire of his bike. He always locked the room to prevent the staff from walking into it while he wasn't there, but although he lacked proof he was sure they had been there anyway. His suspicions led to aggressive behaviours as breaking various items going as far as wrecking furniture. His OCD symptoms were severe; he scored 32 points on the Y-BOCS, with somewhat higher scores on compulsions than obsessions, and the maximum15 points on the NIMH OC scale. However he was not severely depressed. In a discussion he had difficulties to get down to the point, loosing himself in extensive and irrelevant discussions. He often made odd repetitive noises as Oh, Oh Oh, Oh etc. He was physically well although he often suffered from stomach pain and was extremely thin with a BMI of 18.6. Cognitive behaviour therapy and consecutive drug treatments with clomipramine 250 mg/days, fluvoxamin 200 mg/day, sertraline 200mg/day, valproate 1000mg/day, fluoxetin 80 mg/day and anti-androgen treatment (flutamide) were all unsuccessful. However he responded marginally to a combination of olanzapine 5 mg/day and nefazodone 600 mg/day.

This young man fits the diagnostic criteria for ASD, OCD and chronic motor tic disorder depending on the perspective of the physician. What was assessed as tics could alternatively be viewed as stereotypies, his obsessional slowness as catatonia and his hoarding and ordering compulsions could be viewed as repetitive behaviours in ASD.

History of Tics, Symmetry and Ordering

A history of tics is present in approximately 20% of the patients with OCD, compared to 3-6% in normal children (Khalifa & von Knorring 2003; Lanzi et al, 2004). Boys are affected at least three times more often than girls. In OCD, tics have repeatedly been shown to indicate a distinct form of the disorder (Holzer et al, 1994), which is strongly inherited and have an earlier onset. Tics are also commonly reported in the sudden pre-pubertal onset of OCD that is associated with streptococcal infection. Tic-related OCD is characterized by OCD symptoms such as symmetry and ordering, blinking, tapping, touching, rubbing, and staring rituals (Mataix-Cols et al, 1999) but also checking, counting, and hoarding are more common symptoms among those with OCD and tics than in non-tic-related OCD, at least among children and adolescents (Leckman et al, 2004). Men scored significantly higher than women on symmetry/ordering and age of onset is significantly negatively correlated with these symptoms (Mataix-Cols et al, 1999).

Conversely OCD is common among persons with tic disorder (Kurlan et al, 2002). Generally, persons with tics are prone to symptoms of impaired impulse control such as disruptive behaviour disorders and ADHD (Kurlan et al, 2002), alcohol and drug dependence and inappropriate sexual activity. However, since a large part of these traits may be counteracted by the conscientiousness, typical of OCD, patients with tics disorder and comorbid OCD can be expected to be less impulsive than other subjects with tics. Although tics tend to fade away in adolescence, a more vulnerable personality seems to persist.

Also patients with ASD frequently exhibit motor and phonic tics (Kadesjo & Gillberg, 200; Ringman & Jankovic, 2000.). In one study 6% met the full criteria for Tourette syndrome (Baron-Cohen et al, 1999). Therefore tics don't imply a closer relationship to OCD than it does to ASD.

OCD Spectrum, Self-Harm and Anorexia Nervosa

In a family study of "spectrum disorders" in OCD, body dysmorphic disorder, hypochondriasis, any eating disorder, and any grooming condition (nail-biting, trichotillomania, and skin picking) occurred more frequently in OCD subjects than in normal controls (Bienvenu et al, 2000). In addition, body dysmorphic disorder, either somatoform disorder, or any grooming condition occurred more frequently in case first-degree relatives, whether or not case probands also had the same diagnosis, than among control first-degree relatives. In a study on skin picking it was found to be more frequent among subjects with obsessive-compulsive personality disorder or borderline personality disorder with or without a comorbid OCD than in controls (Wilhelm et al, 1999). However, the clinical manifestations of an OCD illness combined with skin picking are similar to those of OCD probands without skin picking (Cullen et al, 2001). On the other hand there is a higher prevalence of recurrent depression, body dysmorphic disorder and anxiety disorders in those with skin picking and OCD than among those with only OCD. These disorders seem associated with skin picking independently of OCD and consequently skin picking is not specific to OCD. Indeed, among all relatives, skin picking, is strongly associated with anxiety disorders including social phobia, generalized anxiety disorder and hypochondriasis.

Also anorexia nervosa and bulimia are reported to be related to OCD (Bellodi et al, 2001). In a study of 21 females who met the DSM-III-R criteria for both anorexia nervosa and OCD, were compared with 23 female patients with only OCD (Matsunagaetal, 1999). The patients with anorexia nervosa and OCD were significantly more likely than those with only OCD to have obsessions with need for symmetry or exactness and ordering/arranging compulsions, whereas both aggressive obsessions and checking compulsions tended to be more frequently identified in OCD patients compared with anorexia nervosa patients with OCD. Anorexia nervosa patients with OCD were significantly more likely than those with only OCD to meet the criteria for obsessive-compulsive personality disorder.

In autism self-injury behaviour (Hollander et al, 2003) is a severe problem and it is more common in this group than among persons with OCD (McDougle et al, 1995). Picking was reported to often occur in 12% of the cases and nail biting in 28% of the cases (Kobayashi & Murata, 1998). Anorexia nervosa is clearly overrepresented in ASD (Nilsson et al, 1999), trichotillomania may be as well (Ghaziuddin et al, 1991; Holttum et al, 1994). However it is doubtful if body dysmorphic disorder exists in ASD as many persons with ASD lack interest in their own appearance.

Suicide

Suicide is conspicuously rare in OCD (Apter et al, 2003; Bejerot, 2003) and it is has been suggested that OCD is protecting against suicide attempts (Apter et al, 2003). In a Swedish follow up study of 251 OCD patients treated in a psychiatric hospital at any time between 1947-1953, only 6 patients had committed suicide during a 40 years follow up (Gunnar Skoog, personal communication, 1998). The Swedish OCD foundation, with approximately 1500 members are aware of only two suicides, both were young men.

I have been informed of two young men with OCD who committed suicide; both had indisputably prominent autistic traits. According to the literature suicide is rare in ASD as well, however, premeditated suicide among ASD occur occasionally as a result of a pragmatic decision. I know of a handful persons with ASD who have committed suicide, none of those were known to have OCD. Obsessive-compulsive symptoms seem to protect against suicide, while ASD does not.

Evolutionary Fitness and Treatment Outcome

Evolutionary fitness can be described as the organism's successful strategies. For humans that would mean ability to survive, find acceptance by others in the community, success in finding a mate, thrive in a family setting and have children. For many persons with psychiatric disorder the evolutionary fitness tend to be low, however those with a clear cut anxiety disorder will be able to appeal and find support from others. Persons with OCD can be more or less successful in regard to evolutionary fitness. Some will have clear alexithymic features, appear hostile, have a severe obsessive-compulsive personality disorder or be overly intellectualizing. On the other hand they can benefit from being conscientious, honest and persistent. In the discussion of treatment outcome in OCD, personality disorders and traits are emphasised. The presence of a cluster A personality disorder or obsessive-compulsive personality disorder, along with the total number of personality disorders, predicts a poorer outcome in OCD (Baer et al, 1992; Cavedini et al, 1997). Other negative predictors in OCD are social impairment, being a single male, childlessness, difficulties in interpersonal relations (Fals-Stewart & Schafer, 1993) and hoarding symptoms (Black et al, 1998). This group will not only be non-responders, they will also have a lower ability to find successful strategies in life. Persons with Asperger syndrome are often males, they will often remain single because of their difficulties in social relations and they may be regarded by their peers as socially deviant, peculiar and lacking common sense. A history of being severely bullied at school is extremely common (Little, 2002). Persons with ASD can be expected to have a low capacity to appeal to others, to ask for advice, to accept those given and make fortunate choices in life. A genetic study by Ozaki and co-workers support a link between autistic traits and poor outcome in OCD (2003).

In persons with OCD the outlook on life may therefore vary depending on if the patient has a concomitant obsessive-compulsive personality and/or autistic traits or if the OCD is only related to anxiety. Consequently, affects, beliefs, attitudes and sociability are thought to be associated to certain OCD symptoms, personality and evolutionary fitness, see *Figure 3.*

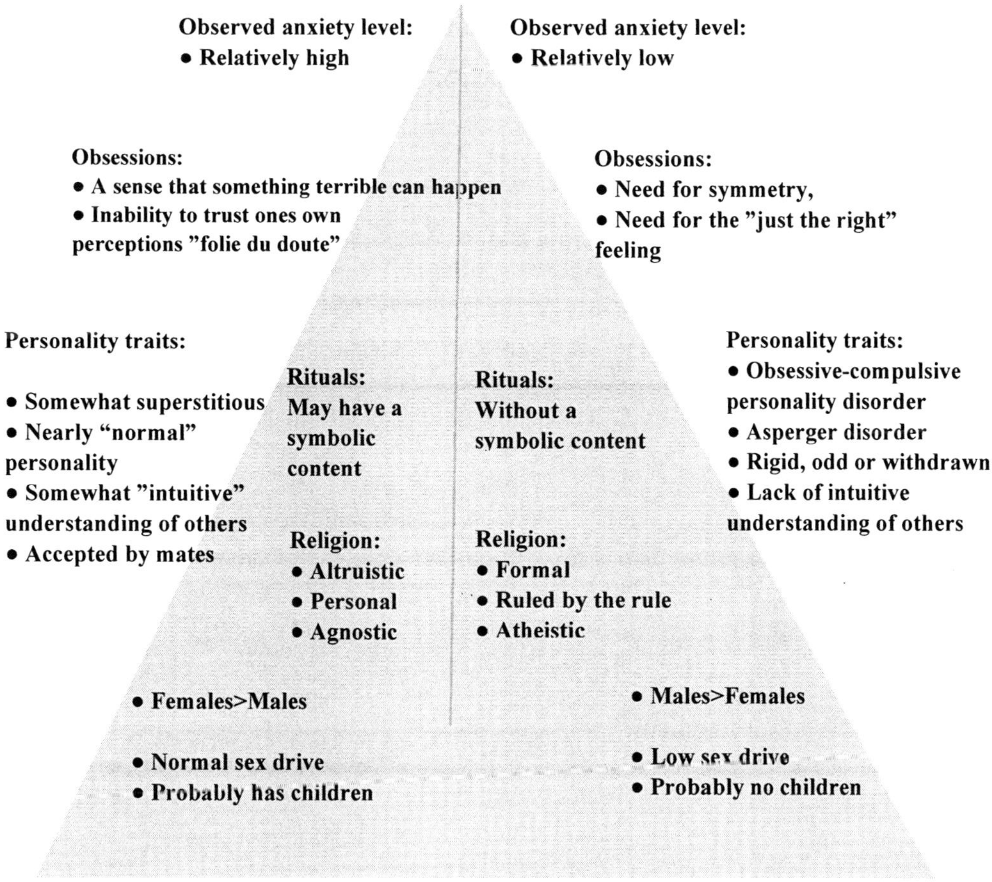

Figure 3. Obsessive-Compulsive Disorder in the shape of an anxiety disorder or in the dimension of Autism Spectrum Disorder

PROSPECTIVE STUDIES OF ASD

In a comprehensive Swedish prospective study (Lindqvist, 2004), 94 persons diagnosed with Minimal brain dysfunction (MBD) in childhood (72 males and 22 females) were followed from 1989 until 2003. The DSM-III and DSM-IV diagnostic criteria of ADHD or ADD were not in use at the time the children had received their diagnosis. Fifty percent of the subjects were between 18-20 years, mean age 22 years, and only 5% were above 35 years in 1989. Information was gathered through the parents of the patients. In 2003, 18 families had dropped out of the study, leaving 76 probands, mean age 36 years (57 males and 19 females). Twenty-four had received additional diagnoses in adolescence or adulthood: Eleven were diagnosed as Asperger syndrome, 2 with other ASD, 3 with Tourette and 9 with personality disorders, in addition 8 of the subjects with ASD or Asperger were also diagnosed with schizophrenia. The remaining subjects were assessed as having ADHD. Additional diagnoses of depression and obsessive-compulsive traits were very common. Twenty-six percent had fixed ideas, rituals, excessive routines, or perfectionism. The men were affected in 59% of the cases and women slightly less, 45%. Besides fixed ideas in more of a quarter of the subjects, obsessive-compulsive symptoms were present in another 14%. However, among those with Asperger syndrome obsessive-compulsive traits were significantly more common as compared to those with ADHD (77% versus 32%). Especially hoarding and washing rituals were reported to be common among those with Asperger syndrome. Interestingly the OCD in this group seemed to have a late onset: In childhood none in the total group reported obsessive-compulsive symptoms, but in adolescence 4% had obsessions or compulsions and in early adulthood the number raised to 10%. In 2003, when the majority of the patients had reached ages between 30 and 40 years, obsessive-compulsive symptoms were reported in 14% (11 persons). The symptoms were chronic in most cases. According to the author, hoarding was the most common symptom, followed by washing and checking. Repeating was also reported as common. In 2003, 6 persons fulfilled the diagnostic criteria for OCD with washing, grooming and hoarding compulsions in 5 of the cases and counting compulsions in one subject. None had sexual obsessions or obsessions about harming others.

In a Danish long term follow-up study of 47 individuals diagnosed with OCD in childhood, 2 met the criteria of Asperger syndrome in adulthood (Thomsen, 1994). Moreover 4 had had anorexia nervosa. In another follow-up study of 24 children with Asperger syndrome and 24 children with high functioning autism, a comorbid OCD was diagnosed in 8, respectively 10% of the cases (Szatmari et al, 1989).

Previous Subtyping of OCD

A number of ways of subtyping OCD patients have been proposed. According to the International classification of diseases (ICD-10) OCD is divided into three subgroups: mainly obsessions, mainly compulsions and mixed obsessions and compulsions. DSM-IV has another subtyping based on the presence or absence of insight. Others have suggested subtypes based on a factor analysis of the Yale-Brown symptom checklist. In the factor analysis performed by Leckman and co-workers (1997) four symptom dimensions emerged: 1) obsessions and checking, (2) symmetry and ordering, (3) cleanliness and washing and (4) hoarding. In a factor analysis obsessions were further divided into aggressive/checking and sexual/religious obsessions which resulted in five subtypes (Mataix-Cols et al, 1999) Another research group have suggested subgroups based on patterns of comorbidity (Nestadt et al, 2003). In a latent class analysis of a population sample, 81 of whom had OCD, four groups emerged. The first three subgroups (with minimal comorbidity, with comorbid generalized anxiety disorder and/or recurrent major depression (60% of OCD subjects), and with conspicuous hypochondriasis or body dysmorphic disorder) were conceptualised as progressively more comorbid variations of related psychopathology. The fourth, purportedly more distinct group was characterized by panic disorder/agoraphobia and to some extent tic disorder, but no history of recurrent depression. Persons with tic disorder, however, were equally distributed between three of the groups.

THE STOCKHOLM STUDY

A study on autistic and other personality traits in patients with OCD was carried out in Stockholm. A total of 64 subjects with obsessive-compulsive disorder according to DSM- IV were included in this study (Bejerot et al, 2001). None of the patients had been investigated for ASD prior to this study. Subjects were excluded if they were diagnosed with schizophrenia, mental retardation or Tourette syndrome. All patients were classified on the basis of autistic traits, through the use of the High functioning autism/Asperger Global Scale (HAGS), se appendix in this chapter. A rating of 1 or 2 was regarded as autistic traits or ASD. Moreover all participants were carefully interviewed for the history of tics. They participated in a 2.5 hours semi structured interview including Y-BOCS for assessing OCD symptoms, general functioning, personality traits, clumsiness, marital status, work situation, age of onset, and relation to peers. The patients were subtyped in accordance with our hypothesis emphasising the importance of autistic traits and a history of tics: (1) "pure" OCD, (2) OCD-autistic traits and (3) OCD-tics. Autistic traits and tics often coexist, but since autistic traits have an earlier onset and represent a more pervasive disorder, the autistic-tics individuals were categorized into the "OCD-autistic traits" group. The result showed that thirty-six (56%) of the patients had "pure" OCD, i.e. they had no obvious autistic traits and no history of tics, thirteen (20%) of the patients were identified as having pronounced autistic traits and four of these (6% of the entire sample) had both autistic traits and tics. Fifteen (23%) of the subjects had OCD and a history of tics but no obvious autistic traits and were defined as the OCD-tics group. Neither the OCD-autistic traits group (n=13) nor the OCD-tics group (n=15) differed from the other groups combined regarding gender, age, age of onset of OCD, Y-BOCS total score, or ability to work/study. However the GAF score was significantly lower in OCD-autistic traits group as compared to the other subjects (Mann-Whitney U=152.0, p=0.0027).

Two of the patients had relatives with ASD; one had two own children diagnosed with Asperger syndrome and another had a sister with autism and mental retardation. None of these two patients were assessed as having autistic traits themselves. In addition, four patients were later diagnosed with ASD by independent clinicians unaware of the current study after its closure.

A history of being severely bullied in school was more common among the OCD-autistic traits group and they fulfilled more diagnostic criteria for various personality disorders than the others. They were also less likely to live with a partner and have children.

THE ROLE OF THE OCD SUBTYPE WITH AUTISTIC TRAITS OR TICS

A substantial subgroup of OCD patients has previously not been adequately understood. The observable fact that approximately 20 percent of the OCD patients have schizotypal, odd, paranoid and/or obsessive-compulsive personality traits in contrast to the much more normal personality among other anxiety patients- and for that matter all other non-psychotic patients-have since long been recognized. Patients with OCD could be characterized by means of a dimension from "normal personality" at one end to severe autistic personality at the other end. OCD with autistic traits and avoidant personality is probably the most common presentation of a "mild form" of HFA in current adult psychiatry.

Table 4. The postulated differences between "pure" OCD, OCD with autistic traits and OCD with only tics.

Characteristics	*"pure" OCD*	*OCD –autistic traits with or without tics*	*OCD-tics without autistic traits*
Symmetry-ordering Need for the "just right" feeling	+	+++	+++
Counting compulsions	-	++	+++
Hoarding	-	+++	+
Washing as the main compulsion	++	+	+
Self-mutilating	-	+	+
Pathological grooming behaviours	-	++	++
Interpersonal ability	+	-	++
Aloof	+	+++	-
Been bullied	+	+++	-
Sexually active	+	-	++
Nicotine dependant	-	-	+
Personality features: avoidant-obsessional –scizoid-schizotypal-paranoid (in various combinations)	+	+++	-
Histrionic/manipulative	-	-	+
Clumsy	+	+++	+
Tics	-	+	+++
Impulsive/hyperactive/ADHD	-	-	+
Response to treatment	+++	+	++

Descriptions of different subtypes of obsessive-compulsive disorder (OCD) characterized by a "pure" OCD, OCD with autistic traits (with or without a history of tics) or OCD with a history of tics, based on the Stockholm study, other clinical experience and accumulated scientific data. - = unexpected finding, + = present to a limited extent, ++ = often present, +++ = very often present

This subgroup of OCD patients is most parsimoniously explained as OCD with autistic traits or ASD with a concomitant OCD although these cases are probably often referred to as OCD with comorbid personality disorders. Hoarding is probably the most predictive indicator of ASD in OCD patients. Rituals are frequently seen in ASD but seldom acknowledged as OCD even when they cause distress, and may be indistinguishable to compulsions seen in OCD.

It should be emphasized that OCD patients with autistic traits will need special approaches and assistance to achieve social functioning, therefore sub-typing is not only of theoretical interest. Subsequently the goals for the treatment should be set at a moderate level.

OCD patients with a normal ability to interact socially and with a history of tics, characterised by motor related, impulsive symptoms, remains a valid subtype. However, tics are common in ASD and autistic traits are always of larger clinical importance than a chronic tic disorder.

Conclusion

It is beyond doubt that obsessive-compulsive personality disorder is related to both OCD and to Asperger syndrome. Schizotypal personality disorder has repeatedly been reported as more common in OCD than in any other non-psychotic psychiatric condition. Moreover, a recent definition of schizotypal personality disorder is identical to the features observed and reported in the broader autism phenotype. Also, OCD subjects with a schizotypal personality disorder are more often non-responders and consequently excluded in most drug- and cognitive behavioural treatment trials on OCD. Subjects with schizotypal personality often display overvalued ideas which are also common in autism (Wing, 1981). Furthermore, avoidant personality disorder, which is closely linked to social phobia is the most common personality disorder diagnosed in OCD and it is also very often observed among persons with ASD. Likewise, obsessive-compulsive personality traits and social phobia are overrepresented among relatives to persons with autism, and autism and Asperger syndrome are probably overly representative in relatives to those with OCD. In addition both ASD and OCD are disorders characterized by low impulsivity, low prevalence of smoking, a history of being severely bullied at, and low evolutionary fitness.

Autistic traits in OCD may be easier to identify than OCD among persons with autism or Asperger syndrome, as autistic symptoms are not included in the diagnostic criteria for OCD in contrast to rituals and repetitive behaviours which are expected in autism and Asperger syndrome.

In summary there is a link between OCD and ASD. Whenever prominent rituals are part of the clinical picture in a person with ASD, OCD should be suspected and the patient should be treated as such. Likewise, if a patient with OCD appears aloof or odd, ASD should be assessed and the patient should be approached and understood as such. Both diagnoses should be acknowledged and treated in their own right.

Appendix

Table 5. High-functioning autism/Asperger syndrome Global Scale (HAGS) (Bejerot et al, 2001).

High-functioning autism/Asperger syndrome Global Scale (HAGS)
1) *Verbal report*: Has a remarkable talent to establish genuine contact with other people, also with those who themselves have difficulties in establishing contact with others. Cares about other people's well being. Has a well-functioning social network with several close friends. Is interested in a variety of topics. *Behaviour*: Empathic. Is neither conceited nor effusive in his/her expressions, nor socially avoidant, though. Has very good capacity for self-reflection, and also normal, relaxed eye-to-eye contact, normal facial expression and body language.
2) Normal communication skills, in between levels 1 and 3. Most individuals in the normal population belong here.
3) *Verbal report*: Often been subjected to mobbing or frozen out at school or at work. Usually lives alone (but may live together with a partner) Has a few friends but regularly experiences difficulties in social situations. May participate in organisations or clubs where special interests are cultivated. May function in a job. *Behaviour*: Somewhat socially awkward, but this is not conspicuous during a short conversation. Presents a blunted emotional contact; may seem reserved, a bit suspicious or rigid, alternatively a little gauche, self-content and garrulous. May have a sense of insight in an intellectual way. Seems at times to lack common sense and does not share "common values". Possibly a clumsy body language. Has more or less normal eye-to-eye contact, facial expression and speech.
4) *Verbal report*: Already perceived as odd in childhood (if such outside information is available). Was objected to bullying/teasing at school or frozen out at work. Has no close friend outside the family, but may have acquaintances who share the same stereotyped, restricted interests. Has no intimate relationships now and never had any long-lasting intimate relations (> 2 years). Can well carry out work if social contacts are not required (i.e. accountant, attendant at a museum, computer consultant etc.). *Behaviour*: Conspicuously socially awkward; a short conversation will reveal peculiarities. Gives poor emotional contact. Seem to lack common sense and does not share "common opinions" about matters. Has strange ideas about things. May appear a little paranoid, or alternatively be gauche or overly cheerful. Is obviously lacking insight and capacity to form a true view of him/herself. Has an awkward body language; odd facial expression and/or strange eye-contact (i.e. staring gaze or avoidant). Speech may be formal or pedantic, or show peculiar prosody (pitch and rhythm), however, language disturbance *is not* required as criterion.

Acknowledgment

I am most grateful to Mats Humble, MD, for his valuable and wise comments on the manuscript.

REFERENCES

Abell F, Krams M, Ashburner J, et al. The neuroanatomy of autism: a voxel-based whole brain analysis of structural scans. *Neuroreport*. 1999;10:1647-1651.

Altemus M, Jacobson KR, Debellis M, et al. Normal CSF oxytocin and NPY levels in OCD. *Biol Psychiatry*. 1999;45:931-933.

American Psychiatric Association. *Diagnostic and Statistical Manual of Mental Disorders*, 4th ed. (DSM-IV). Washington, DC: APA; 1994.

Anderluh MB, Tchanturia K, Rabe-Hesketh S, Treasure J. Childhood obsessive-compulsive personality traits in adult women with eating disorders: defining a broader eating disorder phenotype. *Am J Psychiatry*. 2003;160:242-247.

Apter A, Horesh N, Gothelf D, et al. Depression and suicidal behavior in adolescent inpatients with obsessive-compulsive disorder. *J Affect Disord*. 2003;75:181-189.

Asperger H. Die 'Autistischen Psychopathen' im Kindesalter. Archiv für Psychiatrie und Nervenkrankheiten. 1944;117:76-136. Translated as 'Autistic psychopathy' in childhood. In: Frith U, ed. Autism and Asperger syndrome. Cambridge: Cambridge University Press; 1991:37-92.

Baer L, Jenike MA, Black DW, Treece C, Rosenfeld R, Greist J. Effect of axis II diagnoses on treatment outcome with clomipramine in 55 patients with obsessive-compulsive disorder. *Arch Gen Psychiatry*. 1992;49:862-866.

Bailey A, Luthert P, Dean A, et al. A clinicopathological study of autism. *Brain*. 1998;121:889-905.

Bailey A, Palferman S, Heavey L, Le Couteur A. Autism: the phenotype in relatives. *J Autism Dev Disord*. 1998;28:369-392.

Bankier B, Aigner M, Bach M. Alexithymia in DSM-IV disorder: comparative evaluation of somatoform disorder, panic disorder, obsessive-compulsive disorder, and depression. *Psychosomatics*. 2001;42:235-240.

Baron-Cohen S. Do autistic children have obsessions and compulsions? *Br J Clin Psychol*. 1989;28:193-200.

Baron-Cohen S, Ring HA, Wheelwright S, et al. Social intelligence in the normal and autistic brain: an fMRI study. *Eur J Neurosci*. 1999;11:1891-1898.

Baron-Cohen S, Scahill VL, Izaguirre J, Hornsey H, Robertson MM. The prevalence of Gilles de la Tourette syndrome in children and adolescents with autism: a large scale study. *Psychol Med*. 1999;29:1151-1159.

Baron-Cohen S, Wheelwright S, Skinner R, Martin J, Clubley E. The autism-spectrum quotient (AQ): evidence from Asperger syndrome/high-functioning autism, males and females, scientists and mathematicians. *J Autism Dev Disord*. 2001;31:5-17.

Baron-Cohen S, Wheelwright S. 'Obsessions' in children with autism or Asperger syndrome. Content analysis in terms of core domains of cognition. *Br J Psychiatry*. 1999;175:484-490.

Bauman ML, Kemper TL. Histoanatomic observations of the brain in early infantile autism. *Neurology*. 1985;35:866-874.

Bejerot S. *Obsessive-Compulsive disorders – Personality traits and disorders, autistic traits and biochemical findings* [Thesis]. Uppsala: Uppsala University; 2000.

Bejerot S, Ekselius L, von Knorring L. Comorbidity between obsessive-compulsive disorder (OCD) and personality disorders. *Acta Psychiatr Scand.* 1998;97:398-402.

Bejerot S, Humble M. Low prevalence of smoking among patients with obsessive-compulsive disorder. *Compr Psychiatry.* 1999;40:268-272.

Bejerot S, Nylander L, Lindström E. Autistic traits in obsessive-compulsive disorder. *Nordic J Psychiatry.* 2001;55:169-176.

Bejerot S, Nylander L. Low prevalence of smoking in patients with autism spectrum disorders. *Psychiatry Res.* 2003;119:177-182.

Bejerot S, von Knorring L, Ekselius L. Personality traits and smoking in patients with obsessive-compulsive disorder. *Eur Psychiatry.* 2000;15:395-401.

Bejerot S. Psychosurgery for obsessive-compulsive disorder – concerns remain. *Acta Psychiatr Scand.* 2003;107:241-243.

Bellodi L, Cavallini MC, Bertelli S, Chiapparino D, Riboldi C, Smeraldi E. Morbidity risk for obsessive-compulsive spectrum disorders in first-degree relatives of patients with eating disorders. *Am J Psychiatry.* 2001;158:563-569.

Bienvenu OJ, Samuels JF, Riddle MA, et al. The relationship of obsessive-compulsive disorder to possible spectrum disorders: results from a family study. *Biol Psychiatry.* 2000;48:287-293.

Bishop DV, Norbury CF. Exploring the borderlands of autistic disorder and specific language impairment: a study using standardised diagnostic instruments. *Child Psychol Psychiatry.* 2002;43:917-929.

Black DW, Gaffney GR, Schlosser S, Gabel J. Children of parents with obsessive-compulsive disorder – a 2-year follow-up study. *Acta Psychiatr Scand.* 2003;107:305-313.

Black DW, Monahan P, Gable J, Blum N, Clancy G, Baker P. Hoarding and treatment response in 38 nondepressed subjects with obsessive-compulsive disorder. *J Clin Psychiatry.* 1998;59:420-425.

Bolton D, Raven P, Madronal-Luque R, Marks IM. Neurological and neuropsychological signs in obsessive-compulsive disorder: interaction with behavioural treatment. *Behav Res Ther.* 2000;38:695-708.

Bolton PF, Pickles A, Murphy M, Rutter M. Autism, affective and other psychiatric disorders: patterns of familial aggregation. *Psychol Med.* 1998;28:385-395.

Brattberg G. Enastående. Självbiografisk berättelse om livet med högfungerande autism. Stockholm: Värkstaden; 1999.

Brown WA, Cammuso K, Sachs H, et al. Autism-related language, personality, and cognition in people with absolute pitch: results of a preliminary study. *J Autism Dev Disord.* 2003;33:163-167.

Cath DC, Spinhoven P, Hoogduin CA, et al. Repetitive behaviors in Tourette's syndrome and OCD with and without tics: what are the differences? *Psychiatry Res.* 2001;101:171-185.

Cath DC, Spinhoven P, van Woerkom TC, et al. Gilles de la Tourette's syndrome with and without obsessive-compulsive disorder compared with obsessive-compulsive disorder without tics: which symptoms discriminate? *J Nerv Ment Dis.* 2001;189:219-228.

Cavedini P, Erzegovesi S, Ronchi P, Bellodi L. Predictive value of obsessive-compulsive personality disorder in antiobsessional pharmacological treatment. *Eur Neuropsychopharmacol.* 1997;7:45-49.

Clark T, Feehan C, Tinline C, Vostanis P. Autistic symptoms in children with attention deficit-hyperactivity disorder. *Eur Child Adolesc Psychiatry.* 1999;8:50-55.

Comings DE, Blum K. Reward deficiency syndrome: genetic aspects of behavioral disorders. *Prog Brain Res*. 2000;126:325-341.

Comings DE. *Tourette syndrome and human behaviour*. Duarte, CA: Hope Press; 1990.

Cook EH Jr, Charak DA, Arida J, Spohn JA, Roizen NJ, Leventhal BL. Depressive and obsessive-compulsive symptoms in hyperserotonemic parents of children with autistic disorder. *Psychiatry Res*. 1994;52:25-33.

Courchesne E, Press GA, Yeung-Courchesne R. Parietal lobe abnormalities detected with MR in patients with infantile autism. *Am J Roentgenol*. 1993;160:387-393.

Critchley HD, Daly EM, Bullmore ET, et al. The functional neuroanatomy of social behaviour: changes in cerebral blood flow when people with autistic disorder process facial expressions. *Brain*. 2000;123:2203-2212.

Cullen BA, Samuels JF, Bienvenu OJ, et al. The relationship of pathologic skin picking to obsessive-compulsive disorder. *J Nerv Ment Dis*. 2001;189:193-195.

Damasio A. *Looking for Spinoza*. Joy, Sorrow and the Feeling Brain. FL: Harcourt, Inc.; 2003.

den Boer JA, Westenberg HG. Oxytocin in obsessive-compulsive disorder. *Peptides*. 1992;13:1083-1085.

Dhossche D. Autism as early expression of catatonia. *Med Sci Monit*. 2004;10:RA31-RA39.

Duncan J. *Attention, intelligence and the frontal lobes*. In: Gazzaniga MS, ed. The cognitive neurosciences. Cambridge, MA: MIT Press; 1995:721-733.

Eaves LC, Ho HH, Eaves DM. Subtypes of autism by cluster analysis. *J Autism Dev Disord*. 1994;24:3-22.

Ellis H, Ellis D, Fraser W, Deb S. A preliminary study of right hemisphere cognitive deficits and impaired social judgements among young people with asperger syndrome. *Eur Child Adolesc Psychiatry*. 1994;3:253-263.

Fals-Stewart W, Schafer J. MMPI correlates of psychotherapy compliance among obsessive-compulsives. *Psychopathology*. 1993;26:1-5.

Fazzi E, Lanners J, Danova S, et al. Stereotyped behaviours in blind children. *Brain Dev*. 1999;21:522-528.

Fitzgerald F. *Autism and creativity*. New York: Brunner-Routledge; 2004.

Flament MF, Rapoport JL, Murphy DL, Berg CJ, Lake CR. Biochemical changes during clomipramine treatment of childhood obsessive-compulsive disorder. *Arch Gen Psychiatry*. 1987;44:219-225.

Folstein SE, Rosen-Sheidley B. Genetics of autism: complex aetiology for a heterogeneous disorder. *Nat Rev Genet*. 2001;2:943-955.

Frith U. *Autistic psychopathy in childhood*. In: Frith U, ed. Autism and Asperger syndrome. Cambridge: Cambridge University Press; 1991:37-92.

Frost RO, Steketee G, Williams LF, Warren R. Mood, personality disorder symptoms and disability in obsessive-compulsive hoarders: a comparison with clinical and nonclinical controls. *Behav Res Ther*. 2000;38:1071-1081.

Fulton M, Winokur G. A comparative study of paranoid and schizoid personality disorders. *Am J Psychiatry*. 1993;150:1363-1367.

Gerland G. *A Real Person: Life on the Outside*. London: Souvenir Press Ltd; 1997.

Ghaziuddin M, Butler E. Clumsiness in autism and Asperger syndrome: a further report. *J Intellect Disabil Res*. 1998;42:43-48.

Ghaziuddin M, Greden J. Depression in children with autism/pervasive developmental disorders: a case-control family history study. *J Autism Dev Disord.* 1998;28:111-115.

Ghaziuddin M, Tsai LY, Ghaziuddin N. Brief report: haloperidol treatment of trichotillomania in a boy with autism and mental retardation. *J Autism Dev Disord.* 1991;21:365-371.

Ghaziuddin M, Weidmer-Mikhai E, Ghaziuddin N. Comorbidity of Asperger syndrome: a preliminary report. *J Intellect Disabil Res.* 1998;42:279-283.

Gillberg C, Billstedt E. Autism and Asperger syndrome: coexistence with other clinical disorders. *Acta Psychiatr Scand.* 2000;102:321-330.

Gillberg C, Coleman M. Clinical diagnosis. In: Gillberg C, Coleman M, eds. *The biology of autistic syndromes.* 3rd ed. Cambridge: Cambridge university press; 2000:4-38.

Gillberg C, Kadesjö B. Why bother about clumsiness? The implications of having developmental coordination disorder (DCD). *Neural Plast.* 2003;10:59-68.

Gillberg C. Asperger syndrome and high-functioning autism. *Br J Psychiatry.* 1998;172:200-209.

Gillberg C. *Clinical and neurobiological aspects of Asperger syndrome in six family studies.* In: Frith U, ed. Autism and Asperger syndrome. Cambridge: Cambridge University Press; 1991:122-146.

Gillberg C. *Clinical child neuropsychiatry.* Cambridge: Cambridge University Press; 1995:90-97.

Gillberg C. The Emanuel Miller Memorial Lecture 1991. Autism and autistic-like conditions: subclasses among disorders of empathy. *J Child Psychol Psychiatry.* 1992;33:813-842.

Gillott A, Furniss F, Walter A. Anxiety in high-functioning children with autism. *Autism.* 2001;5:277-286.

Gordon CT, State RC, Nelson JE, Hamburger SD, Rapoport JL. A double-blind comparison of clomipramine, desipramine, and placebo in the treatment of autistic disorder. *Arch Gen Psychiatry.* 1993;50:441-447.

Grandin T. Thinking In Pictures: and Other Reports from My Life with Autism. *Vintage*; 1996.

Green J, Gilchrist A, Burton D, Cox A. Social and psychiatric functioning in adolescents with Asperger syndrome compared with conduct disorder. *J Autism Dev Disord.* 2000;30:279-293.

Greenberg D, Witztum E, Levy A. Hoarding as a psychiatric symptom. *J Clin Psychiatry.* 1990;51:417-421.

Gross-Isseroff R, Hermesh H, Weizman A. Obsessive-compulsive behaviour in autism – towards an autistic-obsessive-compulsive syndrome? *World J Biol Psychiatry.* 2001;2:193-197.

Hack, R. The Private Diaries, Memos and Letters: The Definitive Biography of the First American Billionaire. *New Millennium Press*; 2001.

Happé F, Ehlers S, Fletcher P, et al. "Theory of mind" in the brain: evidence from a PET scan study of Asperger syndrome. *Neuroreport.* 1996;8:197-201.

Happé F, Frith U. The neuropsychology of autism. *Brain.* 1996;119:1377-1400.

Happé F. *The autobiographic writings of three Asperger syndrome adults: problems with implications for theory.* In: Frith U, ed. Autism and Asperger syndrome. Cambridge: Cambridge University Press; 1991:207-242.

Harvey RJ, Cooray SE. The effective treatment of severe repetitive behaviour with fluvoxamine in a 20 year old autistic female. *Int Clin Psychopharmacol.* 1995;10:201-203.

Haznedar MM, Buchsbaum MS, Wei TC, et al. Limbic circuitry in patients with autism spectrum disorders studied with positron emission tomography and magnetic resonance imaging. *Am J Psychiatry.* 2000;157:1994-2001.

Hazneder MM, Buchsbaum MS, Metzger M, Solimando A, Speigel-Cohen J, Hollander E. Anterior cingulate gyrus volume and glucose metabolism in autistic disorder. *Am J Psychiatry.* 1997;154:1047-1050.

Head D, Bolton D, Hymas N. Deficit in cognitive shifting ability in patients with obsessive-compulsive disorder. *Biol Psychiatry.* 1989;25:929-937.

Heden F, Kristiansson M. [Three cases illustrate that there are several possible explanations of erotomania, not only psychosis. In some of the cases autism is the basic problem] *Läkartidningen.* 2003;100:3962-3964, 3967.

Hollander E, DelGiudice-Asch G, Simon L, et al. B lymphocyte antigen D8/17 and repetitive behaviors in autism. *Am J Psychiatry.* 1999;156:317-320.

Hollander E, King A, Delaney K, Smith CJ, Silverman JM. Obsessive-compulsive behaviors in parents of multiplex autism families. *Psychiatry Res.* 2003;117:11-16.

Hollander E, Novotny S, Hanratty M, et al. Oxytocin infusion reduces repetitive behaviors in adults with autistic and Asperger's disorders. *Neuropsychopharmacology.* 2003;28:193-198.

Hollander E, Rossi NB, Sood E, Pallanti S. Risperidone augmentation in treatment-resistant obsessive-compulsive disorder: a double-blind, placebo-controlled study. *Int J Neuropsychopharmacol.* 2003;6:397-401.

Hollander E, Schiffman E, Cohen B, et al. Signs of central nervous system dysfunction in obsessive-compulsive disorder. *Arch Gen Psychiatry.* 1990;47:27-32.

Holttum JR, Lubetsky MJ, Eastman LE. Comprehensive management of trichotillomania in a young autistic girl. *J Am Acad Child Adolesc Psychiatry.* 1994;33:577-581.

Holzer JC, Goodman WK, McDougle CJ, et al. Obsessive-compulsive disorder with and without a chronic tic disorder. A comparison of symptoms in 70 patients. *Br J Psychiatry.* 1994;164:469-473.

Horwitz B, Rumsey JM, Grady CL, Rapoport SI. The cerebral metabolic landscape in autism: intercorrelations of regional glucose utilization. *Arch Neurol.* 1988;45:749-755.

Humble M, Bejerot S, Bergqvist PB, Bengtsson F. Reactivity of serotonin in whole blood: relationship with drug response in obsessive-compulsive disorder. *Biol Psychiatry.* 2001;49:360-368.

Hymas N, Lees A, Bolton D, Epps K, Head D. The neurology of obsessional slowness. *Brain.* 1991;114:2203-2233.

Jenike MA, Breiter HC, Baer L, et al. Cerebral structural abnormalities in obsessive-compulsive disorder. A quantitative morphometric magnetic resonance imaging study. *Arch Gen Psychiatry.* 1996;53:625-632.

Kadesjö B, Gillberg C. Tourette's disorder: epidemiology and comorbidity in primary school children. *J Am Acad Child Adolesc Psychiatry.* 2000;39:548-555.

Kanner L, Eisenberg L. Early infantile autism 1943-1955. *Am J Orthopsychiatry.* 1956;26:55-65.

Khalifa N, von Knorring AL. Prevalence of tic disorders and Tourette syndrome in a Swedish school population. *Dev Med Child Neurol.* 2003;45:315-319.

Kiessling LS, Marcotte AC, Culpepper L. Antineuronal antibodies: tics and obsessive-compulsive symptoms. *J Dev Behav Pediatr.* 1994;15:421-425.

Kim JJ, Lee MC, Kim J, et al. Grey matter abnormalities in obsessive-compulsive disorder: statistical parametric mapping of segmented magnetic resonance images. *Br J Psychiatry.* 2001;179:330-334.

Klim A, Volkmar F. Asperger syndrome. (June 1995) Some guidelines for assessment, diagnosis and intervention. Available at: URL Learning Disabilities Association of America. Accessed June 22, 2004.

Kobayashi R, Murata T. Behavioral characteristics of 187 young adults with autism. *Psychiatry Clin Neurosci.* 1998;52:383-390.

Kraepelin E. Psychiatrie, IV Bd, 8th ed. Leipzig: Verlag von Joh. Ambrosius Barth; 1915.

Kurlan R, Como PG, Miller B, et al. The behavioral spectrum of tic disorders: a community-based study. *Neurology.* 2002;59:414-420.

Kusunoki K, Sato T, Taga C, et al. Low novelty-seeking differentiates obsessive-compulsive disorder from major depression. *Acta Psychiatr Scand.* 2000;101:403-405.

Lanzi G, Zambrino CA, Termine C, et al. Prevalence of tic disorders among primary school students in the city of Pavia, Italy. *Arch Dis Child.* 2004;89:45-47.

LaSalle VH, Cromer KR, Nelson KN, Kazuba D, Justement L, Murphy DL. Diagnostic interview assessed neuropsychiatric disorder comorbidity in 334 individuals with obsessive-compulsive disorder. *Depress Anxiety.* 2004;19:163-73.

Leckman JF, Goodman WK, North WG, et al. Elevated cerebrospinal fluid levels of oxytocin in obsessive-compulsive disorder. Comparison with Tourette's syndrome and healthy controls. *Arch Gen Psychiatry.* 1994;51:782-792.

Leckman JF, Grice DE, Barr LC, et al. Tic-related vs. non-tic-related obsessive-compulsive disorder. *Anxiety.* 1994-95;1:208-215.

Leckman JF, Grice DE, Boardman J, et al. Symptoms of obsessive-compulsive disorder. *Am J Psychiatry.* 1997;154:911-917.

Lindqvist L. Alone on a crooked road. Ten studies of adults and elderly with MBD/DAMP/ADHD, Asperger syndrome and Tourette syndrome (Swedish). Kalmar, Sweden: Kalmar kommun; 2004.

Little L. Middle-class mothers' perceptions of peer and sibling victimization among children with Asperger's syndrome and nonverbal learning disorders. *Issues Compr Pediatr Nurs.* 2002;25:43-57.

Lotspeich LJ, Kwon II, Schumann CM, et al. Investigation of neuroanatomical differences between autism and Asperger syndrome. *Arch Gen Psychiatry.* 2004;61:291-298.

Lucey JV, Burness CE, Costa DC, et al. Wisconsin Card Sorting Task (WCST) errors and cerebral blood flow in obsessive-compulsive disorder (OCD). *Br J Med Psychol.* 1997;70:403-411.

Mataix-Cols D, Alonso P, Hernandez R, et al. Relation of neurological soft signs to nonverbal memory performance in obsessive-compulsive disorder. *J Clin Exp Neuropsychol.* 2003;25:842-851.

Mataix-Cols D, Baer L, Rauch SL, Jenike MA. Relation of factor-analyzed symptom dimensions of obsessive-compulsive disorder to personality disorders. *Acta Psychiatr Scand.* 2000;102:199-202.

Mataix-Cols D, Rauch SL, Manzo PA, Jenike MA, Baer L. Use of factor-analyzed symptom dimensions to predict outcome with serotonin reuptake inhibitors and placebo in the treatment of obsessive-compulsive disorder. *Am J Psychiatry.* 1999;156:1409-1416.

Mataix-Cols D, Wooderson S, Lawrence N, Brammer MJ, Speckens A, Phillips ML. Distinct neural correlates of washing, checking, and hoarding symptom dimensions in obsessive-compulsive disorder. *Arch Gen Psychiatry.* 2004;61:564-576.

Matsunaga H, Kiriike N, Iwasaki Y, Miyata A, Yamagami S, Kaye WH. Clinical characteristics in patients with anorexia nervosa and obsessive-compulsive disorder. *Psychol Med.* 1999;29:407-414.

McAlonan GM, Daly E, Kumari V, et al. Brain anatomy and sensorimotor gating in Asperger's syndrome. *Brain.* 2002;125:1594-1606.

McCauley JL, Olson LM, Dowd M, et al. Linkage and association analysis at the serotonin transporter (SLC6A4) locus in a rigid-compulsive subset of autism. *Am J Med Genet.* 2004;127B:104-112.

McClellan JM, Werry JS. Evidence-based treatments in child and adolescent psychiatry: an inventory. *J Am Acad Child Adolesc Psychiatry.* 2003;42:1388-1400.

McDougle CJ, Epperson CN, Price LH, Gelernter J. Evidence for linkage disequilibrium between serotonin transporter protein gene (SLC6A4) and obsessive-compulsive disorder. *Mol Psychiatry.* 1998;3:270-273.

McDougle CJ, Kresch LE, Goodman WK, et al. A case-controlled study of repetitive thoughts and behavior in adults with autistic disorder and obsessive-compulsive disorder. *Am J Psychiatry.* 1995;152:772-777.

McDougle CJ, Naylor ST, Cohen DJ, Volkmar FR, Heninger GR, Price LH. A double-blind, placebo-controlled study of fluvoxamine in adults with autistic disorder. *Arch Gen Psychiatry.* 1996;53:1001-1008.

McDougle CJ, Naylor ST, Goodman WK, Volkmar FR, Cohen DJ, Price LH. Acute tryptophan depletion in autistic disorder: a controlled case study. *Biol Psychiatry.* 1993;33:547-550.

Micali N, Chakrabarti S, Fombonne E. The broad autism phenotype: findings from an epidemiological survey. *Autism.* 2004;8:21-37.

Moritz S, Fricke S, Jacobsen D, et al. Positive schizotypal symptoms predict treatment outcome in obsessive-compulsive disorder. *Behav Res Ther.* 2004;42:217-227.

Muhle R, Trentacoste SV, Rapin I. The genetics of autism. Pediatrics. 2004;113:e472-86.

Murphy DG, Critchley HD, Schmitz N, et al. Asperger syndrome: a proton magnetic resonance spectroscopy study of brain. *Arch Gen Psychiatry.* 2002;59:885-891.

Nestadt G, Addington A, Samuels J, et al. The identification of OCD-related subgroups based on comorbidity. *Biol Psychiatry.* 2003;53:914-920.

Nestadt G, Samuels J, Riddle M, et al. A family study of obsessive-compulsive disorder. *Arch Gen Psychiatry.* 2000;57:358-363.

Nilsson EW, Gillberg C, Gillberg IC, Råstam M. Ten-year follow-up of adolescent-onset anorexia nervosa: personality disorders. *J Am Acad Child Adolesc Psychiatry.* 1999;38:1389-1395.

Noterdaeme M, Amorosa H, Mildenberger K, Sitter S, Minow F. Evaluation of attention problems in children with autism and children with a specific language disorder. *Eur Child Adolesc Psychiatry.* 2001;10:58-66.

Ozaki N, Goldman D, Kaye WH, et al. Serotonin transporter missense mutation associated with a complex neuropsychiatric phenotype. *Mol Psychiatry*. 2003;8:895, 933-936.

Ozonoff S, Rogers SJ, Pennington BF. Asperger's syndrome: evidence of an empirical distinction from high-functioning autism. *J Child Psychol Psychiatry*. 1991;32:1107-1122.

Pennington BF, Ozonoff S. Executive functions and developmental psychopathology. *J Child Psychol Psychiatry*. 1996;37:51-87.

Piven J, Arndt S, Bailey J, Havercamp S, Andreasen NC, Palmer P. An MRI study of brain size in autism. *Am J Psychiatry*. 1995;152:1145-1149.

Piven J, Berthier ML, Starkstein SE, Nehme E, Pearlson G, Folstein S. Magnetic resonance imaging evidence for a defect of cerebral cortical development in autism. *Am J Psychiatry*. 1990;147:734-739.

Piven J, Chase GA, Landa R, et al. Psychiatric disorders in the parents of autistic individuals. *J Am Acad Child Adolesc Psychiatry*. 1991;30:471-478.

Piven J, Palmer P, Landa R, Santangelo S, Jacobi D, Childress D. Personality and language characteristics in parents from multiple-incidence autism families. *Am J Med Genet*. 1997;74:398-411.

Purcell R, Maruff P, Kyrios M, Pantelis C. Neuropsychological deficits in obsessive-compulsive disorder. A comparison with unipolar depression, panic disorder, and normal controls. *Arch Gen Psychiatry*. 1998;55:415-423.

Ratnasuriya RH, Marks IM, Forshaw DM, Hymas NF. Obsessive slowness revisited. *Br J Psychiatry*. 1991;159:273-274.

Rauch SL, Whalen PJ, Dougherty D, Jenike MA. *Neurobiologic models of obsessive-compulsive disorder*. In: Jenike MA, Baer L, Minichiello WE, eds. Obsessive-compulsive disorders: practical management, 3rd ed. St Louis, MO: Mosby; 1998:222-253.

Retterstøl N, Opjordsmoen S. Erotomania – erotic self-reference psychosis in old maids. A long-term follow-up. *Psychopathology*. 1991;24:388-397.

Ridley RM. The psychology of perseverative and stereotyped behaviour. *Prog Neurobiol*. 1994;44:221-231.

Ringman JM, Jankovic J. Occurrence of tics in Asperger's syndrome and autistic disorder. *J Child Neurol*. 2000;15:394-400.

Rossi A, Daneluzzo E. Schizotypal dimensions in normals and schizophrenic patients: a comparison with other clinical samples. *Schizophr Res*. 2002;54:67-75.

Rumsey JM, Andreasen NC, Rapoport JL. Thought, language, communication, and affective flattening in autistic adults. *Arch Gen Psychiatry*. 1986;43:771-777.

Rumsey JM, Hamburger SD. Neuropsychological divergence of high-level autism and severe dyslexia. *J Autism Dev Disord*. 1990;20:155-168.

Russell AJ, Mataix-Cols D, Anson MA, Murphy DGM. High Prevalence of Obsessions and Compulsions in Asperger's Syndrome and High-Functioning Autism. *Br J Psychiatry*, 2005; 186:525-528.

Rutter M. Temperament, personality and personality disorders. *Br J Psychiatry*. 1987;150:443-458.

Samuels J, Bienvenu OJ 3rd, Riddle MA, et al. Hoarding in obsessive-compulsive disorder: results from a case-control study. *Behav Res Ther*. 2002;40:517-528.

Samuels J, Nestadt G, Bienvenu OJ, et al. Personality disorders and normal personality dimensions in obsessive-compulsive disorder. *Br J Psychiatry*. 2000;177:457-462.

Schneier FR, Blanco C, Antia SX, Liebowitz MR. The social anxiety spectrum. *Psychiatr Clin North Am*. 2002;25:757-774.

Schultz RT, Gauthier I, Klin A, et al. Abnormal ventral temporal cortical activity during face discrimination among individuals with autism and Asperger syndrome. *Arch Gen Psychiatry*. 2000;57:331-340.

Scourfield J, Martin N, Lewis G, McGuffin P. Heritability of social cognitive skills in children and adolescents. *Br J Psychiatry*. 1999;175:559-564.

Sears LL, Vest C, Mohamed S, Bailey J, Ranson BJ, Piven J. An MRI study of the basal ganglia in autism. *Prog Neuropsychopharmacol Biol Psychiatry*. 1999;23:613-624.

Seigel BV Jr, Nuechterlein KH, Abel L, Wu JC, Buschsbaum MS. Glucose metabolic correlates of continuous performance test performance in adults with a history of infantile autism, schizophrenics, and controls. *Schizophr Res*. 1995;17:85-94.

Singh VK, Rivas WH. Prevalence of serum antibodies to caudate nucleus in autistic children. *Neurosci Lett*. 2004;355:53-56.

Smalley SL, McCracken J, Tanguay P. Autism, affective disorders, and social phobia. *Am J Med Genet*. 1995;60:19-26.

Stanley MA, Turner SM, Borden JW. Schizotypal features in obsessive-compulsive disorder. *Compr Psychiatry*. 1990;31:511-518.

Ståhlberg O, Söderström H, Råstam M, Gillberg C.. Bipolar disorder, schizophrenia, and other psychotic disorders in adults with childhood onset AD/HD and/or autism spectrum disorders. *J Neural Transm*. 2004;111:891-902.

Swedo SE, Leonard HL, Rapoport JL. The pediatric autoimmune neuropsychiatric disorders associated with streptococcal infection (PANDAS) subgroup: separating fact from fiction. *Pediatrics*. 2004;113:907-911.

Szatmari P, Bartolucci G, Bremner R. Asperger's syndrome and autism: comparison of early history and outcome. *Dev Med Child Neurol*. 1989;31:709-720.

Szatmari P. Asperger's syndrome: diagnosis, treatment, and outcome. *Psychiatr Clin North Am*. 1991;14:81-93.

Szcszko PR, Robinson D, Alvir JM, et al. Orbital frontal and amygdala volume reductions in obsessive-compulsive disorder. *Arch Gen Psychiatry*. 1999;56:913–919.

Söderström H, Nilsson A. Childhood-onset neuropsychiatric disorders among adult patients in a Swedish special hospital. *Int J Law Psychiatry*. 2003;26:333-338.

Söderström H, Råstam M, Gillberg C. Temperament and character in adults with Asperger syndrome. *Autism*. 2002;6:287-297.

Takeuchi T, Nakagawa A, Harai H, et al. Primary obsessional slowness: long-term findings. *Behav Res Ther*. 1997;35:445-449.

Tani P, Lindberg N, Joukamaa M, et al. Asperger syndrome, alexithymia and perception of sleep. *Neuropsychobiology*. 2004;49:64-70.

Tantam D. *Asperger syndrome in adulthood.* In: Frith U, ed. Autism and Asperger syndrome. Cambridge: Cambridge University Press; 1991:147-183.

Thomsen PH. Obsessive-compulsive disorder in children and adolescens. A 6-22-year follow-up study. Clinical descriptions of the course and continuity of obsessive-compulsive symptomatology. *Eur Child Adolesc Psychiatry*. 1994;3:82-96.

Thorén P, Åsberg M, Bertilsson L, Mellström B, Sjöqvist F, Träskman L. Clomipramine treatment of obsessive-compulsive disorder. II. Biochemical aspects. *Arch Gen Psychiatry*. 1980;37:1289-1294.

Turner M. Annotation: Repetitive behaviour in autism: A review of psychological research. *J Clin Psychol. Psychiat.* 1999;40:839-849.

Volkmar FR, Klin A, Schultz RT, Rubin E, Bronen R. Asperger's disorder. *Am J Psychiatry.* 2000;157:262-267.

Weimer AK, Schatz AM, Lincoln A, Ballantyne AO, Trauner DA. "Motor" impairment in Asperger syndrome: evidence for a deficit in proprioception. *J Dev Behav Pediatr.* 2001;22:92-101.

Westen D, Shedler J. Revising and assessing axis II, Part II: Toward an empirically based and clinically useful classification of personality disorders. *Am J Psychiatry.* 1999;156:273-285.

Wilhelm S, Keuthen NJ, Deckersbach T, et al. Self-injurious skin picking: clinical characteristics and comorbidity. *J Clin Psychiatry.* 1999;60:454-459.

Williams D. Nobody Nowhere: The Extraordinary Autobiography of an Autistic. *Times Books*; 1993.

Wing L, Shah A. Catatonia in autistic spectrum disorders. *Br J Psychiatry.* 2000;176:357-362.

Wing L. Epidemiology, symptoms and diagnosis of autistic spectrum disorders. Unpublished manuscript; 2002.

Wing L. The autistic spectrum – A guide for parents and professionals. *Constable and Company Limited*; 1996.

Wing L. The autistic spectrum. *Lancet.* 1997;350:1761-1766.

Wing L. *The relationship between Asperger's syndrome and Kanner's autism.* In: Frith U, ed. Autism and Asperger syndrome. Cambridge: Cambridge University Press; 1991:93-121.

Wing, L. Asperger´s syndrome: a clinical account. *Psychol Med.* 1981;11:115-129.

Wolff S, McGuire RJ. Schizoid personality in girls: a follow-up study – what are the links with Asperger's syndrome? *J Child Psychol Psychiatry.* 1995;36:793-817.

Wolff S. 'Schizoid' personality in childhood and adult life. I: The vagaries of diagnostic labelling. *Br J Psychiatry.* 1991;159:615-20, 634-5.

Yuwiler A, Shih JC, Chen CH, et al. Hyperserotoninemia and antiserotonin antibodies in autism and other disorders. *J Autism Dev Disord.* 1992;22:33-45.

Zilbovicius M, Garreau B, Samson Y, et al. Delayed maturation of the frontal cortex in childhood autism. *Am J Psychiatry.* 1995;152:248-252.

In: Obsessive-Compulsive Disorder and Comorbidity
Editors: R. Gross-Isseroff and A. Weizman, pp. 103-129
ISBN 1-59454-884-6

Chapter 7

NEUROLOGICAL DISORDERS OF THE BASAL GANGLIA AND OBSESSIVE-COMPULSIVE DISORDER

Roberto Cavallaro,[*] Cristina Cavallini
Department of Neuropsychiatric Sciences, S. Raffaele Hospital Scientific Institute, Milano, Italy;
and Laura Bellodi
Vita-Salute University School of Psychology, Milano, Italy

ABSTRACT

A number of apparently heterogeneous disorders share the clinical, epidemiological-genetic and pharmacological features leading in the last decade to the biological and psychopatological concept of 'Obsessive - Compulsive Disorder (OCD) Spectrum', the most striking clinical interface between psychiatric and neurological sciences. Disorders like Tics and Tourette's syndrome are classified within the so called 'neurological OCD spectrum' due to prevailing motor aspects obsessive manifestations and common familial patterns. Nevertheless obsessive symptoms or syndromes are extensively described during basal ganglia degenerative disorders like Huntington disease or other lenticulostriatal diseases, but also after toxical or lesional pathology in this brain area. These evidences led to more recent clinical, epidemiological, genetic and family research, which results suggest high comorbidity with OCD and high familial morbidity risk for OCD and OCD spectrum diseases transmission in some neurological illnesses of the basal ganglia, like focal dystonia, Tic disorder and Tourette's syndrome. A common, basal ganglia-related, biological background seems to be implied at some level at least in the development of clinically appreciable manifestations of OCD and neurological disorders.

[*] Correspondence should be sent to Dr. Roberto Cavallaro, Department of Neuropsychiatric Sciences, S. Raffaele Hospital Scientific Institute, via Stamira D'Ancona,20, 20127, Milano, Italy, E-Mail cavallaro.roberto@hsr.it

INTRODUCTION

A number of apparently etherogeneous disorders share the clinical, epidemiological-genetic and pharmacological features leading in the last decade to the biological and psychopatological concept of 'Obsessive - Compulsive Disorder (OCD) Spectrum' (Hollander and Wong 95), the most striking clinical interface between psychiatric and neurological sciences. Following this concept a number of these disorders like Tics and Tourette's syndrome, were classified as belonging to the 'neurological' OCD spectrum, in which the motor aspects are so prevailing that for long time have been assessed and treated by neurologists. Nevertheless a number of neurological disorders arising from basal ganglia pathology (idiopathic, toxical or lesional) do show obsessive and compulsive symptoms and signs or show a coexisting OCD. The clinical observation is also supported by epidemiological data on increased OCD prevalence among samples of patients affected by some of these disorders: neuropsychiatric disorders like Tourette Syndrome and Sydenham Corea show high rates of comorbidity with OCD and high familial morbidity risks for OCD (Hollander and Wong 1995).

Obsessive-Compulsive (OC) symptoms or syndromes are extensively described during basal ganglia secondary (toxical or lesional) pathology and degenerative disorders like Huntington disease or other lenticulostriatal diseases, suggesting that basal ganglia pathology, at any level is implied at least in the development of clinically appreciable manifestations of OCD and its spectrum (table1) (Calabresi et al 97, Lauterbach et al 98). This manuscript will take into account data supporting the existence of a common biological background between OCD and some neurological disorders of the basal ganglia, with a selective attention to epidemiological and genetic-familial data supporting a shared biological background for OCD and some neurological illnesses like tic disorder, Tourette's syndrome and idiopathic dystonia.

THE BASAL GANGLIA-THALAMO-CORTICAL-BASAL LOOPS: A MODEL OF INTERACTION OF MOTOR AND COGNITIVE-BEHAVIOURAL PATHWAYS

Nowadays a basal ganglia disease is considered an illness arising from pathology occurring in a wide number of brain structures and not only the large subcortical nuclear masses comprising the striatum (caudate nucleus and the putamen), and the lentiform nucleus (globus pallidus and putamen). The modern concept and understanding of basal ganglia composition and of their inner structures interactions takes into account the high level of integration of motor and emotional-cognitive functions, probably responsible of many psychopathological manifestations of neurological basal ganglia disorders and motor manifestations of psychiatric disorders like OCD.

The high level of integration between motor, cognitive and emotional brain activities passing through the basal ganglia is possible, in a general model of functioning, by the gathering of information from a number of cortical areas which downstreams pass through the basal ganglia and, after integration and processing are directed via the thalamus to one or more other cortical areas. This interpretative model presupposes the existence of cortical-subcortical circuits or loops able to use each station of the loop as a possible area of integration. The development of the real model of functioning of these circuits is still moving on as far as knowledge of neuroanatomical circuitry and functional patterns is still limited and some what uncertain.

Striatum receives a high number of inputs from many cortical and subcortical areas. The basal ganglia along with their connected cortical and thalamic areas, are viewed as components of a family of 'basal ganglia-thalamocortical circuits' that are organized in a parallel manner and remain largely segregated from one another, both structurally and functionally.

Each circuit receives input from several separate, but functionally related cortical areas, traverses specific regions of the striatum, Gpi, SNR, and thalamus, and projects back to one of the frontocortical areas providing input to the circuit (Figure 1). This hypothesis from Alexander et al follows the first ones suggesting two distinct, parallel loops, a motor one including the putamen and an associative one, including the caudate nucleus. Alexander et al.(1986) described evidence for 5 circuits, two motor and three associative: the "motor circuit", the "oculomotor circuit", the "dorsolateral prefrontal circuit", the "lateral orbitofrontal circuit" and the "anterior cingulate circuit" (Figure 2), but these circuits were thought to be segregated from each other and to project to restricted portions of the frontal lobe. In the Alexander view each of these loops starts with multiple corticostriate inputs integrated in their passage through the basal ganglia, ultimately projects to a restricted area of the thalamus and from there back to a single cortical area. Cortical areas inputting the single circuit should be integrated as functionally related and the same organization pattern should be present also in the basal ganglia (Alexander et al 1986). This pattern of organization is believed to be replicated also in the pars reticulata of the substantia nigra, the other output nucleus from the basal ganglia (Middleton and Strick 1997).

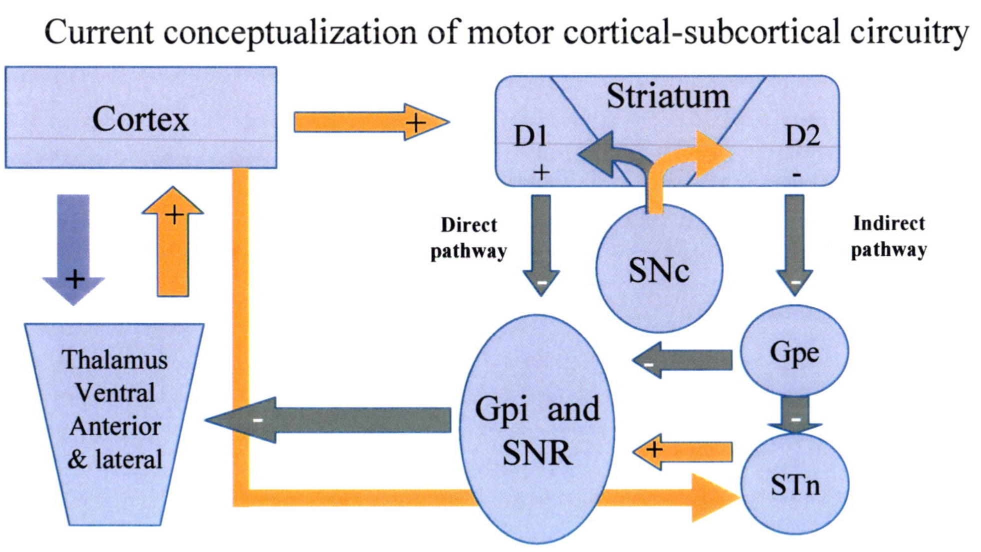

Figure 1. Current Conceptualization of motor cortical-subcortical circuity. Modified from Cavallaro et al 2000.

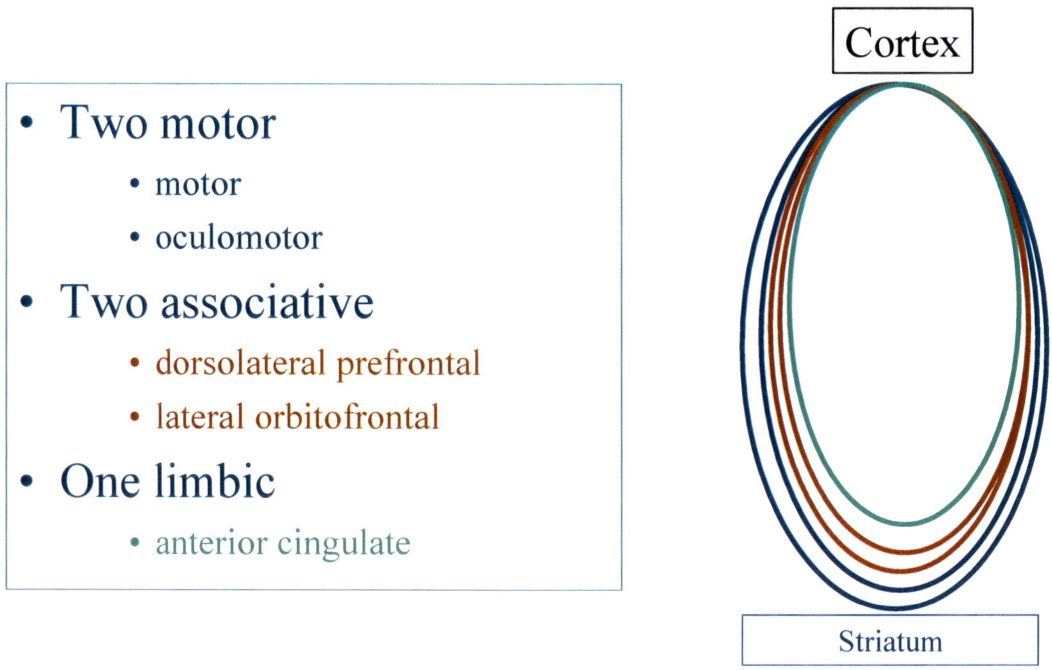

Figure 2. Alexander et al (1986-90) basal gangliathalamocortical segregated circuits.

Nevertheless the high levels of segregation hypothesized would not be compatible with the well known above reported coexistence of clinically relevant cognitive, motor and emotional aspects of basal ganglia illnesses or lesions.

Moreover research on primates, while confirming broad functional subdivisions within the basal ganglia, suggest that that it is probably the case that motor, cognitive, and motivational systems can interact within the caudate and putamen (Kimura and Matsumoto 1997), when looking at patterns of neural activity in various conditioning tasks.

Rigidity of the interpretation of the level of segregation of motor, cognitive and emotional strio-thalamic-cortico-striatal loops was improved by other more recent approaches keeping into account new findings from basic and clinical research. Parent and Hazrati (1995) mantained in their model the Alexander's segregated circuits, but suggested a tripartite organization of the cortex and striatum, resulting in an associative, a limbic and a motor area, distributed at the two ends of the circuit that was still closed in each of its components (Figure 3). According to this view the tripartite organization is mantained in the striatum, in the subthalamic nuclei, in the globus pallidus, and in the cortex (Figure 4).

More recently other neuroanatomical and functional findings suggested further possibilities of functional ingration of the Alexander's circuits in open loops. Joel and Weiner (1994-97) model improved between-circuits connectivity beside the closed circuits within the three areas of the Parent's tripartite distribution, suggesting open circuits at different levels. In this model the first, extrastriatal, link, is the so- called 'split circuit'. The ‘split circuit’ is a closed circuit including a striofrontocortical pathway reentering the frontocortical area of origin, that also includes another circuit that leads in an open way from the striatum to a frontocortical area which is the source of another, closed circuit. At present time a split circuit for each striofrontocortial area seems to fit better the strio-thalamo-cortical circuitry (Joel and Weiner 1994) (Figure 5).

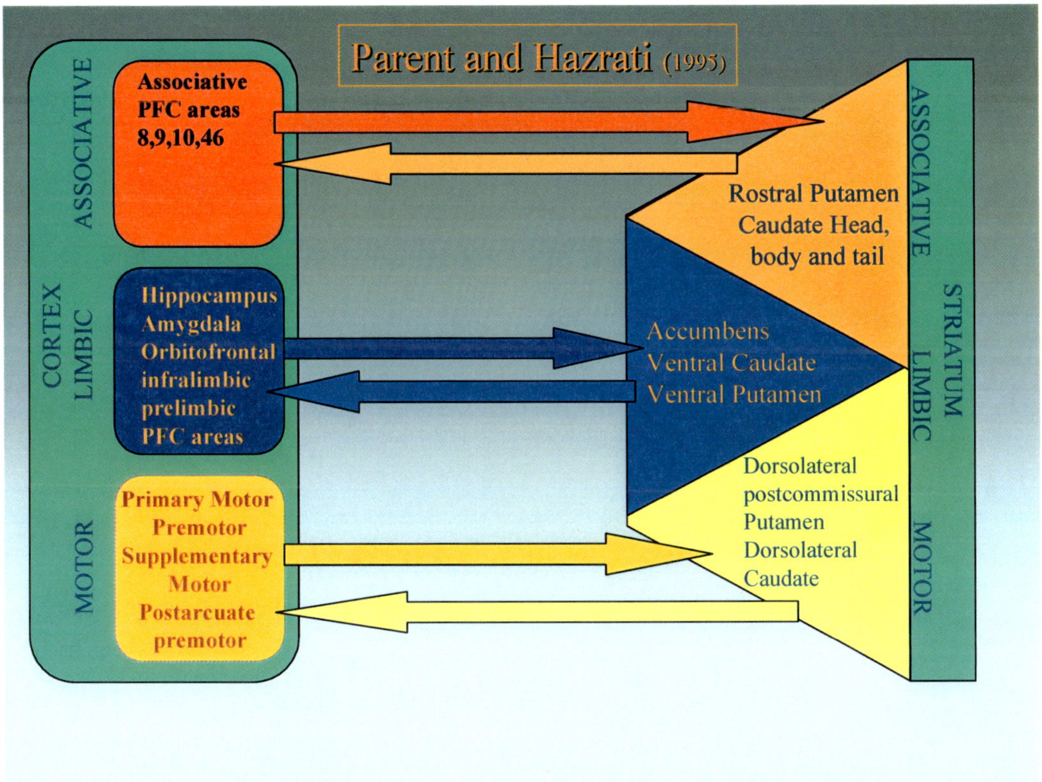

Figure 3. A tripartite organization of the cortex and striatum (Parent and Hazrati 1995)

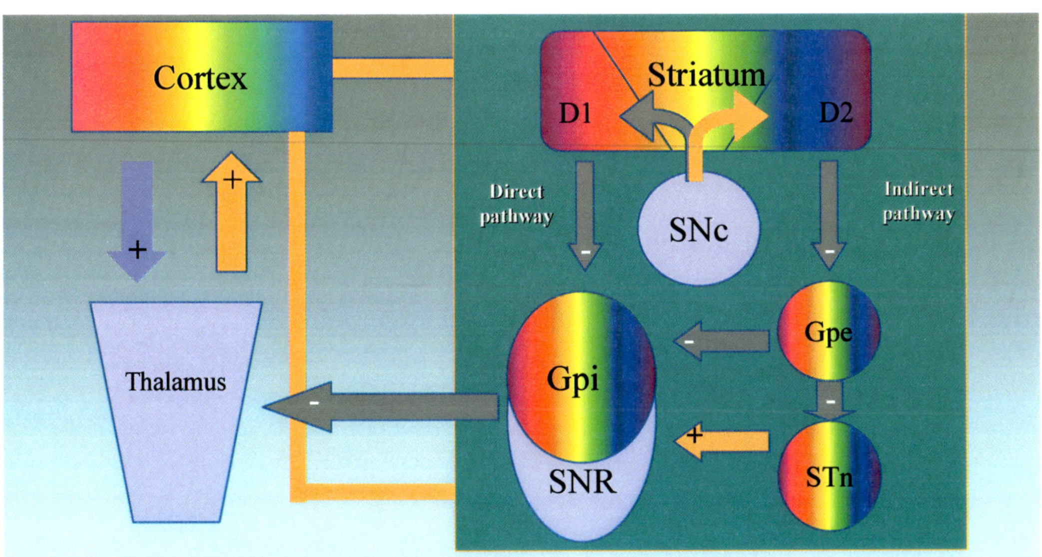

Figure 4. Conceptualization of motor cortical-subcortical circuitry

The second level of open circuitry is hypothesized to be intrastriatal, and in particular pertaining the indirect pathway that through the external Globus Pallidus (GPe) and the subthalamic nuclei (STN) converges with the direct way on the internal Globus Pallidus/Substantia nigra pars reticulata complex with a net inhibitory effect on the thalamus. Between these nuclei are hypothesized three closed circuits cornesponding to the tripartite functional organization (motor, associative and limbic) and two open pathways, one from the associative striatum to the motor GPi, via the associative Gpe and the motor STN, and the other connecting the associative striatum to the VP, via the associative GPe and limbic STn (Figure 5). This model, that surely best fits to the complex integrative activity of the striatum and its inhibitory effects on thalamocortical circuits, allows to understand the possibility of holding 'on line' informations of another functional area of importance for a given program organization and execution, and, in case of dysfunction, also the cooccurrece of both neurological and psychiatric symptomatology.

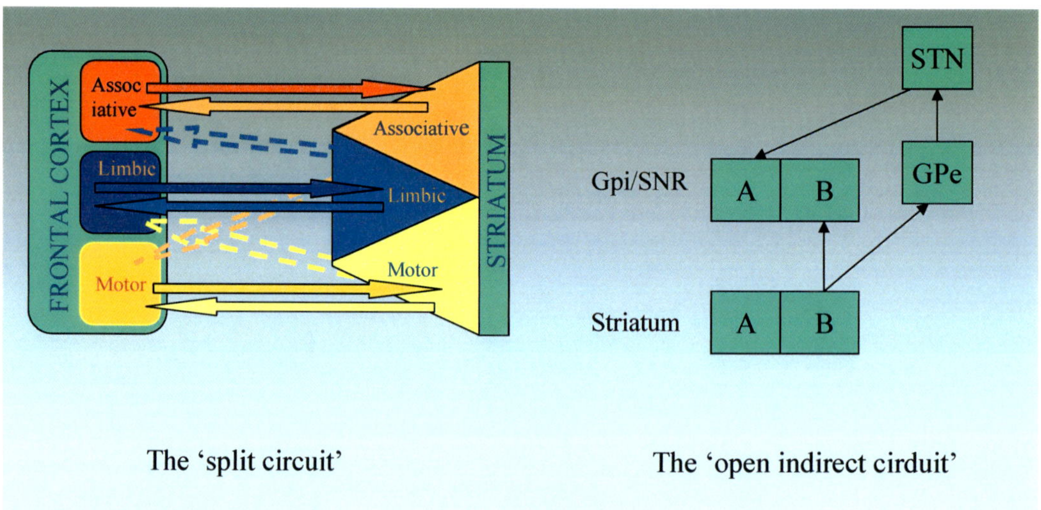

Figure 5. The split circuit and the open pathways (Joel and Weiner 1994, 1997)

At present time, lesional studies, brain circuitry knowledge and functional brain imaging, drove many authors to formulate the hypothesis that OCD just derives from thalamo-cortical disfunction, and in particular from thalamic dishinibition of basal-cortical circuitry induced by direct/indirect strio-pallido-thalamic pathways unbalance (Saxena et al 1998; Eidelberg et al 1995; Hallet 1993).

This brief evaluation of the evolution of interpretative models of basal-cortical circuitry leads to an evident support to the existence of so called 'neurological' or 'psychiatric' conditions arising from pathology of each of the structures involved, but sharing signs and symptoms. A number of common anatomical and functional nodes are evident in all the stages of the development of these models. Some of these disorders like idiopathic dystonia and OCD share similar results at functional imaging and high probability of comorbidity (see below in detail) which point to common pathways of illness. This is supported by lesional studies, but the most striking support to consider the spectrum of neurological-OCD conditions as a real, genetically controlled or influenced illness comes from epidemiological and familial studies on some of these neuropsychiatric conditions.

OC Manifestations during Neurological Disorders of the Basal Ganglia

The clinical manifestations of all basal ganglia disorders include, along the course of illness and depending from its severity and stage, abnormal movements, psychiatric symptoms, and cognitive impairment. The interaction of these pathological manifestations lead to a peculiar degree of severity given from impaired motor and mental performance, but also severe psychological suffering. We will briefly summarize neurological illnesses of the basal ganglia presenting frequently with OC signs and symptoms or OCD comorbidity for which different pathology (lesional/toxic, inflammatory/autoimmune or ereditary/idiopathic) has been shown to affect the striatal 'station' of the strio-thalamo-cortico-striatal loop.

Focal Lesions in the Basal Ganglia

Rarely in psychiatry clinical models of an idiopathic illness were strongly supported by lesional studies, like for OCD, but none can state that OCD as an illness can be experimentally observed with specific lesions: what we can find in lesional literature is probably the neurological functional architecture of part of the OCD manifestations. The first reports of OCD symptoms in patients with lesional, inflammatory or toxic dysfunctions of the basal ganglia date the '30s of the past century. One of these clinical observations came from Schilder (1938) who observed OC symptoms in patients with post encephalitic parkinsonism, together with other clinicians of that period. The common autoptical finding in those cases was of lesional pathology in the pallidum and substantia nigra (Schilder 1938). With the birth of brain imaging, from the '80s of the last century more cases were presented in the clinical literature and more knowledge was added in this field. Most of cases reported pointed to putaminal and caudate lesions mono- or, more frequently, bilateral, with ischaemical or toxic origin, including CO and manganese intoxications. Among all the reports of lesional cases showing clinical manifestations of obsessions and compulsions or stereotyped acts or vocalizations there is a general trend to attribute a repetitive behaviour to symptoms of OCD in a most frequently completely absent psychopathological description of all features making a repetitive behaviour a real symptom of an obsessive-compulsive disorder. All the reports seem to describe a list of repetitive motor and psychological activities, undoubtly pathological, but far to be a complete sign of OCD. OCD symptomatology probably needs this neurological 'skeleton', but the real expression of the OC illness can be appreciated only when other psychopathological features like the feeling of intrusiveness of ideas, the feeling of being obliged, the discomfort and lack of resistance and the core phobic features, variously combine with a mental content or a motor behaviour. About this it is interesting that these reports of neurological conditions (and some of the data that will be treated later) frequently describe a reduced or lacking emotional participation to symptoms or lack of egodystonic feelings about described pathological behaviours (Laplane 1981). Probably what makes the difference with OCD stands in this peculiarity. The other failure of the reports of OC symptoms after lesional pathology consists in a rare and poor descriptions of the possible effects of treatments known to be effective in OCD. In one case (Stowe et al 1991) with a clear and large bilateral pallidal lesion following CO intoxication clear OC signs developed across years after the early occurrence of simply repetitive behaviours. Contents (obsessive preoccupations for dirt and order) and behaviours (compulsions of controlling, touching, washing, counting, hoarding) were resistant to dopaminergic and antidopaminergic drugs, while a clear response was obtained with fluoxetine, a SSRI used to treat OCD. This case too lacked of clear emotional consequences of symptomatology, but OC symptoms appeared with increasing severity along many years, like if the basal ganglia lesions were a necessary, but not directly and causally related factor in their development, while repetitive motor behaviour appeared immediately after lesions. Another interesting case, among the many ones in the literature was reported by Weilburg et al (1989), who reported a case of a young man who developed OCD after infancy, but who suffered since its birth, due to perinatal suffering, from a caudate-putaminal lesion. Also in this case the lesional pathology seems to be a strong acquired vulnerability factor, on which across time, with loss of other functions or interaction with other genetic vulnerabilities (first case), or development of the brain (second case), an OCD syndrome more similar to the idiopathic one develops, following also its rules, like the response to specifical pharmacological interventions. Lesional studies seem then, in our opinion, to be of absolute interest to construct and validate physiopathological models of OCD and promote research on candidate biological structures expressed in the lesioned areas that may contribute to the origin or clinical manifestations and development of the illness, but cannot be considered phenocopies of the illness.

OC Symptoms in Neurological Disorders

Huntington Corea

Huntington corea is a autosomical dominant degenerative disease characterized by choreic movements and progressive dementia, often presenting or associated with psychiatric symptoms, with an onset ranging from the fourth to the fifth decade of life. Outcomes relative to psychiatric symptoms are quite different among subjects and kind of psychiatric manifestation is highly variable. The main brain area involved by degeneration is striatum, especially the caudate, while cortex is also involved with mild atrophy. Neuronal populations undergoing degeneration in the striatum are various with consequent decrease in the neostriatal concentration of GABA, acetylcholine, acetylcholinetransferase, but also enkephalines and other neurotransmitters. Conversely dopamine concentrations are increased in striatum, substantia nigra and accumbens nuclei. It should be noted that in many pathological conditions of the caudate dopamine is increased. A number of cases of OC symptomatology have been described in literature (Cummings 1993, Rapoport 1988). Biological interpretation of these OC symptoms during chorea point at the possible increased dopaminergic inhibition of the substantia negra on the pallidum and the caudate. Against the dopamine hypothesis must be considered that antidopaminergic drugs while effective in treating motor aspects of chorea are uneffective in treating emerging OC symptoms. Caudate degeneration itself may also be responsible of a reduced pallido-thalamical inhibiting activity, with altered communications in the strio-thalamic-cortical-striatal loops hypothesized to be involved in OCD symptomatology.

Sydenham Chorea and PANDAS

Sydenham Chorea is a basal ganglia illness presenting with choreic or ballistic movements of the arms and legs, with onset during infancy or adolescence in subjects who were affected by rheumatic fever. Pathological findings include striatal and cortical abnormalities and the finding of elevated concentrations of anticytoplasm autoantibodies directed toward cytoplasm of caudate and subthalamic nuclei cells. Recently specific autoantigens have been considered a key factor for thc development of the illness. Autoimmune reactions seem to be crucial for damage in the putaminal area explaining the motor disorders and damagebin the strio-thalamo-cortico-striatal loop (Swedo et al 1993) for the psychiatric signs of the OC series frequently observed in these patients. OC symptoms in patients affected by Sydenham Chorea range from single symptoms and signs to complete syndromes that satisfy DSM IV criteria for OCD. It has been reported that OCD symptoms are significantly more frequent among subjects with Sydenham Chorea than among subjects who just suffered from uncomplicated rheumatic fever (Swedo 1989,1993). It is interesting that OC symptoms often precede motor signs, get their maximum intensity with chorea signs and dissolve before chorea signs. It has been extimated that OC symptoms during Sydenham Chorea last, as chorea, from 2 to 16 months and that no more signs are present after 18 months (Swedo 1993). This time window within which OC symptoms appear and disappear is interesting, as it is an inflammatory model of the involvement of basal ganglia in the pathogenesis of OCD symptoms. It remains to be demonstrated if patients with OCD have a more frequent history of Sydenham Chorea and how many subjects with OC symptoms during chorea show a chronic evolution of psychiatric symptoms. OC symptoms during post-streptococcal chorea started a new line of research about the psychiatric sequelae of streptococcal infections inducing autoimmune response, the PANDAS. This clinical entity has been recently proposed to include a number of OCD cases with prepuberal onset, in which tics are clearly appreciable with OCD or alone, a sudden onset after a streptococcical infection and a long term development with phases of remission and reexacerbation. PANDAS stands for Pediatric Autoimmune Neuropsychiatric Disorders Associated with Streptococal infections. Although this pathological entity is still controversial, a number of evidences show the specifical presence of autoantibodies directed towards the neurons of caudate and putamen, including the same 60Kda autoantigen found in Sydenham Chorea (Church et al 2003). Again this disorder may be a good model to study OCD and candidate biological structures supporting illness development, but studies about the familial status for OCD and OCD disorders spectrum to explain why only some subjects having streptococcal infections do develop OC symptoms or an OCD during their adolescence or adulthood are lacking. These studies would disconfirm or confirm the role of autoimmune response or direct toxic effect of streptococcical infections as a vulnerability or precipitating factor for OCD, or neither. On the other hand basal ganglia and again caudate-putaminal areas are confirmed as a crucial anatomical and functional node for the development of OC spectrum signs and symptoms.

Tourette Syndrome

Gilles de la Tourette's (GTS) syndrome or disorder is charachterized by multiple vocal and motor tics, psychopathological manifestations, deficit in attention, and is well known in particular for the peculiarity of some vocal and motor tics, like coprophenomena, echophenomena, palilalia, and comorbidity with OCD and ADHD. It is now thought that

GTS is a familial illness in at least half cases, with a most plausible transmission model of SML with incomplete penetrance (see below for details). An intersting detail about GTS transmission and its relationship to OCD is that beside the observation of 37 to 49% comorbidity with OCD or OC symptoms, the prevalence of OCD in first-grade relatives of GTS patients is significantly higher than in the general population, in particular for female relatives (see below). Without any doubt GTS is the neuropsychiatric disorder comorbid with OCD and included into the OCD spectrum with the greatest number of familial studies in relation to OCD transmission. OC symptoms where included by Gilles de la Tourette in his first descriptions of his syndrome and nowadays some authors suggest that OCD, OCD with tics and GTS are different phenotypical manifestations of a common genetic background. Some difference in the clinical presentation of the OC symptoms during GTS may lead to think that the major component to be affected in the cortical-subcortical loop is predominantly striatal, as the typical cognitive/emotional charachterization of OCD symptoms, probably related to disturbed activity in the prefrontal cortex is quite limited among the OCD/GTS. OC symptoms in GTS could then be interpreted as a sort of 'pre-verbal' pathological behaviour, more probably related to basal ganglia-thalamic disease than to the cortical stations of the cortical-subcortical loop. Functional brain imaging supports the involvement of the loop with images of decreased activity in striatum and subcortical limbic areas and increased activity in the motor-sensitive superior cortex (Stoetter et al 92). MR studies suggest a decreased volume of basal ganglia. Recently high levels of antineuronal antibodies towards basal ganglia neurons and high antistreptolisinic titles have been found among GTS patients as well as the same 60kDa autoantigen found among subjects with Sydenham Chorea and PANDAS: these findings suggest that at least part of the GTS syndromes may be included among basal ganglia diseases related to streptococcical infections.

A Model of Neuropsychiatric Condition Sharing Both Clinical, Epidemiological, Familial and Brain Imaging Research Findings: Idyiopathic Dystonia and OCD

Among neurological disorders with striatal involvement, torticollis, a form of idiopathic dystonia, was included within the OCD spectrum since the birth of the concept (Hollander and Wong 1995): clinical brain imaging and epidemiological-familial studies supported and confirmed the inclusion in the spectrum.

Idiopathic dystonia is a disorder of unknown origin, with a prevalence of 330 per million, that may be both familial or sporadic (Richter and Loscher 1998). It is characterised by sustained muscle contractions, causing twisting, repetitive movements or abnormal postures, aggravated by stress and emotional states, that may involve specific muscular groups like in idiopathic focal dystonia , (IFD) (i.e. blepharospasm or torticollis,) or be generalised. Primary dystonias represent about two thirds of the dystonias and may be both familial, both sporadic.

At least five different hereditary backgrounds have been suggested for dystonia. Different causative mutations have been described for early-onset primary torsion dystonia. On chromosome 9 at DYT1 locus (Ozelius et al 1989) sporadic or familial forms of focal dystonias (writer's cramp) did not appear to be related to any mutation in this genomic area (Brassat et al 2000; Kamm et al 2000). Familial studies suggest that the much more frequent focal dystonia follows an autosomal dominant inheritance with reduced penetrance. Nevertheless, two loci causing late onset primary torsion dystonia (PTD), which tends to begin in craniocervical muscles or an arm and usually remains focal or segmental in distribution and is not DYT1 related, have been mapped. Leube et al (1996) mapped DYT7, tracing adult-onset focal PTD to chromosome 18p, and Almasy et al (1997) mapped DYT6, tracing an "intermediate" phenotype with features common to both early- and late-onset PTD to the pericentromeric region of chromosome 8.

Dystonia is the most frequent movement disorder related to basal ganglia lesions in humans, particularly when putamen is involved (Bhatia and Marsden 1994, Lee and Marsden 1994), is frequently associated with basal ganglia diseases like Parkinson, Huntington and Wilson diseases, but may be also induced by exogenous factors like chronic antidopaminergic treatment (tardive dystonia), dopamine agonist treatment, toxins or carbon monoxide intoxications (Richter and Loscher 1998 for review). The basal ganglia area more frequently lesioned in secondary dystonias are the lentiform nuclei (formed by the putamen and the globus pallidus) (Bhatia and Marsden 1994), the caudate nuclei and the thalamus (Lee and Marsden 1994), all areas involved in the basal ganglia-thalamo-cortical loop, the circuitry supposed to be altered in OCD. At present time, based on the lesional studies and brain circuitry knowledge, many authors think that a great part of dystonias derives from thalamo-cortical dysfunction, and in particular from thalamic dishinibition of basal-cortical circuitry induced by dyrect/indirect strio-pallido-thalamic pathways unbalance, the same hypothesis of basal-prefrontal dysfunction suggested for OCD (Eidelberg et al 1995; Hallet 1993; Saxena 1998).

Functional brain imaging with PET and fMRI studies, including two previous studies from our group, supports the hypothesis that patients with IFD (Eidelberg et al 1995; Galardi et al 1996; Playfordet al 1998) and OCD (Baxter et al 1987, 1988; Breiter et al 1996; Perani et al 1995; McGuire et al 1994; Rauch et al 1994; Swedo et al 1989), share similar dysfunctions with regard to brain localization such as the basal ganglia (putamen and caudate or lenticular nuclei), thalamus, and in the frontal and cingulate cortex. Very recently Carbon et al (2004) found a genotype-specific increases in metabolism in the putamen, anterior cingulate, and cerebellar hemispheres of DYT1 gene carriers, the idiopathic early onset dystonia gene, and concluded that, metabolic abnormalities in subcortical structures may represent trait features that are specific for individual dystonia genotypes.

Again very recently, in an animal model of dystonia Kohling et al (2004) found that while striatal projection neurones behave normally in terms of neuronal discharge patterns and intrinsic membrane properties there are strong indications that network excitability in the striatum in response to neocortical activation is raised. An increase in excitability within the cortico-striatal pathway in these animal is considered to contribute significantly to the expression of dystonic symptoms. In humans a neurophysiological study performed with transcranial magnetic stimulation also found that intracortical inhibition was similarly decreased in Tourette's syndrome (TS), a known OCD spectrum disorder, IFD, and OCD patients (Greenberg et al 2000).

The above biological data, suggest a similar and possibly shared dysfunction in basal ganglia-thalamic-cortico-basal neuronal loops (Richter et al 1998; Saxena et al 1998) for both IFD and OCD. In particular, a candidate area for the study of a shared dysfunction might be the striopallidal portion of the loop, because of the strong and multilevel interaction between motor, associative, and limbic projections above reported in the more recent literature models of cortical-subcortical circuitry suggested in the literature (Joel and Weiner 1997).

Dystonia, as other basal ganglia disorders above reported, has clinical features recalling OC signs patterns and may be associated to OC symptoms and OCD. Stress and emotional states worsen dystonic movements, like in OCD and Tic disorder, and frequently patients develop motor strategies, called antagonistic gestures or 'sensory tricks' (Fahn 1988) consisting of voluntary movements (like touching the cheek or the eyelid or singing) that alleviate dystonia. These voluntary movements, often presenting with the features of a ritualized, compulsive behaviour, are found from patients themselves to really alleviate the intensity and frequency of the dystonic movement, like compulsions alleviate obsessions-induced anxiety in OCD.

More stringently, the frequent evidence of obsessive behaviours (more clearly identifiable as a co-occurring condition rather than a psychopathological consequence of distress like anxiety and depressive symptoms) suggested to evaluate the occurrence of OC symptoms or OCD in IFD. In two separate focal dystonia subtypes, blepharospasm and torticollis, Bihari et al (1992a, 1992b) found higher obsessionality ratings than in control subjects. Broocks et al (1998) confirmed these results more recently, whereas Wenzel et al (1998) found a 6.8% prevalence of DSM-III-R OCD in a population of 44 patients affected by torticollis. These papers showed an increased frequency of the disorder or highest levels of the psychopathological dimension of obsessionality relative to controls suggesting a common vulnerability for OCD and IFD, but did not search for biological validators of the clinically–based hypothesis in the same samples.

Among biological validators in psychiatry, familiarity seems to be one of the most stable across different diagnoses. This happens also for OCD and OCD spectrum disorders (see below), so that we decided to make a study to evaluate the prevalence and familial risk of DSM IV OCD diagnosis as a validator of shared biological background of the two disorders in a population of IFD patients (Cavallaro et al 2002). Among 57 patients suffering from IFD 19.7% fulfilled the DSM-IV diagnostic criteria for OCD and 3.5% for obsessive–compulsive spectrum disorders (anorexia/bulimia and one with a tic disorder), while 10.5% were diagnosed as subclinical OCD because they did not satisfy the distress or interference criteria. OCD prevalence was significantly higher ($p<.001$) than in a control group (.77%) of 129 surgical patients age and sex matched.

When we studied family history for OCD and neurological conditions up to first-degree relatives, using the Family History Method (Andreasen et al 1977), the MR among first-degree relatives of IFD patients with comorbid OCD was significantly higher than that of IFD patients without OCD diagnosis(13.8% vs. 0.55%; $p< .01$). We found no significant difference between MR for OCD of 97 first-degree relatives from families of IFD/OCD patients and data available in the literature for OCD families (MR for OCD 11.7%; Nestadt et al 2000). In addition, MR for OCD in families of IFD/OCD patients was higher than MR found among 638 firstdegree relatives of control subjects ($p<.001$). On the contrary neurological family study found only one IFD (non OCD) patient with a a doubtful familial dystonia and one patient with a family history of essential tremor.

Findings of a concomitant significantly higher prevalence of OCD among IFD and of a significantly higher MR for OCD among first-degree relatives of these IFD subjects with OCD comorbidity, in comparison to general population, together with the findings of OCD MR not significantly different from figures found among first degree relatives of OCD probands supports the hypothesis of a biological relationship between the two disorders. Nevertheless IFD was not familial among these patients and the familial connection between the liabilities of the two disorders pointed by MR values is valid only for subjects with IFD and OCD comorbidity. The interpretative model nearest to these findings may be that that IFD generally does not share the same genetic liability with OCD, but that a specific subgroup of IFD subjects, those with comorbid OCD, has a higher probability of a diagnosis of a familial form of OCD (and possibly a shared biological mechanism for IFD and OCD), being then their IFD a spectrum manifestation of OCD.

An interesting feature of patients studied in that sample was that most patients with a OCD diagnosis showed poor insight and reduced egodystonia regarding OCD symptoms, a feature already noted when OC symptoms present after the neurological lesions or degeneration processes of various nature in the basal ganglia above summarized. This peculiarity made impossible to assess the exact age of onset of OCD, but clearly all patients stated that this kind of symptoms started from the second decade of life, several years or decades before dystonia onset (well remembered due to physical impairment). Lack of smooth data did not allow to verify the inverse effect of proband's age of onset on familial MR, a well known effect in OCD (Bellodi et al 1992; Pauls et al 1995), but the delay of the clinical manifestations of IFD relative to OCD onset in comorbid patients may suggest that in this subgroup OCD is an early-onset manifestation of a basal ganglia circuitry instability, expressed as OCD alone in the families. Idiopathic focal dystonia may be a tardive, motor-shifted expression of this instability, linked to a co-occurring biological condition.

Another peculiarity worth to note concerns clinical presentation: as could be expected by a prevailing 'neurological' basal ganglia component, with analogies with the above cited ceurological lesions and disorders associated with OC symptoms, mean Y-BOCS values of both obsessions and compulsions subscales of time spent as symptomatic, interference, and anxiety were low, while mean values of resistance and control were severe, if compared with a sample of age and sex-matched OCD patients without IFD. In the same comparison that IFD/OCD patients compared with pure OCD patients were particularly charachterized by ordering and hoarding obsessions and compulsions, a feature frequent in GT comorbid OCD (Eapen et al 1997), in which basal ganglia and dopaminergic function involvement in symptoms is rather clear.

Our results epidemiological and familial results support furtherly the relationship between the two disorders already hypothesized by current neurofunctional theories suggesting a dysfunction in basal ganglia-thalamic-cortico-striatal loop both in OCD, both in IFD (Saxena et al 98, Richter et al 98), with a possibly shared mechanisms in the strio-pallidal portion of the loop where the most recent theories above reported (Joel and Weiner 94-97 for review) suggest a high and multiple level of interactions between motor, associative and limbic projections. The brain localization might be more probably lenticular and in particular pallidal as PET studies and lesional/degenerative studies suggest.

Analysis of clinical patterns of symptoms of the two disorders together with familial data suggests in OCD to be the leading genetic motor of this dysfunction in our IFD/OCD patients, but it looks like if OCD phenotypical, clinical features (or what we aknowledge to be?) have been stopped in their evolution in terms of severity by the motor 'shifting' of symptoms based on a same dysfunction.

Nevertheless other hypotheses should be considered outside the basal ganglia, i.e the possibility of a dysfunction in the anterior cyngulate cortex.

AC cortex seems critical in Tourette disorder and shows abnormal metabolic activity in OCD (Busatto et al 2000), while among its functions there is a significant involvement in the outflow of limbic computations to motor regions. About this, a function of frontal/subcortical circuits passing through the striatum is the execution of 'macros' that must be executed rapidly in response to specific stimuli, untill the need is judged to have passed (Saxena et al 1998). Moreover AC cortex appears to be particularly involved in avoidance responses to noxious stimuli (Koyama et al 2000,; Freeman et al 1996), a function that ideally may fit the origin of both OCD psychopathology (phobic harm avoidance) and the motor facts of IFD (closing eyes and turning the face aside by turning the neck are common automatic responses to facing of sudden frontal dangers!)

In summary our data point to the possible existence of a clinical entity of comporbid OCD/IFD with peculiar presentation features and familial risk within the OCD spectrum: findings support the hypothesis of possible shared biological dysfunction with a most candidate neuroanatomical and functional area corresponding to basal ganglia.

Genetic analysis of these disorders seems then helpful to increase the understanding of the possible interactions between motor and psychological activities of the basal ganglia, probably 'best' expressed in their pathology.

Genetics of the Neurological Spectrum of OCD

The etiology of OCD is to date an intriguing question: the available information may be useful, but incomplete to understand the structure of this complex disorder. Obsessive symptoms, even though quite easily recognizable, are not specific of OCD: mood and psychotic diseases, neurological conditions may present Obsessive-Compulsive aspects. We reviewed above a number of disorders where obsessive-compulsive features are predominant in some phases of illness or coexist with neurological disorders of the basal ganglia. Nevertheless in a number of cases the psychopathological features are part of a fully expressed and coexisting OCD. This led to study models of transmission of OCD and OCD neurological spectrum disordersin the families of both OCD patients and of neurological patients.

Familial Studies on OCD and OCD Neurological Spectrum Disorders

OCD is a familial disorder (Pauls et al. 1995, Nestadt et al. 2000) with a higher morbidity risk for OCD among first degree relatives of OCD patients than among relatives of control subjects.

To date there are three different segregation studies of OCD. The first segregation study was conducted on a small sample of 24 families (Nicolini et al. 1991) and an autosomal dominant model of transmission was found with 80% of penetrance of AA and Aa genotypes was the most compatible with the observed patterns of transmission. Cavallini et al. (1999) recruited 107 families of Italian OCD probands without other co-diagnoses, with the exception of tic disorder. In this sample the best fit was for a Mendelian Dominant model of transmission considering OCD diagnosis as the affected phenotype, while after the inclusion of CMT and TS as affection status a no Mendelian model of transmission became the best fit. Conclusions of this study are that additional data needed to establish whether OCD and TS share a common etiology.

A further complex segregation analyses of 153 families (80 case and 73 control), ascertained in the Johns Hopkins OCD Family Study (Nestadt et al. 2000) provided strong evidence for a major gene. A Mendelian-dominant model, with significant sex effects and with residual familial effects, best explained the observed data. Stratification of the sample by the sex of probands provided further evidence of heterogeneity with respect to familial aggregation. Segregation analyses of 86 families with a female proband and of the 67 families with a male proband suggested that a Mendelian-dominant model with familial residual effects was the most parsimonious model explaining the inheritance of OCD in both subgroups.

Alsobrook et al. (1999) applying complex segregation analysis to a sample of OCD families rejected the no transmission hypothesis. Selection of OCD families with at least a secondary case of OCD (the "true" familial OCD cases) allowed acceptance of mixed model of transmission including the effect of a SML and a multifactorial background. In the same study, probands were reclassified on the basis of results of factor analysis on their YBOCS symptoms contents and the choice of families with high scores on symmetry/ordering factor then indicates the involvement of a major locus in transmission of OCD.

Phenotype definition is a key point in psychiatric genetics analysis. A better definition of the true phenotypic boundaries of OCD may help to individuate different etiological forms of OCD and to separately analyze the different forms of OCD. For example in the Alsobrook et al.'s study the authors chose to analyze only families of probands with a positive family history for OCD, considering these patients as a specific sub-group. In this research, positive family history represents an additional criterion to discriminate among subgroups of OCD probands with homogeneous etiology. Co-morbidity of tics or Tourette's syndrome represents the other criterion more frequently used with the aim to select more homogeneous sub-group of OCD patients.

Strong evidences are available that OCD shares common genetic basis with Tourette Syndrome (TS), characterized by disordered movement. As above anticipated, frequently subjects affected with TS have a co-diagnosis of OCD and OC behaviors and the prevalence of OCD in first-degree relatives of TS patients is significantly higher than that in general population.

Segregation studies have been performed to evaluate the role of transmissible components in the heritability of TS. The aim of these studies is the evaluation if a Single Major Locus (SML) accounts for transmission of the disorder: segregation analyses testing different transmission models may help to quantify the familial risk and to determine gene frequency of SML, penetrances of genotypes at risk and phenocopies rates. A SML with incomplete penetrance seems to be the most plausible hypothesis for TS (Comings et al. 1984; Devor et al. 1984; Pauls et al. 1986, 1990; Eapen et al. 1993; Hasstedt et al. 1995, Walkup et al. 1996; Seuchter et al. 2000).

In several cases the inclusion of OCD as affected phenotype in TS segregation analyses allows for a best parametric definition in tested models and gives further supports to the idea of a genetic continuum between OCD and TS, taking also into account Chronic Motor Tic (CMT) diagnosis. Generally a major locus with a dominant mode of transmission was invoked for TS families, while the last segregation study on TS, that to date represents the largest one, found that a no Mendelian model of transmission has the best fit for 108 TS families (Seuchter et al. 2000).

Further supports to the genetic link between OCD and TS derived from epidemiological studies on OCD probands. TS is a rare condition in the general population (5/10000). Leonard et al. (1992) found rates equal to 14% for CMT and to 6% for TS among the first-degree relatives of 52 probands with primary OCD, Pauls et al. (1995) found a rate equal to 4.6% for TS and CMT among relatives of 100 OCD probands, Grados et al.(2001) found a prevalence of any tic disorders in relatives of 80 OCD patients of 6.2% versus 1.7% in relatives of 73 controls indicating that in families of OCD probands the risk for CMT/TS is specifically increased. Offspring of individuals affected with OCD have an increased risk for OC spectrum disorders: 37% of OCD offspring are affected with OC spectrum disorder, that is chronic motor tics (14%), TS (9%) and OCD (31%) (Bajo et al. 1999).

As we previously discussed TS is a complex movement disorder with several evidences favoring its link to OCD, but other movement disorders may show some link with obsessive-compulsive area, among these we concentrated our research efforts on Tic disorder and focal dystonia.

It is well documented that some forms of idiopathic dystonia are familial, generally with an autosomal dominant model of transmission and to date several genetic loci have been involved in the etiology of different forms of dystonia (DYT1, DYT5, DYT6, DYT7).

Data from our group above reported (Cavallaro et al 2002) and previous literature observed that patients affected with Idiopathic Focal Dystonia (IFD), having torticollis and blepharospasm (Bihari et al. 1992, Bihari et al. 1992b, Wenzel et al. 1998, Broocks et al. 1998) have an augmented recurrence of Obsessive-Compulsive symptoms when compared with controls. Also TS and dystonia may coexist (Stone et al 1991): Nemeth et al. (1999) described a three generation pedigree in which TS and dystonia cosegregate. The identification of this family further strengthens the evidence in favor of an etiologic relationship between some cases of TS and IFD.

Furthermore it has been described an association between OCD and the myoclonus dystonia syndrome (MDS). MDS is an autosomal dominant disorder characterized by myoclonic and dystonic muscle contractions, associated with psychiatric manifestations. MDS is usually considered as a benign disease. In most of the families, the MDS phenotype in proband is associated to several psychiatric features, characterized by obsessive-compulsive disorder, depression, and anxiety in relatives and is linked to chromosome 7q21 and mutations within epsilon-sarcoglycan (SGCE) gene have been described (Marechal et al. 2003).

Both OCD, dystonia, tourette syndrome and tic disorder have been studied with positive results as genetically transmitted illnesses with different models found according to the probands and family members phenotype.

Starting from these evidences, we focused our attention on the hypothesis of a common genetic background for OCD and related movement disorders, moving throughout patients with OCD/tic and getting patients with IFD at the opposite side.

We collected four sample of patients affected by OCD or OC spectrum syndromes:

1) Fifty eight patients with IFD from the study above described (Cavallaro et al 2002).

2) A sample of 110 OCD patients (60.9% with positive family history of OCD) without any co-diagnosis at the time of the ascertainment. No differences in age at onset for OCD or in actual age have been observed between sexes.
3) 47 Patients with OCD and CMT co-diagnosis have been grouped (59.97% of positive family history of OCD). These patients were analyzed separately, since the presence of tics in these patients suggests they are an intermediate phenotype between OCD and TS, while in the previous segregation paper (Cavallini et al. 1999) we considered all patients with and without tic together (18.7% of CMT rate).
4) A sample of 39 TS subjects: 43.58% of TS patients have a co-diagnosis of OCD, 33.33% have a positive family history for OCD. The age at onset both for tic and for OCD is younger than in the case of OCD plus tic patients (see table 1).

Table 1 summarizes demographic characteristics of all recruited samples.

Table 1: Non-motor symptoms in neurological diseases which involve the neostriatum

Disease	Symptoms
Parkinson's disease	Cognitive slowing (bradyphrenia)
	Deficits in learning process
	Mood syndromes
Huntington's disease	Schizophrenic-like symptoms
	Obsessive-compulsive symptoms
	Manic-depressive symptoms
	Memory dysfunctions
Sydenham chorea	Obsessive-compulsive symptoms
Choreoacanthocytosis	Personality alterations and disinhibited behaviour
Gilles de la Tourette	Obsessive-compulsive disorder
Focal lesions	Depression
	Abulia
	Disinhibition
	Memory dysfunctions
Dystonia	Obsessive-compulsive symptoms (disorder ?)

Adapted from Calabresi et al 1997.

All these patients have been diagnosed following the DSM IV diagnostic criteria: their family history has been collected directly from the probands and in the majority of cases (75%) from at least another first-degree relative.

Before applying the complex segregation procedures to this sample we evaluated the familial Morbidity Risk (MR for OCD and for OCD/tic disorder.

MRs were computed as ratios of affected individuals versus affected plus at-risk individuals. An appropriate age correction for unaffected relatives at risk was introduced (see for details of the method Bellodi et al. 2001).

No differences in MR for OCD and for OCD+tics have been observed between samples of OCD, OCD/tics, TS probands and IFD with OCD probands (table 2). On the contrary a significant difference between IFD patients without OCD and the other clinical groups of patients was observed. Comparing MR in first degree relatives of probands with IFD/OCD with relatives of patients with IFD, Z value is 2.59 with p=0.01. In the case of TS patients we remark this interesting aspect: in families of TS patients the MR for tic is higher than MR for OCD and these rates are symmetric to those observed in OCD probands without tics (higher rates for OCD than for tics). Dividing TS into two groups on the basis of OCD co-diagnosis we found in TS with OCD a MR for OCD equal to 12.97%, while patients without OCD have a risk of 6.08%. MR for tics is similar in the two subgroups: 28.84% versus 17.87%.

Table 2: Demographic characteristics of recruited samples

Diagnosis	N	OCD	Males	Actual Age	Onset of OCD	Onset of Tic	Onset of dystonia
OCD	110	100%	46.78%	32.73±10.74	17.44±7.83	-	-
OCD+tic	47	100%	74.46%	31.02±8.35	17.65±7.36	13.34±4.95	-
TS/OCD	17	100%	52.9%	27.88±8.55	15.76±9.64	8.29±3.9	-
TS	22	-	68.18%	30.36±15.17	-	9.25±7.64	-
Distonia/OCD	12	100%	35.29%	50.82±14.52	Not available	-	42.56±15.95
Distonia	46	-	34.78%	56.12±14.97	-	-	45.96±14.49

MR for OCD and tic in the three samples of probands (OCD, OCD/tic and TS) are higher than that expected in the general population, suggesting the presence of a familial diathesis for these disorders. In IFD patients with full OCD the MR is 13.8%, while in considering IFD patients with full and sub-threshold forms of OCD we found a MR of 10.33%. The MR for OCD is not different from those evaluated in the samples of psychiatric patients (OCD and TS).

These results encouraged us to explore if this common familial diathesis for OCD spectrum disorders (OCD and tics) may be due to the transmission of a single major gene and the parameters of this major gene. We performed a complex segregation analysis using regressive logistic models (statistical package SAGE, Sorant et al. 1991). In a previous segregation study performed with the same statistical method we observed that a genetic component account for OCD transmission in 107 OCD families (Cavallini et al. 1999). In the analyses we conditioned the ascertainment of families to the diagnosis of proband and we assumed that there is one proband per family (single ascertainment). We included in the analysis first and second-degree relatives. In this exploratory analysis we introduced a raw age correction, considering the actual age of each subject like a covariate in the model. The use of regression logistic models allows us to estimate in transmission models the effect of different types of relevant co-variates in addition to SML effect. In all the analyses we considered as affected phenotype OCD, Tics and TS.

None of IFD patients show a positive family history for dystonia, with the exception of patients having two relatives affected with essential tremor. To our knowledge no secondary cases of dystonia have been observed in first and second-degree relatives of OCD and TS probands.

We analyzed the following data samples derived from different grouping of recruited families:

1) 110 families of OCD probands.
2) 47 families of OCD/tics probands.

3) 110 families of OCD+47 OCD/tic probands.
4) 39 families of TS probands.
5) 110 OCD+47 OCD/tic families+39 TS families
6) 110 OCD+47 OCD/tic families+39 TS families + 17 families of IFD patients with full and sub-threshold OCD.
7) 47 OCD/tic families+39 TS families + 17 families of IFD patients with full and sub-threshold OCD.

OCD sample had an appropriate dimension for the segregation analysis. Even though TS and OCD/tic samples are small, we analyzed them separately from OCD families. Our aim was to establish if OCD/tic/TS are genetically transmitted in these families and if a SML accounts for this transmission.

Table 3 shows the distribution of OCD and tic disorder in first and second-degree-relatives.

Table 3: Morbidity Risks for OCD and tics in families of recruited patients

Sample	DIAGNOSIS	N	MR for OCD	MR for tics	MR for OCD+tics
1	OCD	110	15.55%	1.98%	17.86%
2	OCD+TIC	47	12.354%	7.32%	19.19%
3	TOURETTE'S	22	6.08%	17.87%	24.69%
4	TOURETTE'S with OCD	17	12.97%	28.84%	33.88%
5	DYSTONIA+ OCD	12	13.8%	6.84%	20.5%
6	DYSTONIA	46	0.55%	2%	2.54%

OCD and tic are considered the affected phenotypes in segregation analysis of OCD families. Then in the following analyses we added to families of OCD probands also families of patients with motor abnormalities, that is tics or dystonic movements, in order to estimate the degree of homogeneity in the analysis.

In the segregation analysis, the hypothesis of genetic transmission versus the hypothesis of no genetic transmission was tested, that is the distribution of cases in families is due mainly to genetic component and specifically to a major gene. We can make this, conditioning some parameters inside the model (for example transmission probabilities). Then, the presence of Mendelian transmission was evaluated in our data. Under this hypothesis transmission probabilities, that is probabilities that a parent transmits a specific allele A to his/her offspring, have specific values: 1 in the case of AA genotype, 0.5 in the case of Aa genotype and 0 in the case of aa genotype.

The comparison among/between models allows us to select the model with the best fit for our data. The test of significance applied in comparison among models is a chi square test. When chi square does not allow to chose among proposed solutions the Akaike Information Criterion (AIC) was applied, which allows to chose the most parsimonious model (Akaike 1974) as the most probable model of transmission. Table 4 summarizes results.

Table 4: Distribution of OCD and tic diagnoses in first- and second-degree relatives of recruited samples

Diagnosis	N	Cases among I° Relatives		N	Cases among II° Relatives	
		Males	Females		Males	Females
OCD	443	46(10.4%)	31(6.99%)	1119	6(0.5%)	14(1.25%)
OCD+tic	165	18(10.9%)	16(9.69%)	493	5(1.01%)	12(2.43%)
TS	146	22(15.1%)	13(8.9%)	357	16(4.48%)	9(2.52%)
Dystonia+OCD*	97	10(10.3%)	3(3.43%)	163	0(0%)	1(0.61%)

* In segregation analysis we considered only Dystonic probands with OCD co-diagnosis.

For the 110 OCD families the no transmission hypothesis was rejected, the best fit was for a no Mendelian model of transmission for OCD spectrum diagnosis. The parameters of the model are respectively gene frequency=0.168, penetrance of AA genotype is 36.51%, without phenocopies and the prevalence in the general population estimated by the model is 0.1%. Differently from a previous segregation study (Cavallini et al. 1999) we did not found a Mendelian solution for our data, but these findings are in accord with Alsobrook et al's (1999) results. In the Alsobrook's study, when families of OCD probands are analyzed all together the analysis allowed the rejection of only the no transmission model.

For 47 families of OCD/tic probands the best fit was for a no Mendelian model of transmission with gene frequency =0.003 and AA penetrance =10%.

Considering the overall sample of OCD patients (OCD and OCD/tic patients) the best fit was for a no Mendelian model with gene frequency = 0.108 and AA penetrance = 29.28%.

For 39 TS families the best fit was for a dominant model of transmission with gene frequency =0.046 and AA and Aa penetrances = 24.08%. This model predicts population prevalence for OCD/tic of 0.021 (2.1%). The more recent paper on TS transmission was performed on 108 families and a different type of age correction was introduced, aspects that could justify differences in results.

In fact, Seuchter et al. (2000) found that the pattern of Tourette and other related tic disorders in their data sample is not consistent with Mendelian inheritance even after modeling explanatory variables such as obsessive-compulsive symptoms.

Merging the three samples of OCD, OCD+tics and TS families the best fit was for a Mendelian additive model of transmission. The gene frequency is 0.08 and the AA genotype penetrance is 100% and the Aa penetrance is 11.28%. No phenocopies have been estimated. Population prevalence predicted by the model is 1.67%. Grouping the three types of families altogether allows the determination of the best fit for a Mendelian model of transmission.

In families of IFD patients without OCD the MR for OCD and tic is low and equal to the prevalence in general population. Generally IFD patients with OCD co-diagnosis who we ascertained have an early age at onset for IFD. Furthermore some of these patients clearly remember that the onset of Obsessive-compulsive symptoms was antecedent to dystonic problems and sometimes OC symptoms disappeared or lowered after onset of IFD.

Because of the hypothesized relationship between OCD spectrum disorders and IFD we extended the segregation analysis also to 17 families of IFD/OCD patients. To date the small number of families did not allow us to perform a separate segregation analysis on these families. For this reason we added these families to the overall sample of patients. The best model of transmission is an additive Mendelian model of transmission: the gene frequency is

0.07 and AA genotype penetrance is 100% and Aa penetrance is 14.09%. The model has estimated no phenocopies. Considering only patients with motor dysfunction (that is patients with tics, TS and IFD) the best fit is for a general Mendelian model of transmission. The gene frequency is 0.034 and AA genotype penetrance is 100%.

Our results support the idea of a transmissible factor accounting for the liability to OCD, tics and specific neurological disorders in our families. However some interesting observations are possible. The extension of the analysis to all OCD families produced a best fit for a no Mendelian model of transmission. This means that not only a major gene with Mendelian feature may account for OCD transmission under the hypothesis that all families of OCD patients have the same genetic liability. When probands having some motor disturbance (that is tics or IFD) are grouped all together the best fit is for an Additive Mendelian model of transmission. These findings may indicate that the presence of motor dysfunction individuates a more homogeneous liability due to the transmission of a single major gene with additive features.

To date the lack of clear knowledge about OCD etiology is due to the complexity of this disorder. This complexity may be due to:

1) OCD is heterogeneous as clinical presentation. Contents, age of onset, course, drug response vary across patients even though from etiological point of view there is a unique liability.
2) OC symptoms are present in different disorders. We focused our attention on the relationship with movement disorders. Alterations in basal ganglia which are structures involved also in tics and in IFD may be related to the presence of neural abnormalities in OCD. Both the disorders show OC symptoms in the lifetime course. The link, ascertained from a clinical point of view, has been further explored under an etiological perspective. The increased rate of OCD and tics in relatives of IFD patients with OCD suggests the presence of a common liability for these disorders. However, we did not observed an increased rate of IFD cases either in relatives of OCD patients and in IFD probands. Nevertheless, we are not completely sure that not interviewed subjects classified as tic disorders in families of OCD probands may be affected with some forms of dystonia. The presence of dystonia is not incompatible with tics: even though to date tics have been described as sudden, quick, involuntary phenomena the observation of patients affected with TS highlighted also the presence of slow and sustained movements, namely dystonic or tonic tics (Jankovic 1997). We found that families of IFD patients with OCD have a morbidity risk for OCD and related disorders that overlap that of OCD patients. We hypothesized that a SML may account for the transmission of a common liability (OCD and IFD).

We found that the OCD spectrum disorders are genetically conditioned, but in different way. Specifically, some forms of dystonia may be clinically and etiologically related to OCD. OC characteristics of these patients have been described elsewhere in this book.

The main consequence of our findings may be the potential extension of genetic hypotheses formulated at the molecular level for dystonia to OCD or vice versa.

For OCD and TS several genes have been candidate in the past, starting from evidences from neuropharmachological field. The involvement of genes controlling for serotonergic, dopaminergic, cathecolaminergic pathways was explored without definitive results. Genomic scan of a wide number of markers in TS families is not conclusive (Barr et al. 1999). On the contrary, in the case of some familial forms of dystonia, causative mutations have been isolated: for idiopathic early onset dystonia (DYT1 locus, Ozelius et al. 1989) and for dopa responsive dystonia (DYTY5 locus: Nygaard et al. 1993, Ichinose et al. 1994).

Table 5: Segregation analysis results

	Affected phenotypes in relatives OCD spectrum disorders
110 OCD families	*No Mendelian model:* qA=0.168, AA penetrance=36.51%
47 OCD/TIC families	*No Mendelian model:* qA=0.0.004 AA penetrance=10 %
110 OCD+47 OCD/TIC families	*No Mendelian model:* qA=0.108 AA penetrance=29.28%
39 TS families	*Dominant model:*qA=0.046, AA and Aa penetrances =24.08%
157 OCD families + 39 TS families	*Additive model:*qA=0.088, AA penetrance=100% and Aa penetrance=11.28%
196 OCD-OCD/TIC-TS families and 17 DYSTONIA/OCD families	*Additive model:*qA=0.071, AA penetrance=100% and Aa penetrance=14.09%
104 OCD/TIC, TS families and 17 DYSTONIA/OCD families	*Mendelian model:* qA=0.034, AA penetrance=100%

CONCLUSION

Genetic data and clinical reviews ond comorbidity of OCD and neurological disorders presented, as well as genetic analysis of the so called Neurological spectrum of OCD, share a common suggestion about the probable high level of integration of motor and psychological functioning in the basal ganglia. This suggestion is clearly supported by lesional and degenerative studies of the basal ganglia, but the most striking (and euristically useful) finding is that these different illnesses seem to share part of their genetic control as supported by the study of models of transmission and their sensitivity to neurological phenotypes data treatment. The most intriguing hypotheses is that it is possible that we are dividing in 'neurological' or 'psychiatirc' clinical conditions that are, in the biological reality, a single natural entity and not the coexistence of two disorders. Among the families 'spectrum' manifestations may become other single illnesses, and among the probands diverse aspects (motor and psychological) may get differential relative importance depending o the genetic load of the different variants of a same illness (pathology) of the basal ganglia and their thalamo-cortical circuitry. A next step in the work of the international research community may include, after the smoothing of neuropharmacological hypotheses about these disorders, the evaluation of the clinical response of psychiatric symptoms to 'neurological' agents (and/or the contrary) using psychopharmacological response as a tool of further phenotype definition.

REFERENCES

Akaike HA. (1974): New look at the statistical model identification IEEE *Trans Autom Control* 19:716-723.

Alexander G, DeLong M, Strick P (1986): Parallel organization of functionally segregated circuits linking basal ganglia and cortex. *Ann Rev Neurosci* 9: 357-381.

Almasy L, Bressman SB, Raymond D, et al. (1997): Idiopathic torsion dystonia linked to chromosome 8 in two Mennonite families. *Ann Neurol* 42(4):670-3.

Alsobrook II JP, Leckman JF, Goodman WK et al (1999): Segregation analysis of obsessive-compulsive disorder using symptom-based factor scores. *Am J Med Genet* 88(6):669-75.

Andreasen NC, Endicott J, Spitzer RL, Winokur G. (1977): The family history method using diagnostic criteria. Reliability and validity. *Arch Gen Psychiatry* 34(10):1229-35

Bajo S, Albertazzi M, Henin MP (1999): La familiarità per lo spettro DOC e risposta clinica. In atti del IV Congresso Nazionale della Società Italiana di Psicopatologia. *Giornale Italiano di Psicopatologia* 5:50.

Barr CL, Wigg KG, Pakstis AJ et al (1999): Genome scan for linkage to Gilles de la Tourette syndrome. *Am J Med Genet* 88(4):437-45.

Baxter LR Jr., Phelps ME, Mazziotta JC et al (1987): Local cerebral glucose metabolic rates in obsessive-compulsive disorder. A comparison with rates in unipolar depression and in normal controls. *Arch Gen Psychiatry* 44(3):211-8.

Baxter LR Jr., Schwartz JM, Mazziotta JC et al (1988): Cerebral glucose metabolic rates in nondepressed patients with obsessive-compulsive disorder. *Am J Psychiatry* 145(12):1560-3.

Bellodi L, Sciuto G, Diaferia G, Ronchi P, Smeraldi E. (1992): Psychiatric disorders in the families of patients with obsessive-compulsive disorder. *Psychiatry Res* 42(2):111-20.

Bellodi L, Cavallini MC, Bertelli S et al (2001): Morbidity risk for obsessive-compulsive spectrum disorders in first-degree relatives of patients with eating disorders. *Am J Psychiatry* 158(4):563-9.

Bhatia, K. P. and Marsden, C. D. (1994): The behavioural and motor consequences of focal lesions of the basal ganglia in man. *Brain* 117: 859-876.

Bihari K, Hill JL, Murphy DL. (1992a): Obsessive-compulsive characteristics in patients with idiopathic spasmodic torticollis. *Psychiatry Res* 42(3):267-72.

Bihari K, Pigott TA, Hill JL, Murphy DL. (1992b): Blepharospasm and obsessive-compulsive disorder.*J Nerv Ment Dis* 180(2):130-2.

Brassat D, Camuzat A, Vidailhet M et al (2000): Frequency of the DYT1 mutation in primary torsion dystonia without family history. *Arch Neurol* 57(3):333-5.

Breiter HC, Rauch SL, Kwong KK et al (1996): Functional magnetic resonance imaging of symptom provocation in obsessive-compulsive disorder. *Arch Gen Psychiatry* 53(7):595-606.

Broocks A, Thiel A, Angerstein D, Dressler D.Higher (1998): Prevalence of obsessive-compulsive symptoms in patients with blepharospasm than in patients with hemifacial spasm. *Am J Psychiatry* 155(4):555-7.

Busatto GF, Zamignani DR, Buchpiguel CA et al. (2000): A voxel-based investigation of regional cerebral blood flow abnormalities in obsessive-compulsive disorder using single photon emission computed tomography (SPECT). *Psychiatry Res* 99(1):15-27

Calabresi P, De Murtas M, Bernardi G. (1997): The neostriatum beyond the motor function:experimental and clinical evidence. *Neuroscience* 78 (1): 39–60.

Cavallaro R, Cavallini C, Henin MP et al. (2000) The basal ganglia talamo-cortico loop and the neurological OCD spectrum disorders: OCD comorbidity and family history in idiopathic focal distonia. In: Bellodi L, Cavallaro R (Eds) *The Basal-Cortical Function in Obsesssive Compulsive Disorder Spectrum*. Pacini Editore Pisa pp 149-165.

Cavallaro R, Galardi G, Cavallini MC, et al (2002): Obsessive-compulsive disorder among idiopathic focal dystonia patients: an epidemiological and family study. *Biol Psychiatry* 52(4):356-61.

Cavallini MC, Pasquale L, Bellodi L, Smeraldi E. (1999): Complex segregation analysis for obsessive-compulsive disorder and related disorders. *Am J Med Genet* 88(1):38-43

Carbon M, Su S, Dhawan V et al. (2004) Regional metabolism in primary torsion dystonia: effects of penetrance and genotype. *Neurology* 27;62(8):1384-90.

Church AJ, Dale RC, Lees AJ et al (2003) Tourette's syndrome: a cross sectional study to examine the PANDAS hypothesis. *J Neurol Neurosurg Psychiat* 74:602-7

Comings DE, Comings BG, Devor EJ, Cloninger CR. (1984) Detection of major gene for Gilles de la Tourette syndrome. *Am J Hum Genet*. 36(3):586-600.

Cummings JL (1993) Frontal-subcortical circuits and human behaviour. *Archives of Neurology*, 50: 873-880

Devor J. (1984) Complex segregation analysis of Gilles de la Tourette syndrome: further evidence for a major locus mode of transmission. *Am J Hum Genet*. 36(3):704-9.

Eapen V, Robertson MM, Alsobrook JP 2nd, Pauls DL (1997): Obsessive-compulsive symptoms in Gilles de la Tourette syndrome and obsessive-compulsive disorder: differences by diagnosis and family history. *Am J Med Genet* 74(4): 432-438.

Eapen V, Pauls DL, Robertson MM. (1993) Evidence for autosomal dominant transmission in Tourette's syndrome. United Kingdom cohort study. *Br J Psychiatry* 162:593-6.

Eidelberg, D, Moeller, JR, Ishikawa, T et al (1995) The metabolic topography of idiopathic torsion dystonia. *Brain* 118: 1473-1484.

Fahn, S. (1988) Concept and classification of dystonia. *In: Dystonia 2. Advances in neurology*, Vol. 50, pp. 1-8, Eds S. Fahn, C. D. Marsden and D. B. Calne. Raven Press: New York.

Freeman Jr., J., Cuppernell, C., Flannery, K. Gabriel, M. (1996):Context-specific multi-site cingulate cortical, limbic thala-mic, and hippocampal neuronal activity during concurrent discriminative approach and avoidance training in rabbits. J. Neurosci 16: 1538-1549.

Galardi G, Perani DP, Grassi Fet al (1996): Basal ganglia and talamo-cortical hypermetabolism in patients with spasmodic torticollis. *Acta Neurol Scand* 94(3):172-176.

Grados MA, Riddle MA, Samuels JF et al (2001) The familial phenotype of obsessive-compulsive disorder in relation to tic disorders: the Hopkins OCD family study. *Biol Psychiatry* 50(8):559-65

Greenberg BD, Ziemann U, Cora-Locatelli G et al (2000) Altered cortical excitability in obsessive-compulsive disorder. *Neurology* 54(1):142-7.

Hallett, M. (1993) Physiology of basal ganglia disorders: an overview. *Can J Neurol Sci* 20: 177-183.

Hasstedt SJ, Leppert M, Filloux F (1995) Intermediate inheritance of Tourette syndrome, assuming assortative mating. A*m J Hum Genet* 57(3):682-9

Hollander E, Wong CM (1995) Obsessive-compulsive spectrum disorders. *J Clin Psychiatry* 56 Suppl 4:3-6.

Ichinose H, Nagatsu T (1997): Molecular genetics of hereditary dystonia-mutations in the GTP cyclohydrolase I gene. *Brain Res Bull* 43(1): 35-8.

Kohling R, Koch UR, Hamann M, Richter A. (2004) Increased excitability in cortico-striatal synaptic pathway in a model of paroxysmal dystonia. *Neurobiol Dis* 16(1):236-45.

Jankovic J. (1997) Tourette syndrome. Phenomenology and classification of tics. *Neurol Clin* 15(2):267-75.

Joel D, Weiner I (1994) The organization of the basal ganglia-thalamocortical circuits: open interconnected rather than closed segregated. *Neuroscience*. 63(2):363-79.

Joel D, Weiner I (1997) The connections of the primate subthalamic nucleus: indirect pathways and the open-interconnected scheme of basal ganglia-thalamocortical circuitry. *Brain Res Brain Res Rev* 23(1-2):62-78

Kamm C, Naumann M, Mueller J (2000) The DYT1 GAG deletion is infrequent in sporadic and familial writer' s cramp. *Mov Disord* 15(6):1238-41.

Kimura M, Matsumoto N (1997) Neuronal activity in the basal ganglia. Functional implications. *Adv Neurol* 74: 111-18

Koyama T, Kato K, Mikami A (2000) During pain-avoidance neurons activated in the macaque anterior cingulate and caudate *Nuroscience Letters* 283:17-20

Laplane D, Degos JD, Baulac M, Gray F.(1981) Bilateral infarction of the anterior cingulate gyri and of the fornices. Report of a case. *J Neurol Sci.* 51(2):289-300.

Lauterbach EC, Cummings JL, Duffy J et al. (1998) Neuropsychiatric correlates and treatment of lenticulostriatal diseases: a review of the literature and overview of research opportunities in Huntington's, Wilson's and Fahr's diseases. Report of the ANPA Committee on Research. American Neuropsychiatric Association. *J Neuropsychiatry Clin Neurosci* 10 (3):249-266.

Lee, M. S. and Marsden, C. D. (1994) Movement disorders following lesions of the thalamus or subthalamic region. *Movement Dis* 9: 493-507.

Leube B, Rudnicki D, Ratzlaff T et al. (1996) Idiopathic torsion dystonia: assignment of a gene to chromosome 18p in a German family with adult onset, autosomal dominant inheritance and purely focal distribution. *Hum Mol Genet* 5(10):1673-7.

Marechal L, Raux G, Dumanchin C et al. (2003)Severe myoclonus-dystonia syndrome associated with a novel epsilon-sarcoglycan gene truncating mutation. *J Med Genet* 19B(1):114-7.

McGuire PK, Bench CJ, Frith CD et al. (1994). Functional anatomy of obsessive-compulsive phenomena. *Br J Psychiatry* 164(4):459-68.

Midleton FA, Strick PL. (1997) New concepts about the organization of basal ganglia outputs. *Adv Neurol* 74: 57-68

Nemeth AH, Mills KR, Elston JS, et al. (1999): Do the same genes predispose to Gilles de la Tourette syndrome and dystonia? Report of a new family and review of the literature. *Mov Disord* 14(5): 826-31.

Nestadt G, Samuels J, Riddle M et al. (2000) A family study of obsessive-compulsive disorder. *Arch Gen Psychiatry*. 57(4):358-63.

Nicolini H, Hanna G, Baxter L et al. (1991): Segregation analysis of obsessive-compulsive disorders: preliminary results. *Ursus Medicus* 1: 25-28.

Nygaard TG, Wilhelmsen KC, Risch NJ et al. (1993): Linkage mapping of dopa-responsive dystonia (DRD) to chromosome 14q. Nat Genet 5(4): 386-91.

Ozelius L, Kramer PL, Moskowitz CB et al (1989) Human gene for torsion dystonia located on chromosome 9q32-q34. *Neuron* 2(5):1427-34

Parent A, Hazrati LN. (1995) Functional anatomy of the basal ganglia. I. The cortico-basal ganglia-thalamo-cortical loop. *Brain Res Brain Res Rev* 20(1):91-127

Pauls DL, Towbin KE, Leckman JF, Zahner GE, Cohen DJ (1986) Gilles de la Tourette's syndrome and obsessive-compulsive disorder. Evidence supporting a genetic relationship. *Arch Gen Psychiatry* 43(12):1180-2

Pauls DL, Alsobrook JP 2nd, Goodman W, Rasmussen. S, Leckman JF (1995): A family study of obsessive-compulsive disorder. *Am J Psychiatry* 152(1): 76-84.

Pauls DL, Pakstis AJ, Kurlan R et al. (1990) Segregation and linkage analyses of Tourette's syndrome and related disorders. *J Am Acad Child Adolesc Psychiatry*. 29(2):195-203.

Perani D, Colombo C, Bressi S et al. (1995): [18F] FDG PET Study in obsessive-compulsive disorder: A clinical metabolic correlation study after treatment. *Br J Psychiatry* 166:244-250.

Playford ED, Passingham RE, Marsden CD, Brooks DJ.(1998) Increased activation of frontal areas during arm movement in idiopathic torsion dystonia. *Mov Disord* 13(2):309-18.

Rapoport JL, Wise SP (1988). Obsessive-compulsive disorder: evidence for basal ganglia dysfunction. *Psychopharmacol Bull* 24:380-4

Rauch SL, Jenike MA, Alpert NM et al.(1994). Regional cerebral blood flow measured during symptom provocation in obsessive-compulsive disorder using oxygen 15-labeled carbon dioxide and positron emission tomography. *Arch Gen Psychiatry* 51(1):62-70.

Richter A, Loscher W (1998): Pathophysiology of idiopathic dystonia: findings from genetic animal models *Prog Neurobiol* 54:633-677.

Saxena S, Brody AL, Schwartz JM, Baxter LR (1998). Neuroimaging and frontal-subcortical circuitry in obsessive-compulsive disorder. *Br J Psychiatry* Suppl.35:26-37.

Schilder P. (1938) The organic background of obsessions and compulsions. *Am J Psychiatry*; 94: 1397-1416

Seuchter SA, Hebebrand J, Klug B et al. (2000) Complex segregation analysis of families ascertained through Gilles de la Tourette syndrome. *Genet Epidemiol* 18(1):33-47.

Sorant AGM, Bonney GE, Elston RC (1991): Segregation analysis of a discrete trait under a class A regressive logistic model. (REGD version 4.0) *LSU Medical Center*, New Orleans.

Stoetter B, Braun AR, Randolph C et al. (1992) Functional neuroanatomy of Tourette syndrome. Limbic-motor interactions studied with FDG PET. *Adv Neurol* 58:213-26.

Stowe RM, Barnas DM, Diamond MS (1991) OCD associated with pallidal lesions responds to serotonergic manipulation. *Biol Psychiatry* (S) 11: 312 s

Swedo SE, Schapiro MG, Grady CL et al. (1989) Cerebral glucose metabolism in childhood onset obsessive-compulsive disorder. *Arch Gen Psychiatry* 46: 518-523

Swedo SE, Leonard Hl, Shapiro MB, Casey BJ et al (1993) Sydenham's Chorea: physical and psychopathological symptoms of St. Vitus dance. *Pediatrics* 91:706-13

Stone LA, Jankovic J (1991): The coexistence of tics and dystonia. *Arch Neurol* 48(8): 862-5.

Walkup JT, LaBuda MC, Singer HS, Brown J, Riddle MA, Hurko O. (1996) Family study and segregation analysis of Tourette syndrome: evidence for a mixed model of inheritance. *Am J Hum Genet* 59(3):684-93

Weilburg JB, Mesulam M, Weintraub S et al (1989): Focal striatal abnormalities in a patient with obsessive-compulsive disorder. *Arch Neurol* 46:233-235

Wenzel T, Schnider P, Wimmer A, Steinhoff N, Moraru E, Auff E (1998): Psychiatric comorbidity in patients with spasmodic torticollis. *J Psychosom Res* 44:687-690.

In: Obsessive-Compulsive Disorder and Comorbidity ISBN 1-59454-884-6
Editors: R. Gross-Isseroff and A. Weizman, pp. 131-144

Chapter 8

ANTIPSYCHOTICS IN OCD

Joseph Zohar,* Leah Fostick, Rachel Sonnino, Eran Harari and Yehuda Sasson
Division of Psychiatry, The Chaim Sheba Medical Center, Tel Hashomer, Israel

ABSTRACT

The accepted medication of choice in OCD is serotonin reuptake inhibitors (SRI). The use of antipsychotics, both typical and atypical, has been attempted in treating various anxiety disorders, among them OCD. Certain types of OCD in particular may be candidates for treatment with antipsychotics, and these will be the focus of this chapter. In OCD with psychotic features, despite speculation as to the potential benefit of antipsychotics, no studies have been carried out to date. In addition, there is no conclusive evidence to suggest that SRIs are less beneficial in this subset of patients. For OCD with comorbid tic disorder, a combination of SRI and antipsychotic has been noted to improve both OC and tic symptoms. OCD refractory to an adequate trial of SRI was found to benefit from augmentation with risperidone and olanzapine. Finally, in comorbid schizophrenia and OCD, data is mixed, with some studies reporting improvement, and others noting exacerbation, of OC symptoms during treatment with antipsychotic medication. It emerges that, although SRIs are still the treatment of choice in OCD, certain subgroups may potentially benefit from antipsychotic augmentation.

INTRODUCTION

OCD is a unique disorder, since so far it seems to respond specifically to only one type of medications, namely, medications that block serotonin reuptake (Zohar et al., 2004). In this sense, OCD is different from other anxiety related disorders, which seem to respond to both noradrenergic and serotonergic medications (Davidson, 2004).

* jzohar@post.tau.ac.il

The introduction of atypical neuroleptics has been associated with the use of these medications in other indications, including some of the anxiety disorders (Barnett, 2002; Ahearn, 2003; Butterfield, 2001). In this chapter we will review whether or not there is a role for antipsychotics in OCD, and will touch upon typical as well as atypical antipsychotics. We will cover four different areas that might be relevant for potential uses for OCD, namely OCD with psychotic features, OCD and tic disorder, refractory OCD and schizophrenia and OCD. We will suggest to the reader that each of these four conditions needs to be thought of differently when one is contemplating use of antipcychotics in OCD.

OCD WITH PSYCHOTIC FEATURES

According both to the DSM-IV (1994) and ICD-10 (2003), one of the hallmarks of OCD is that it is ego-dystonic, i.e., the patient recognizes his behavior as "excessive and unreasonable" (DSM-IV, 1994). However, there is, according to the DSM-IV, a subtype of OCD which is called "poor insight type". The definition of this is that most of the time the patient does not recognize that the obsessions and compulsions are excessive and unreasonable. The emphasis in the definition is on the *current* episode, and the criteria to differentiate obsessions with poor insight from delusion are by the *past history* of the patient. As defined in DSM-IV: "*at some point* during the course of the disorder the person has recognized that the obsessions or compulsions are excessive or unreasonable". Hence, the way to differentiate obsession from delusion is actually based not on the mental status examination carried out upon seeing the patient, but on careful history taking (table 1).

Table 1. A comparison of ego-dystonic features and reality testing in obsessions with and without insight, and in delusions

	Obsessions	Obsessions with poor insight	Delusions
Ego-dystonic	+	–	–
Reality testing	+	+*	–

* In the past

This concept of OCD which conceptualises poor insight as being on the severe end of obsessive-compulsive disorder, rather than schizophrenia, is actually based, among others, on a study by Weiss et al. (1969). In this study, they followed up 36 patients with what was then called "obsessional psychosis". In this long term follow up it was found that "there was not impairment in the affect, no loss of association, no hallucination and no intellectual decline". Namely, these patients did not develop characteristics that are typical of schizophrenia, and in this sense the natural course of the disorder was more related to OCD than to schizophrenia. Some years later, Insel and Akiskal (1986), in their paper "obsessive-compulsive disorder with psychotic features – a phenomenologic analysis", proposed that "OCD represents a psychopathologic spectrum varying along a continuum of insight", and that "this 'obsessional' delusion did not signify a schizophrenia diagnosis".

Based on these two observations, among other things, the DSM-IV (1994) came up with the category of "poor insight type". The idea behind this is that OCD with psychotic features is a severe form of OCD and not schizophrenia.

Is there a role for antipsychotics in OCD with poor insight?

This issue was specifically addressed in an elegant paper by Eisen et al. (2001) entitled: "insight and treatment outcome in OCD". In this study, 14 patients with poor insight at start were compared to 57 patients with good insight, in a 16 week open label treatment with Sertraline. Degree of insight at baseline did not predict response to Sertraline. Patients with poor insight were just as likely to respond as patients with good insight. It seems, therefore, based on this study, that there is no additional benefit of adding antipsychotic. However, a more recent study (Ravi-Kishore et al, 2004) found that OCD with poor insight responded considerably less (33% response) as compared to OCD patients with insight (64%). Unfortunately, the question of whether adding antipsychotics will have a beneficial effect was not tested. It seems, therefore, that one should probably focus on proper antiobsessive treatment, namely treatment with medium to high doses of SSRI in OCD patients with poor insight, for at least 8 weeks, before adding on antipsychotic.

OCD and Tic Disorder

A substantial number of OCD patients have tic disorder. The reported figures include 38% (McDougle et al., 1994) and 31% (Leckman et al., 1995). It is of interest to know whether these patients, namely with both OCD and tic, would require different therapeutic approach, as compared to OCD patients without tic. Or, putting it differently, whether, in the cases of OCD and tic disorder, the addition of antipsychotic is the treatment of choice? McDougle et al. (1994) address this issue in an important double-blind, placebo-controlled four-arm study. In this study, all the patients received, prior to recruitment, an adequate dose of fluvoxamine but did not respond to it. While continuing fluvoxamine treatment, the patients were divided to four groups, in order to test the clinical utility of haloperidol augmentation. The four groups were: patients with tic who got fluvoxamine and haloperidol, patients with tic who got fluvoxamine and placebo, patients without tic who got fluvoxamine and haloperidol and patients without tic who got fluvoxamine and placebo. Only the subset of OCD patients with tics who received haloperidol augmentation responded, both in terms of a significant reduction of their OC symptoms, as well as a significant improvement in their tics. The obsessive-compulsive symptoms of the other 3 groups, namely patients with tic who got fluvoxamine and placebo, and patients without tic who had already failed on fluvoxamine treatment, who got either haloperidol or placebo augmentation, did not change.

Based on this study, addition of small doses of classical potent neuroleptics (haloperidol or pimozide) seems to be the treatment of choice in case of OCD and tic disorder. It is, therefore, of utmost importance for the clinician to inquire specifically, and in detail, about the presence of a tic disorder, as if it is not diagnosed and treated accordingly (with addition of small doses of typical neuroleptic), the patient will probably not respond to adequate treatment with SSRI alone.

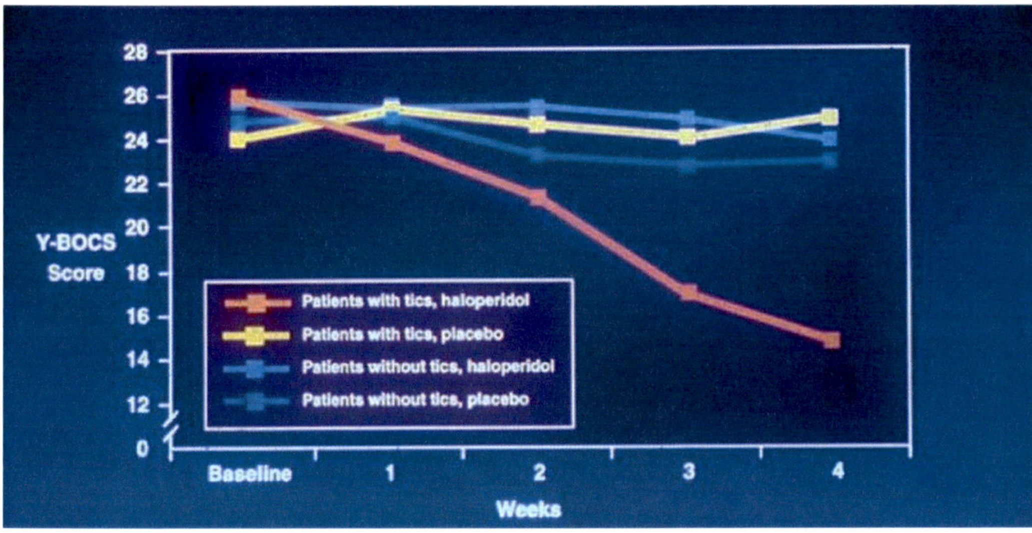

Figure 1. Mean YBOCS of fluvoxamine refractory OCD patients, with or without tics, treated with haloperidol or placebo (by McDougle et al., 1994).

REFRACTORY OCD

The introduction of the second generation antipsychotics (SGA), which are also known as atypical antipsychotics, drew attention in regard to their possible role in OCD. The serotonergic component in these medications, on top of the classical dopamine blocking properties, were one of the motives to look at their potential role in refractory OCD.

We will review the current knowledge in regard to the role of different neuroleptics in refractory OCD and cover the following neuroleptics: clozapine, risperidone, olanzapine, clothiapine, quetiapine, amisulpiride, and ziprasidone.

Clozapine

Clozapine was studied in refractory OCD (McDougle, 1995). In this open label, 10 week study, 20 treatment resistant OCD patients were treated with clozapine doses ranging between 300mg and 600mg daily. However, no significant improvement was noticed.

Risperidone

The picture in regard to risperidone augmentation in refractory OCD is entirely different. Several open studies (McDougle, 1995; Saxena et al., 1996; Stein et al., 1997; Ravizza et al., 1996; Pfanner et al., 2000) reported on a potential benefit of risperidone in treatment refractory OCD. Convincing evidence came from a double-blind study (McDougle, 2000) in which augmentation with a small dose of risperidone (from 0.5 mg twice a day to 3 mg twice a day) was compared to augmentation with placebo. Risperidone was found to be superior to placebo from the third week up to the end of the study (week 6).

This study was replicated in another double-blind, placebo-controlled study (Hollander et al., 2003). In this particular study, 0.5 to 3 mg risperidone daily were added to SSRI in 10 treatment refractory OCD patients, while another six treatment refractory OCD patients got placebo augmentation. Four patients out of the 10 risperidone treated patients responded with clinical global improvement of 1 or 2 points, and with more than 25% reduction in YBOCS. Although the results were not statistically significant from the control (possibly due to the small sample size), they are in line with previous reports. Erzegovesi et al. (2005) recently performed a double-blind, placebo-controlled study on 39 drug naïve OCD patients. Following a twelve-week open label fluvoxamine phase, patients were randomly assigned to risperidone (0.5mg die) or placebo augmentation for 6 weeks. In the patients who had not responded to the fluvoxamine (YBOCS decrease < 35%, CGI < much improved, N=20), risperidone augmentation was found to be effective, with an average decrease of 7.9 on YBOCS, compared with a decrease of 1.8 for placebo. In addition, the authors reported that the effects of risperidone augmentation were no different to placebo in fluvoxamine responders (N=19), thus strengthening the case for a specific subtype of refractory OCD. Hence, augmentation with small dose of risperidone, is probably currently the first augmentation strategy to be employed for treatment refractory patients.

Olanzapine

Weiss et al. (1999) conducted an open label augmentation study with olanzapine. They reported a beneficial effect for seven out of the nine refractory OCD patients who completed the study. Other open studies (Koran et al., 2000; Bogetto et al., 2000; Francobandiera, 2001; Shapira et al, 2004; D'Amico et al, 2003) also reported similar findings.

The first double-blind placebo-controlled study was published by Bystritsky (2004). In this study, a mean YBOCS score decrease of 4.2 points was observed when patients were treated with olanzapine augmentation, as compared to a decrease of 0.54 points in mean YBOCS score for the placebo treated patients.

Quetiapine

Quetiapine addition to SSRI, in patients with treatment refractory OCD, was studied both in open label (Denys et al., 2002) and double-blind studies (Denys et al., 2004a). In the double-blind, placebo-controlled study, 40 OCD patients participated, who were found to be non responsive to an adequate treatment with serotonin reuptake inhibitor. For 8 weeks, patients received either quetiapine, titrated up to 300 mg (n=20), or placebo (n=20). Significant differences between quetiapine and placebo groups were observed in YBOCS score in weeks 4, 6 and 8 (the end of the study), and in clinical global improvement in weeks 6 and 8. However, these findings were not replicated by Sevincok and Topuz (2003), in an open label study with quetiapine 150 mg a day.

Amisulpiride

Amisulpiride augmentation in OCD has been reported only in an open trial (Metin et al., 2003). Flexible doses of amisulpiride (up to 600 mg per day) were given to 12 treatment refractory OCD patients for 12 weeks. A decrease of mean YBOCS score was consequently observed.

Ziprasidone

As there might be a specific role for $5HT_{1D}$ in OCD (Zohar et al., 2004), the affinity of ziprasidone to the $5HT_{1D}$ receptor should be noted. Ziprasidone's affinity to $5HT_{1D}$ is markedly higher than the affinity of the other neuroleptics (affinity of 4+, as compared to the 1+ binding affinity of olanzapine and risperidone, and compared to quetiapine and clozapine which have no receptor binding affinity to $5HT_{1D}$)(Schmidt, 2001; Sprouse et al., 1999).

Although preliminary reports on ziprasidone augmentation in refractory OCD patients were not encouraging (Hollander et al., personal communication), we believe that further work still needs to be done.

Conclusion

The role of second generation antipsychotics in refractory OCD has been studied since the introduction of the atypical antipsychotics. When this chapter was written (2005), there is, based on double-blind placebo-controlled studies, a role for augmentation with risperidone and probably with olanzapine in these patients. There are also conflicting data regarding quetiapine; negative study with clozapine; one open study with amisulpiride; and no published data on ziprasidone.

Schizophrenia and OCD

In DSM-III (1980), schizophrenia was a part of the exclusion criteria for diagnosing OCD. So, it was impossible (according to the DSM-III) to diagnose both schizophrenia and OCD. This was of course an obstacle in regards to recognition and studying co-morbidity of schizophrenia and OCD. With the introduction of DSM-IV (1994), this attitude changed, as it was specified that "some individuals manifest symptoms of both obsessive-compulsive disorder and schizophrenia, warranting both diagnoses" and "if another Axis I disorder is present, the content of the obsessions or compulsions is not restricted to it; e.g., paranoid delusions in schizophrenic-paranoid type" (DSM-IV, 1994). The sort of patients ("schizo-obsessive" patients) that we are referring to is, for example, like Mr. AC.

Mr. AC, a 34 year-old single male, has a 15 year history of paranoid schizophrenia with inappropriate affect, and grandiose and paranoid delusions. Mr. AC is still living with his mother and cannot live without continuous and extensive support. On top of the abovementioned symptomatology, Mr. AC also suffers from washing obsessions, and is preoccupied with his laundry. i.e., his OC symptoms are not related to his delusional symptoms.

The prevalence of co-morbidity of OCD and schizophrenia are presented in table 2.

Table 2. Prevalence of co-morbidity of Schizophrenia and OCD

Paper	Prevalence of co-morbidity of Schizophrenia and OCD
Muller et al., 1953	12.5%
Rudin et al., 1953	10%
Ingram et al., 1961	6.3%
Rasmussen et al., 1986	10%
Karno et al., 1988	12.2%
Berman et al., 1995	25%
Eisen et al., 1997	7.8%
Poyurovsky et al., 1999	14%
Tibbo et al., 2000	25%
Fabisch et al., 2001	10% (male patients)
Poyurovsky et al., 2001	23.5%
Ohta et al., 2003	18.3%
Nechmad et al., 2003	26% (adolescents)
Zohar et al., submitted	15%

Looking at these figures, it is clear that in studies that were carried out from year 2000 and on, the co-morbidity ranged from 10% (Fabisch et al., 2001) up to 26% (Nechmad et al., 2003). Our own findings (Zohar et al., submitted) are in line with these figures (15%). It is therefore clear that the co-morbidity of OCD and schizophrenia is more prevalent than the prevalence that would be expected by the lifetime prevalence of each illness separately (Tibbo and Warneke, 1999). This high prevalence of OCD and schizophrenia suggests a potential involvement of the dopaminergic system in OCD, more than its role in schizophrenia (Denys et al., 2004).

The prognosis of schizophrenia and OCD subset of patients was studied by Fenton and McGlashan (1986). Their initial finding was that "persistent obsessive-compulsive symptoms appear to be a powerful predictor for poor prognosis in schizophrenia". This finding was also confirmed by other studies (Berman et al, 1995; Berman et al., 1998; Hwang et al, 2000; Lysaker et al, 2000). As obsessive-compulsive symptoms in schizophrenia patients are not rare, and since this specific comorbidity is associated with poor prognosis, this subset of patients ("schizo-obsessive" patients) might deserve a specific therapeutic approach.

This specific approach might be a treatment which focuses on symptomatic approach rather than a syndromatic approach. Or, to put it differently, treating the relevant symptoms, rather than focusing on treating the disorder (namely schizophrenia).

The symptomatic approach essentially suggests treating with both antipsychotic (for the schizophrenia symptoms) and with anti-obsessive medication (for the OC component). This kind of approach was performed by Zohar et al. (1993) in an ABA type of study. In this study, patients with co-morbid schizophrenia and OCD were treated initially with neuroleptics (phase A), then switched to a combination of neuroleptic and antipsychotic medications (clomipramine, phase B). Lastly, participants were switched back to neuroleptics (phase A). Measures of psychotic symptoms severity (via BPRS) and of obsessive-compulsive symptomatology (via YBOCS) were carried out every 2 weeks throughout the 18 weeks duration of the study.

The addition of an anti-obsessive medication was associated with significant decrease in the severity of OC symptomatology, during the period in which the patients were treated with a combination of antipsychotics and antiobsessive medication (Phase B). This reduction in the severity of OC symptoms was also associated with a decrease in the BPRS score. After discontinuing the anti-obsessive medication, patients experienced again exacerbation of their OC symptoms. This finding was also replicated by a small double-blind study (Berman et al., 1995), and by other open studies (Pulman et al., 1986; Stroebel et al., 1984). Moreover, the findings were not restricted only to augmentation with clomipramine. The anti-obsessive fluvoxamine was also found to be therapeutically effective in the treatment of OC symptoms in schizophrenia patients in an add-on open study (Poyurovsky et al, 1999). It seems, therefore, that if a patient has schizophrenia and OCD, this patient should receive antipsychotic medication for the schizophrenic symptoms, and anti-obsessive medication for the OC angle.

The Role of Second Generation Antipsychotics for Schizophrenic Patients with OCD

The introduction of atypical neuroleptic with mixed dopaminergic and serotonergic profile suggests, at least theoretically, that these medications might have specific therapeutic edge in the treatment of schizophrenia patients with OCD. In this paragraph we will review the role of second generation antipsychotics in the treatment of "scizobsessive" patients.

Clozapine

Clozapine has been associated with exacerbation of OC symptoms in schizophrenic patients. The first report came from Baker et al. (1992). Baker and his colleagues reported either exacerbation of preexisting OC symptoms, or de-novo surfacing of OC symptoms, in five out of 59 schizophrenia patients treated with clozapine. This report was also replicated by others (Patel and Tandon, 1993; Levkovich et al., 1995). However, in a larger study (Ghaemi et al., 1995) the extent of this phenomenon was found to be less prevalent; exacerbation of OC symptoms in this retrospective study was observed only in two out of 142 inpatients. In another report of four patients, spontaneous decrease in OC symptoms was observed in two patients, and adding anti-obsessive medication was reported to be therapeutically beneficial in the other two (Poyurovsky et al., 1996).

Olanzapine

The reports about the effect of olanzapine in this subset of patients are mixed. An initial report (Baker et al., 1996) showed no exacerbation of OC symptoms in 25 patients. However, a few years later Morrison et al. (1998) and Lykouras et al. (2000) reported symptom exacerbation in some isolated cases.

Augmentation of olanzapine in treatment resistant "schizobsessive" patients was reported to be beneficial in three resistant patients (Poyurovsky et al., 2000). Based on this study, and another unpublished report (Amiaz et al., submitted), addition of olanzapine to SSRI might be therapeutically effective for "schizobsessive" patients who did not respond to other antipsychotic while getting concommittant SSRI.

Risperidone

The role of risperidone in schizophrenic patients with OC symptoms was evaluated in a retrospective study of 113 patients (de Haan et al., 2002). 39 patients were randomly assigned to olanzapine, and 23 to risperidone. The patients treated with olanzapine had significantly more severe OC symptoms at week 6, as compared to the patients treated with risperidone. Based on this indirect finding the authors suggest that risperidone might be preferable in this subset of patients. However, more studies are clearly required.

Quetiapine

Khullar et al. (2004) reported exacerbation of OC symptoms of OCD in a male patient who had co-morbid trichotillomania, bipolar II, and delusional disorders. The authors suggest that "pure OCD and OCD comorbid with a psychotic disorder represent very different disorders in terms of neurobiology" and that "the primary syndrome is a key determinant in whether atypical induced OC symptoms occur".

Ziprasidone

The potential role of Ziprasidone in treating patients with schizophrenia and OCD derives from the high affinity of ziprasidone to $5HT_{1D}$ (which has already been discussed in the refractory OCD paragraph). By the same rationale, the unique role of $5HT_{1D}$ in OCD on one hand, and the high affinity of ziprasidone to this specific receptor on the other hand may suggest a potential role for ziprasidone in this subset of patients. However, this has not been studied as of yet.

Conclusion

The role of antipsychotics in OCD was examined in four different conditions: OCD with psychotic features; OCD and tic disorder; refractory OCD; and schizophrenia and OCD. It seems that in OCD with psychotic features what is needed is (at least initially) a high effective dose of anti-obsessive medication. In the case of OCD with tic, current data suggest that a small dose of high potency classical neuroleptics (haloperidol or pimozide) might be effective. For patients with refractory OCD, the strongest data is related to risperidone, although there are some data suggesting a potential role for olanzapine, conflicting data on the role of quetiapine, and theoretically (but not yet studied) a role for ziprasidone. Finally, for schizophrenic patients with OCD, studies suggest a possible role for risperidone. There are also open data about a potential beneficial role of olanzapine, and not yet studied, but potentially of interest, is the role of ziprasidone. Hence, we conclude that there is a role for antipsychotics in OCD. However, the role, and the specific medication to be chosen, depends (as always) on the diagnostic entity, and in this case, on the different subtypes, namely OCD and tics, refractory OCD and the comorbidity of schizophrenia and OCD. As for poor insight OCD, it is not clear whether or not augmentation with antipsychotics actually works.

References

Ahearn EP, Krohn A, Connor KM, Davidson JR. (2003) Pharmacologic treatment of posttraumatic stress disorder: a focus on antipsychotic use. *Ann Clin Psychiatry*, *15*, 193-201.

American Psychiatric Association (1990) *Diagnostic and Statistical Manual of Mental Disorders*, Third Edition, American Psychiatric Association, Washington D.C.

American Psychiatric Association (1994) *Diagnostic and Statistical Manual of Mental Disorders*, Fourth Edition, American Psychiatric Association, Washington D.C.

Baker RW, Ames D, Umbricht DS, Chengappa KN, Schooler NR, (1996) Obsessive-compulsive symptoms in schizophrenia: a comparison of olanzapine and placebo. *Psychopharmacol Bull*, *32*, 89-93.

Baker RW, Chengappa KN, Baird JW, Steingard S, Christ MA, Schooler NR., (1992) Emergence of obsessive-compulsive symptoms during treatment with clozapine. *J Clin Psychiatry*, *53*, 439-442.

Barnett SD, Kramer ML, Casat CD, Connor KM, Davidson JR. (2002) Efficacy of olanzapine in social anxiety disorder: a pilot study. *J Psychopharmacol*, *16*, 365-368.

Berman I, Merson A, Viegner B, Losonczy MF, Pappas D, Green AI. (1998) Obsessions and compulsions as a distinct cluster of symptoms in schizophrenia: a neuropsychological study. *J Nerv Ment Dis*, *186*, 150-156.

Berman I, Kalinowski A, Berman SM, Lengua J, Green AI. (1995) Obsessive and compulsive symptoms in chronic schizophrenia. *Compr Psychiatry*, *36*, 6-10.

Bogetto F, Bellino S, Vaschetto P, Ziero S. (2000) Olanzapine augmentation of fluvoxamine-refractory obsessive-compulsive disorder (OCD): A 12-week open trial. *Psychiatry Res*, *96*, 91-98.

Butterfield MI, Becker ME, Connor KM, Sutherland S, Churchill LE, Davidson JR. (2001) Olanzapine in the treatment of post-traumatic stress disorder: a pilot study. *Int Clin Psychopharmacol*, *16*, 197-203.

Bystritsky A, Ackerman DL, Rosen RM, Vapnik T, Gorbis E, Maidment KM, Saxena S. (2004) Augmentation of serotonin reuptake inhibitors in refractory obsessive-compulsive disorder using adjunctive olanzapine: A placebo-controlled trial. *J Clin Psychiatry*, *65*, 565-568.

D'Amico G, Cedro C, Muscatello MR, Pandolfo G, Di Rosa AE, Zoccali R, La Torre D, D'Arrigo C, Spina E. (2003) Olanzapine augmentation of paroxetine-refractory obsessive-compulsive disorder. *Prog Neuropsychopharmacol Biol Psychiatry*, *27*, 619-623.

Davidson JR. (2004) Generalized Anxiety and Panic: Common, Costly, and Challenging Disorders and their Pharmacologic Management. *CNS Spectr*, *9*(6 Suppl 13), 1-7.

de Haan L, Beuk N, Hoogenboom B, Dingemans P, Linszen D. (2002) Obsessive-compulsive symptoms during treatment with olanzapine and risperidone: a prospective study of 113 patients with recent-onset schizophrenia or related disorders. *J Clin Psychiatry*, *63*, 104-107.

Denys D, Zohar J, Westenberg HGM. (2004a) The Role of Dopamine in Obsessive-Compulsive Disorder: Preclinical and Clinical Evidence. *J Clin Psychiatry*, *65* (Suppl 14), 11-17.

Denys D, de Geus F, van Megen HJ, Westenberg HG. (2004b) A double-blind, randomized, placebo-controlled trial of quetiapine addition in patients with obsessive-compulsive disorder refractory to serotonin reuptake inhibitors. *J Clin Psychiatry*, *65*, 1040-1048.

Denys D, van Megen H, Westenberg H. (2002) Quetiapine addition to serotonin reuptake inhibitor treatment in patients with treatment-resistant obsessive-compulsive disorder: An open label study. *J Clin Psychiatry*, *63*, 700-703.

Eisen JL, Beer DA, Pato MT, Venditto TA, Rasmussen SA. (1997) Obsessive-compulsive disorder in patients with schizophrenia or schizoaffective disorder. *Am J Psychiatry*, *154*, 271-273.

Eisen JL, Rasmussen SA, Phillips KA, Price LH, Davidson J, Lydiard RB, Ninan P, Piggott T. (2001) Insight and treatment outcome in obsessive-compulsive disorder. *Compr Psychiatry*, *42*, 494-497.

Eisen JL, Rasmussen SA. (1993) Obsessive-compulsive disorder with psychotic features. *J Clin Psychiatry*, *54*, 373-379.

Erzegovesi S., Guglielmo E., Siliprandi F., Bellodi L. (2005) Low-dose risperidone augmentation of fluvoxamine treatment in obsessive-compulsive disorder: A double-blind, placebo-controlled study. *Eur. Neuropsychopharmacol*, *15*, 69-74.

Fabisch K, Fabisch H, Langs G, Huber HP, Zapotoczky HG. (2001) Incidence of obsessive-compulsive phenomena in the course of acute schizophrenia and schizoaffective disorder. *Eur Psychiatry, 16*, 336-341.

Fenton WS, McGlashan TH. (1986) The prognostic significance of obsessive-compulsive symptoms in schizophrenia. *Am J Psychiatry*, *143*, 437-441.

Francobandiera G. (2001) Olanzapine augmentation of serotonin uptake inhibitors in obsessive-compulsive disorder: An open study. *Can J Psychiatry*, *46*, 356-358.

Ghaemi SN, Zarate CA Jr, Popli AP, Pillay SS, Cole JO. (1995) Is there a relationship between clozapine and obsessive-compulsive disorder?: a retrospective chart review. *Compr Psychiatry*, *36*, 267-270.

Hollander E, Baldini Rossi N, Sood E, Pallanti S. (2003) Risperidone augmentation in treatment-resistant obsessive-compulsive disorder: A double-blind, placebo-controlled study. *Int J Neuropsychopharmacol*, *6*, 397-401.

Hwang MY, Morgan JE, Losconzcy MF. (2000) Clinical and neuropsychological profiles of obsessive-compulsive schizophrenia: a pilot study. *J Neuropsychiatry Clin Neurosci*, *12*, 91-94.

Ingram IM. (1961) Obsessional illness in mental hospital patients. *J Ment Sci*, *107*, 382-402.

Insel TR, Akiskal HS. (1986) Obsessive-compulsive disorder with psychotic features: A phenomenologic analysis. *Am J Psychiatry*, *143*, 1527-1533.

International Statistical Classification of Diseases and Related Health Problems, 10th Revision, World Health Organization, 2003

Karno M, Golding JM, Sorenson SB, Burnam MA. (1988) The epidemiology of obsessive-compulsive disorder in five US communities. *Arch Gen Psychiatry*, *45*, 1094-1099.

Khullar A, Chue P, Tibbo P. (2001) Quetiapine and obsessive–compulsive symptoms (OCS): case report and review of atypical antipsychotic-induced OCS. *J Psychiatry Neurosci*, *26*, 55-59.

Koran LM, Ringold AL, Elliot MA. (2000) Olanzapine augmentation for treatment-resistant obsessive-compulsive disorder. *J Clin Psychiatry*, *61*, 514-517.

Leckman JF, Grice DE, Barr LC, de Vries AL, Martin C, Cohen DJ, McDougle CJ, Goodman WK, Rasmussen SA. (1994) Tic-related vs. non-tic-related obsessive-compulsive disorder. *Anxiety*, *1*, 208-215.

Levkovich Y, Kronnenberg Y, Gaoni B. (1995) Can Clozapine trigger OCD? *J Am Acad Child Adolesc Psychiatry*, *34*, 263.

Lykouras L, Zervas IM, Gournellis R, Malliori M, Rabavilas A. (2000) Olanzapine and obsessive-compulsive symptoms. *Eur Neuropsychopharmacol*, *10*, 385-387.

Lysaker PH, Marks KA, Picone JB, Rollins AL, Fastenau PS, Bond GR. (2000) Obsessive and compulsive symptoms in schizophrenia: clinical and neurocognitive correlates. *J Nerv Ment Dis*, *188*, 78-83.

McDougle CJ, Barr LC, Goodman WK, Pelton GH, Aronson SC, Anand A, Price LH. (1995) Lack of efficacy of clozapine monotherapy in refractory obsessive-compulsive disorder. *Am J Psychiatry*, *152,* 1812-1814.

McDougle CJ, C. Epperson N, Pelton GH, Wasylink S, Price LH. (2000) A Double-blind, placebo-controlled study of risperidone addition in serotonin reuptake inhibitor–refractory obsessive-compulsive disorder. *Arch Gen Psychiatry*, *57*, 794-801.

McDougle CJ, Goodman WK, Leckman JF, Lee NC, Heninger GR, Price LH. (1994) Haloperidol addition in fluvoxamine-refractory obsessive-compulsive disorder. A double-blind, placebo-controlled study in patients with and without tics. *Arch Gen Psychiatry*, *51*, 302-308.

Metin O, Yazici K, Tot S, Yazici AE. (2003) Amisulpiride augmentation in treatment-resistant obsessive-compulsive disorder: An open trial. *Human Psychopharmacology*, *18*, 463-467.

Morrison D, Clark D, Goldfarb E, McCoy L. (1998) Worsening of obsessive-compulsive symptoms following treatment with olanzapine. *Am J Psychiatry*, *155*, 855.

Muller C. (1953) The transition of obsessional neurosis into schizophrenia in the light of catamnesis. *Schweiz Arch Neurol Psychiatr*, *72*, 218-225.

Nechmad A, Ratzoni G, Poyurovsky M, Meged S, Avidan G, Fuchs C, Bloch Y, Weizman R. (2003) Obsessive-compulsive disorder in adolescent schizophrenia patients. *Am J Psychiatry*, *160*, 1002-1004.

Ohta M, Kokai M, Morita Y. (2003) Features of obsessive-compulsive disorder in patients primarily diagnosed with schizophrenia. *Psychiatry Clin Neurosci*, *57*, 67-74.

Patel B, Tandon R. (1993) Development of obsessive-compulsive symptoms during clozapine treatment. *Am J Psychiatry*, *150*, 836.

Pfanner C, Marazziti D, Dell'Osso L Presta S, Gemignani A, Milanfranchi A, Cassano GB. (2000) Risperidone augmentation in refractory obsessive-compulsive disorder: An open-label study. *Int Clin Psychopharmacol*, *15*, 297-301.

Poyurovsky M, Hermesh H, Weizman A. (1996) Fluvoxamine treatment in clozapine-induced obsessive-compulsive symptoms in schizophrenic patients. *Clin Neuropharmacol, 19*, 305-313.

Poyurovsky M, Fuchs C, Weizman A. (1999a) Obsessive-compulsive disorder in patients with first-episode schizophrenia. *Am J Psychiatry*, *156*, 1998-2000.

Poyurovsky M, Isakov V, Hromnikov S, Modai I, Rauchberger B, Schneidman M, Weizman A. (1999b) Fluvoxamine treatment of obsessive-compulsive symptoms in schizophrenic patients: an add-on open study. *Int Clin Psychopharmacol*, *14*, 95-100.

Poyurovsky M, Dorfman-Etrog P, Hermesh H, Munitz H, Tollefson GD, Weizman A. (2000) Beneficial effect of olanzapine in schizophrenic patients with obsessive-compulsive symptoms. *Int Clin Psychopharmacol*, *15*, 169-173.

Poyurovsky M, Hramenkov S, Isakov V, Rauchverger B, Modai I, Schneidman M, Fuchs C, Weizman A. (2001) Obsessive-compulsive disorder in hospitalized patients with chronic schizophrenia. *Psychiatry Res*,*102*, 49-57.

Pulman J, Yassa R, Ananth J. (1984) Clomipramine treatment of repetitive behavior. *Can J Psychiatry*, *29*, 254-255.

Rasmussen SA, Tsuang MT. (1986) Clinical characteristics and family history in DSM-III obsessive-compulsive disorder. *Am J Psychiatry*, *143*, 317-322.

Ravi-Kishore V, Samar R, Janardhan-Reddy YC, Chandrasekhar CR, Thennarasu K. (2004) Clinical characteristics and treatment response in poor and good insight obsessive-compulsive disorder. *Eur Psychiatry*, *19*, 202-208.

Ravizza L, Barzega G, Bellino S, Bogetto F, Maina G. (1996) Therapeutic effect and safety of adjunctive risperidone in refractory obsessive-compulsive disorder (OCD). *Psychopharmacol Bull*, *32*, 677-682.

Richter MA, Summerfeldt LJ, Antony MM, Swinson RP. (2003) Obsessive-compulsive spectrum conditions in obsessive-compulsive disorder and other anxiety disorders. *Depression and Anxiety*, *18*, 118-127.

Rudin E. (1953) On the problem of compulsive disease with special reference to its hereditary relations. *Arch Psychiatr Nervenkr Z Gesamte Neurol Psychiatr*, *191*, 14-54.

Saxena S, Wang D, Bystritsky A, Baxter LR Jr. (1996) Risperidone augmentation of SRI treatment for refractory obsessive-compulsive disorder. *J Clin Psychiatry*, *57,* 303-306.

Schmidt AW, Lebel LA, Howard HR Jr, Zorn SH. (2001) Ziprasidone: A novel antipsychotic with a unique human receptor binding profile. *Eur J Pharmacol*, *425*, 197-201.

Sevincok L, Topuz A. (2003) Lack of efficacy of low doses of quetiapine addition in refractory obsessive-compulsive disorder. *J Clin Psychopharmacol*, *23*, 448-450.

Shapira NA, Ward HE, Mandoki M, Murphy TK, Yang MC, Blier P, Goodman WK. (2004) A double-blind, placebo-controlled trial of olanzapine addition in fluoxetine-refractory obsessive-compulsive disorder. *Biol Psychiatry*, *55*, 553-555.

Sprouse JS, Reynolds LS, Braselton JP, Rollema H, Zorn SH. (1999) Comparison of the novel antipsychotic ziprasidone with clozapine and olanzapine: inhibition of dorsal raphe cell firing and the role of $5HT_{1A}$ receptor activation. *Neuropsychopharmacol*, *21*, 622-631.

Stein DJ, Bouwer C, Hawkridge S, Emsley RA. (1997) Risperidone augmentation of serotonin reuptake inhibitors in obsessive-compulsive and related disorders. *J Clin Psychiatry*, *58*, 119-122.

Stroebel CF, Szarek BL, Glueck BC. (1984) Use of clomipramine in treatment of obsessive-compulsive symptomatology. *J Clin Psychopharmacol*, *4*, 98-100.

Tibbo P, Warneke L. (1999) Obsessive-compulsive disorder in schizophrenia: epidemiologic and biologic overlap. *J Psychiatry Neurosci*, *24*, 15-24.

Tibbo P, Kroetsch M, Chue P, Warneke L. (2000) Obsessive-compulsive disorder in schizophrenia. *J Psychiatr Res*, *34*, 139-146.

Tibbo P, Warneke L. (1999) Obsessive-compulsive disorder in Schizophrenia: epidemiologic and biologic overlap. *J. Psychiatry Neuroscience*, *24*, 15-24.

Weiss AA, Robinson S, Winnik HZ. (1969) "Obsessive psychosis"--psychodiagnostic findings.*Isr Ann Psychiatr Relat Discip*, *7*, 175-178.

Weiss EL, Potenza MN, McDougle CJ, Epperson CN. (1999) Olanzapine addition in obsessive-compulsive disorder refractory to selective serotonin reuptake inhibitors: An open-label case series. *J Clin Psychiatry, 60*, 524-527.

Zohar J, Kaplan Z, Benjamin J. (1993) Clomipramine treatment of obsessive-compulsive symptomatology in schizophrenic patients. *J Clin Psychiatry*, *54*, 358-388.

Zohar J, Tzfoni A, Sirota P, Chopra M, Sasson Y. Chronic Schizophrenia with Obsessive-Compulsive Symptoms: Comorbidity or a subtype? Submitted.

Zohar J, Kennedy JL, Hollander, E, Koran, LM. (2004) Serotonin-1D Hypothesis of Obsessive-Compulsive Disorder: An Update. *J Clin Psychiatry*, *65* Suppl 14, 18-21

In: Obsessive-Compulsive Disorder and Comorbidity
Editors: R. Gross-Isseroff and A. Weizman, pp. 145-160
ISBN 1-59454-884-6

Chapter 9

STATE OF THE ART AND FUTURE DIRECTIONS IN THE PATHOPHYSIOLOGY OF OBSESSIVE-COMPUSIVE DISORDER

Donatella Marazziti,* Francesco Mungai and Bernardo Dell'Osso
Dipartimento di Psichiatria, Neurobiologia, Farmacologia e Biotecnologie, Section of Psychiatry, University of Pisa, Pisa, Italy

INTRODUCTION

OCD has been considered for a long time a rare and treatment-refractory psychiatric condition, while is now considered as a relatively common desease, with a lifetime prevalence of about 2.5 %, and as a major cause of long-term disability to patients and their families. The treatment of OCD has changed substantially over the last decade following the introduction of selective serotonin (5-HT) re-uptake inhibitors (SSRIs), such as fluoxetine, fluvoxamine, paroxetine, sertraline, citalopram, which provide symptom remission in about 60% of the patients. Intensive pharmacological investigation has demonstrated that OCD is unique in the response to serotonergic agents and furthermore that non-serotonergic antidepressants such as desipramine have no effect. The specific response of OCD patients to SSRIs has emphasized the possible role of the main target of these drugs, namely the 5-HT system in the pathophysiology of the disorder. In fact, although it seems unlikely that one transmitter system can explain all the complexities of OCD, recent efforts to elucidate the pathophysiology of OCD have centered largely around the role of this neurotransmitter.

For more than a decade the 5-HT hypothesis has represented a frame of reference for approaching the biology and pathophysiology of this mental condition. The main evidences were those related to the effectiveness of clomipramine, a tricyclic which blocks

* Correspondence: Dipartimento di Psichiatria, Neurobiologia, Farmacologia e Biotecnologie", Section of Psychiatry, University of Pisa, via Roma 67, 56100 Pisa, Italy; tel. + 39 050/835412; fax: + 39 050/21581; e-mail address: dmarazzi@psico.med.unipi.it

preferentially the 5-HT reuptake, as compared with other tricyclics or placebo, subsequently confirmed by the superiority of selective 5-HT uptake inhibitors (SSRI's), such as fluoxetine, fluvoxamine, paroxetine, sertraline and citalopram (Montgomery et al.,1995; Greist et al., 1995; Piccinelli et al., 1995; Fineberg et al., 1996). Moreover, indications of a 5-HT involvement came also from cerebrospinal fluid (CSF) studies of 5-hydroxyindoleacetic acid (5-HIAA) in OCD, which have shown that a positive response to clomipramine was associated with high CSF 5-HIAA levels (Thoren et al., 1980; Insel et al., 1985), while low levels correlate negatively with response to clomipramine and positively with OC symptom severity (Asberg et al., 1981). Other supporting evidences, showing the exacerbations of OC symptoms with 5-HT agonists somministration, have led to the hypothesis of hypersensitivity of postsynaptic 5-HT receptors in OCD, a hypothesis that is still considered valid (Zohar et al., 1987; Hollander et al., 1988; Zohar et al., 1988).

In any case, If the role of 5-HT in OCD is not questionable, future studies should be directed towards the elucidation of the 5-HT receptor subtypes involved, of the second messengers transducing the signal, as well as of the interactions between 5-HT and the other neurotransmitters.

Platelet Studies

The main target of clomipramine and SSRI's, that is the 5-HT transporter, have been deeply investigated in OCD for its presence in blood platelets: in fact, the active uptake for 5-HT in these cells is similar to that present in the brain, as demonstrated by the cloning of the two structures (Lesch et al., 1993; Rausch et al., 1995). For some years, ^{3}H-imipramine (^{3}H-IMI), has been mainly used to label it (Meyerson et al., 1987). However, pharmacological studies in this field have shown heterogeneity of IMI binding sites when desipramine is used to define "specific" binding (Hrdina, 1989): desipramine-defined IMI binding appears to be constituted by two sub-populations: only that of protein nature, 5-HT-sensitive and Na-dependent would be present in serotonergic neurons and related to the 5-HT transporter (Marcusson et al., 1985). Insel et al. (1985) found no difference in both 5-HT uptake and ^{3}H-IMI binding between healthy controls and OC patients, and Weizman et al. (1986) and Marazziti et al. (1992) observed normal 5-HT uptake coupled with a reduced number of ^{3}H-IMI binding sites. Black et al. (1990) replicated Insel et al.'s data of no change in ^{3}H-IMI binding, except for a decrease in such binding sites in clomipramine-treated patients, while other studies have shown a decreased number of ^{3}H-IMI binding sites and a decreased affinity for 5-HT uptake (Bastani et al., 1991), as well as an increased velocity of 5-HT uptake, with no change in ^{3}H-IMI binding (Vitiello et al., 1991). Subsequently, it has been demonstrated that the more selective ligand ^{3}H-paroxetine (^{3}H-Par) binds to a single site, probably corresponding to the neuronal transporter (Mellerup et al., 1983; Mann et al., 1992) and a significant decrease in the number of ^{3}H-Par binding sites, as compared with healthy controls, has been reported by two groups (Marazziti et al., 1996; Sallee et al., 1996). Such a decrease appears to constitute a state-dependent marker, as it is reverted by a successful treatment with different SRI's (Hollander et al., 1998). In addition, this and other reports suggest that the patients showing the most "severe" serotonergic abnormalities are those who respond better to the drugs and, therefore, link the serotonergic alteration to a positive response to serotonergic drugs (Marazziti, 1997; Hollander et al., 1998; Zohar et al., 1998).

PHARMACOLOGICAL RESPONSES

The identification of at least 17 5-HT receptor subtypes (Hoyer et al., 1997) has led to the question of which subtype or subsystem might be primarily implicated in OCD. Besides the blockade of the 5-HT transporter, clomipramine enhances the responsiveness of the postsynaptic 5-HT_{1A} receptor and provokes a desensitization of 5-HT_{2C} receptors, while SSRI's cause a decrease in somatodendritic and terminal autoreceptor responsiveness (Blier et al., 1998). The net increase in 5-HT release provoked by the two actions is particularly evident in the orbitofrontal cortex, an area that appears primarily implicated in OCD, after a time lag (8 weeks) consistent with the delayed response to these drugs typical of OCD patients, at variance with depression. In addition, high doses of SSRI's are required to elicit this effect in agreement with clinical observation that OCD patients need higher doses than depressed patients. The effect of 5-HT in the orbitofrontal cortex has been linked to 5-HT_2-like receptors, since it is reverted by a long administration of 5-HT_2 antagonists. Clinical observation support the notion that drugs blocking the 5-HT transporter display anti-obssesional properties by increasing the serotonergic transmission: both metergoline and ritanserin, non-selective 5-HT antagonists, seems to provoke symptoms in drug-remitted patients (Benkefalt et al., 1989; Erzegovesi et al., 1992). The role of 5-HT_2-like receptors is supported by preliminary observations of the antiobsessional effect of psilocybin, a hallucinogen with 2-HT agonist properties (Moreno et al., 1997) and by the clinical utility in resistant OCD of atypical neuroleptics, such risperidone with a $5\text{-HT}_2/D_2$ profile (Mc Dougle, 1987).

DRUG CHALLENGE TESTS

Another useful approach for exploring receptor subtypes is represented by drug-challenge tests. Although the related findings are questionable because no sufficiently selective compounds is currently available, nevertheless they provide dynamic studies of the receptors and interesting suggestions. The most employed challenge is that with m-chlorophenylpiperazine (m-CPP) (Zohar et al., 1987; Hollander et al., 1988; Pigott et al., 1991), a partial 5-HT agonist with 5-HT_{1A}, $5\text{-HT}_{1B/D}$, 5-HT_{2C}, 5-HT_2 receptor agonist and 5-HT_2 receptor antagonist properties, which also inhibits 5-HT re-uptake and displaces ^{3}H-Par binding to the 5-HT transporter, that provokes exacerbation of OC symptoms. On the contrary MK-212, a 5-HT_{1A} and 5-HT_{2C} receptor agonist provokes no behavioral effect in OCD (Bastani et al., 1990). The main difference between m-CCP and MK-212 is represented by the fact that this last compound shows no affinity for $5\text{-HT}_{1B/D}$ receptors. The possible role of $5\text{-HT}_{1B/D}$ receptors was investigated by means of sumatriptan, an agonist at this level, but data are still meager and controversial: while Zohar's group (1998) reported exacerbation of obsessive symptoms, others did not observe any change in 15 patients except a significant increase in growth hormone response (Pian et al., 1998). Certainly, the matter needs to be furtherly investigated maybe with $5\text{-}HT_{1B/D}$ receptor agonists with better brain penetrating properties than sumatriptan that does not easily pass the blood-brain barrier.

Receptors Subtypes

In order to summarize the overall data, they suggest the involvement of the following 5-HT receptor subtypes: $5\text{-}HT_{1A}$ receptors, $5\text{-}HT_{2A}$ receptors, $5\text{-}HT_{2C}$ and $5\text{-}HT_{1B/D}$ receptors. With regard to the $5\text{-}HT_{1A}$ receptor subtype, it does not appear altered in OCD patients, as shown by no effect of the challenge with ipsapirone, a $5\text{-}HT_{1A}$ receptor agonist, in the patients (Lesch et al., 1991), and by the lack of clinical efficacy of buspirone (Mc Dougle et al., 1993), so that the use of this drug in augmentation strategies is no longer recommended. The question of the role of the $5\text{-}HT_{2A}$, $5\text{-}HT_{2C}$ and $5\text{-}HT_{1B/D}$ receptors in OCD is still open and deserves further investigation. However, we cannot disregard the potential involvement of other receptor subtypes for which a few or no possibility of exploration does exist at the moment. We refer, in particular, to the $5\text{-}HT_{5A}$ and $5\text{-}HT_6$ subtypes where clomipramine seems to interact, or to $5\text{-}HT_{1F}$ where sumatriptan displays an agonistic activity at the same degree of that exerted at the level of $5\text{-}HT_{1D}$ receptors. With regard to other receptor subtypes, the status of the $5\text{-}HT_3$ receptors, was explored with ondansetron, a drug which display a high affinity at its level, given to 11 OCD patients (Broock et al., 1998) before intravenous administration of m-CPP. The findings of this study, showing that m-CPP provoked exacerbation of OCD symptoms and that pretreatment with ondansetron did not change this response, seem to exclude the involvement of $5\text{-}HT_3$ receptors in OCD, although further data, in particular comparisons with control groups, are needed. Given the existence of one or more receptor abnormalities, are these due to a genetic defect, or to an altered expression of the gene products, or rather to changes in the environment surrounding the receptor? Our group is actually focusing on the of $5\text{-}HT_{2C}$ and $5\text{-}HT_{5A}$ subtype expression for the abundance of their mRNA in lymphocytes (Marazziti et al., 2001): the preliminary results of a study which still in progress suggest an over-expression of the $5\text{-}HT_{2C}$ mRNA in OCD patients, as compared with controls.

Intracellular Mechanisms

Since a receptor is just the first step of a subsequent cascade of events, from a biochemical point of view, currently, much interest is focused on the intracellular regulation of the 5-HT transporter and receptors. Some reports have underlined a link between 5-HT reuptake and protein kinase of type C (PKC) (Anderson et al., 1992) that inhibits the process, and PKA that, on the contrary, exerts a positive influence on 5-HT re-uptake (De Vivo et al., 1985). PKC is a class of phosphorylases present at high concentration in the brain (Nishizuka et al., 1986; Kikkawa et al., 1989; Wilkinson et al., 1994). Diacylglycerol, derived from the hydrolysis of phosphatidylinositol-4,5-bisphosphate (PIP2), stimulates PKC by increasing its affinity for calcium and membrane phospholipids deriving from receptor-mediated hydrolysis and by promoting its translocation from the cytosol to the particulate fraction (Berridge et al., 1982; Ashendel et al., 1985; Weiss et al., 1989). We investigated the effect of the activation of PKC on the 5-HT reuptake in a group of patients with OCD vs controls and observed the velocity of the re-uptake decreased significantly in both OCD patients and healthy controls, but to a greater degree in OCD patients. This decrease in Vmax of OCD patients was significantly more robust than in healthy controls, indicating that the mechanism is "more active" in OCD (Marazziti et al., 2000). This phenomenon could perhaps be attributed either to a hyper-responsiveness of the 5-HT reuptake system, or to a hyperactivation of PKC in OCD. Such a latter condition might in turn reflect increased endogenous production of dyacylglycerol as a result of hyperactive phosphatidylinositol (PI) pathway. A stimulation of the PI pathway in OCD is congruent with data showing a worsening of OCD symptoms following 5-HT_{2C} receptor agonist such as m-CPP (Zohar et al., 1987; Hollander et al, 1998), a non specific 5-HT_{2C} receptor agonist, and it is well known that 5-HT_{2C} receptors are linked with a G-protein activating phospholipase C (Wang et al., 1989). However, other receptors are linked with phospholipase C, including 5-HT_{2A}, dopamine and muscarinic receptors: interstingly atypical neuroleptics are agonist at 5-HT_{2A} receptor level. Hyperactivity of the PI pathway might provoke an alteration in the normal balance existing between the PI pathway and the cAMP pathway and currently increased PKA activity in OCD patients has been demonstrated (Perez et al., 2000). On this line, there is also evidence of the therapeutic effect of inositol, a naturally occurring isomer of glucose that acts as a precursor in the PI pathway in OCD (Fux et al., 1996). The hyperactivity of the PI pathway has been supported by a recent paper showing inreased inositol 3-phoshate and 5-HT2a binding sites in OCD patients that normalized after specific treatments (Delorme et al., 2004). It can, therefore, be hypothesized that OCD may perhaps be due to a dysbalance of the two main transductory pathways, cAMP and PI, with a prevalence of the second and a consequently higher activation of PKC, relative to that of PKA, given the cross-talk between the two main second messengers at the level of different effectors (Marazziti et al., 2001). Besides the PI pathway, SSRI's and antidepressants have been shown to up-regulate the cyclic adenosine monophosphate (cAMP)-cAMP response element binding protein (CREB, a transcription factor) cascade, as well as the expression of the brain-derived neurotrophic factor (BDNF) (Duman, 1998). Interestingly, CREB is a substrate for both PKA and PKC and 5-HT_{2C} agonists seem to influence CREB and BDNF expression. Therefore, we strongly believe that the elucidations of these mechanisms will shed new lights in those disorders, such as OCD, where SSRI's are effective.

WHAT BEYOND 5-HT?

Although the current bulk of findings 5-HT in the pathophysiology of OCD, is increasing at a level and with a convergence that is not found in any other psychiatric disorder, the hypothesis that this disorder might be due to a unique neurochemical abnormality, contrasts with the observation that at least 30% of patients do not respond to SSRI's (Montgomery et al., 1994; Sasson et al., 1996). In addition, it is plausible the overall clinical heterogeneity of the patients might be underlied by different biological mechanisms. In these years evidences have been accumulating of disturbances in other neurotransmitters, such as dopamine, norepinephrine and in some neuropeptides in the etiology of OCD: however, in some cases, the findings are meager and controversial. On the contrary, more agreement exists on the role of immune mechanisms in a subtype of childhood OCD.

OCD and Dopamine

In addition to 5-HT abnormalities, the most consisting findings described up-to-now in OCD are those related to the dopamine system.

The first data derive from the observation of increased stereotyped behaviours in that animals undergoing manipulation of the dopamine system. Subjects with disorders of the basal ganglia, a dopamine area, such as Gilles de la Tourette's syndrome, postencenphalitic Parkinson's disease or tics disorder often present OC symptoms. Cocaine users also suffer from stereotyped and OC behaviours. These observations have led to the use of dopamine blocker, i.e., typical and atypical neuroleptics as augmentation strategies in refractory OCD (McDougle et al., 1990).

The direct evaluation of peripheral dopamine markers is still very difficult. We demonstrated an increased activity of the platelet sulphotransferase, an enzyme involved in the catabolism of dopamine, in a group of drug-free OCD patients, which can reflect an increased level of circulating neurotransmitter (Marazziti et al., 1992).

OCD and Norepinephrine

The findings showing abnormalities in the norepinephrine system are quite a few and based mainly on the positive response of OCD patients to the alpha2-adrenergic agonist clonidine (Knesevich, 1982; Hollander et al., 1988, 1991). On the contrary, the evaluation of the role of the norepinephrine system in OCD by means of challenge tests have been controversial.

An interesting study (Leckman et al., 1995) has shown lower cerebrospinal fluid concentrations of tyramine and homovanilic acid in 44 OCD patients than in normal controls or patients with Tourette's syndrome who also exibited increased levels of norepinephrine. However, CSF findings, as well as those deriving from plasma or urine measurements, should be considered with cautions given the low reliability and sensitivity of the methods that are influenced by different factors.

OCD and Neuropeptides

Recently, much interest has been directed towards two related neuropeptides, arginin vasopressin and oxytocin, as increased levels have been reported in pure OCD patients (Leckman et al., 1994). According to this and other authors, the oxytocin system would be involved in the regulation of affiliative behaviours and parental bonding and they speculate that a disturbance at this level may be related to the pathophysiology of a specific OCD subtype. Altemus et al. (1994) showed that clomipramine increased cerebrospinal fluid oxytocin in OCD children and adolescents.

Another neuropeptide reported to be increased in the cerebrospinal fluid of OCD patients is somatostatin (Altemus et al., 1993) that in experimental animals produces behaviours similar to compulsive acts (Pitman, 1989).

OPIOID PEPTIDES

Amongst the different activities, the opioid system is involved in the regulation of conditioned responses and, therefore, it has been hypothesized that it might have a role in the onset and maintanance of OCD symptoms. On this line, a few clinical observations have suggested the possible usefulness of tramadol, a major analgesic, in refractory OCD patients (Shapira et al., 1997; Goldsmith et al., 1999).

IMMUNOLOGICAL ALTERATIONS IN OCD

Currently, a broad agreement exists regarding the possibility of some forms of childhood OCD being due to immunological alterations, on the basis of the possible shared involvement of basal ganglia abnormalities in OCD and Sydenham's chorea, both resulting from infection-driven autoimmune processes (Swedo, 1994). Sydenham's chorea is a manifestation of rheumatic fever, following an infection provoked by group A ß-haemolytic streptococci, which is thought to derive from the production of antibodies cross-reacting with neurons of the basal ganglia (Bronze et al., 1993). The relationship between OCD and Sydenham's chorea is strenghtened by clinical observations showing that more than 80% of children with this last condition show obsessions and compulsions both before, and concomitantly with, choreic movements (Swedo, 1994), and that one third of OCD children present choreiform movements Denckla et al., 1989). As a result, the hypothesis has emerged that infections with group A ß-haemolytic streptococci might produce conditions grouped together under the name of PANDAS (paediatric autoimmune neuropsychiatric disorders associated with streptococci), including subtypes of paediatric OCD and tics (Swedo, 1997, 1998) but the observation has been made that even viral infections might trigger the autoimmune process leading to OCD (Allen et al., 1995; Khanna et al., 1997). Furthermore, patients with rheumatic fever show a high level of antineural antibodies against the caudate (Husby et al., 1976) and a particular antigen in B lymphocytes reacting with a monoclonal antibody called D8/D17 (Zabriskie, 1986; Gibofsky et al., 1991). Such an antigen has been shown to be stable in different populations and over time and, more interestingly, it is also present in patients with childhood OCD, Tourette's syndrome and chronic tic disorder (Murphy et al., 1997); preliminary data are available also in subjects with autism (Hollander et al., 1999). Although the relationship between the antigen identified by the D8/17 antibody and the pathophysiology of the various disorders is not yet clear, it has been considered either as an immunological marker of susceptibility to rheumatic fever (Gibofsky et al., 1991) or to be linked to the motor component of the various disturbances (Kiessling et al., 1993). It is worth noting that such an antigen has been observed also in other related disorders such as Tourette's syndrome, tic disorder and autism (Murphy et al., 1997; Hollander et al., 1999). The literature regarding immunological factors in adult OCD is quite meager. Cytokine production appears to be normal in OCD patients, at variance with depressed patients (Weizman et al., 1996). Barber et al. (1996) evaluated T-lymphocyte subsets in chronic OCD patients in the acute phase, but were unable to find any difference in comparison with healthy controls, either before or after successful clomipramine treatment. On the other hand, the possible involvement of the immune system in some subtypes of OCD is supported by the finding of a relationship between the severity of the disorder and the interleukin-6 (IL-6) and IL-6 receptor levels (Maes et al., 1994) and by the observation of decreased plasma cytokines, such as interleukin-1 beta and tumor necrosis factor alfa (Brambilla et al., 1997) which has been related to hyperactivity of the noradrenergic system and of the HPA axis. Recently, we showed increased CD8+ and decreased CD4+ lymphocytes, i.e., suppressor and helper lymphocytes, respectively, in adult OCD patients (Marazziti et al., 1999). The role of immune factors in OCD is also supported by the report of increased CSF levels of immunoglobulin G antibodies against herpes virus of type 1 suggestive of a chronic infection, in an indian sample of adult patients (Garvey et al., 1999), but the specificity of these findings needs to be clarified. All these observations are in general very intriguing, but much remains to be done in this area. In particular, it would be helpful to identify familial, clinical or symptomatological features that might be linked to immunological disturbances. The presence of such disturbances suggest the use of non-conventional treatments, in particular antibiotics or immunomodulators (Swedo et al., 1994; Allen et al., 1995), however, the results of the first pilot study of penicillin prophylaxis in children with PANDAS were negative (Garvey et al., 1999).

Relevance of Neurobiology in OCD Comorbidity

It is frequent, in the clinical practice, to observe that patients suffering from OCD also meet criteria for other diagnoses such as mood, anxiety, personality or psychotic disorders. This considerable comorbidity overlap raises the issue of possible common structural and/or functional biological substrates.

Consistent data relative to the neurobiology and the pathophysiology of OCD have underlined the central role played by specific brain circuits such as the orbitofrontal cortex, the caudate nucleus, and the thalamus (Kaplan, 1998; Rauch, 1993): this notion is supported by the observations of OCD symptoms amongst subjects with diseases affecting those areas of the brain, such as Sydenham's chorea, Huntington's chorea, localized brain tumors, strongly support this evidence (Jenike, 1983). Another hypothesis, mainly related to the early-onset OCD, would consider the possible abnormalities involving the normal "pruning" of excess neurons occurring during brain maturation. Morphometric magnetic resonance imaging studies showing increased ventral prefrontal cortical anterior cingulated volumes of OCD paediatric patients has been interpreted as a consequence of this altered process (Rosenberg, 1998). Even in the absence of an identification of a mendelian pattern of inheritance or of an OCD gene, some authors have identified a familial pattern characterized by an early onset and a severe OCD subset of symptoms (Nestadt, 2000).

The advances in OCD neurobiological research has progressively prompted increasing attention to more specific approaches to the assessment of the most frequent OCD comorbid conditions. In particular, the focus of the research has been driven to the identification of possible distinctive clinical features, different course of illness and pharmacological treatment implications of comorbid OCD.

The conceptualisation of an OCD spectrum, gathering together a wide range of different clinical conditions such as body dysmorphic disorder (BBD), impulse control, tic and eating disorders, had lead the research to test the involvement of the serotonergic system as a possible common biological substrate. The available data seem to support the evidence of a common abnormality at the level of the presynaptic 5-HT transporter shared by these clinical condition, in particular, this abnormality would result in a similar decreased density of [3H] paroxetine binding sites (Marazziti et al., 1999).

The strong association between BBD and OCD, as well as, other related disorders such as social phobia, mood, eating and impulse control disorders, suggested to consider these clinical variants as a particularly severe form of the syndrome characterized by a greater load of psychopatology and functional impairment (Frare et al., 2004).

Studies assessing the comorbidity rates of OCD and eating disorders reported a significant higher prevalence of OCD in patients suffering from anorexia nervosa (AN) and bulimia nervosa than in nonclinical groups. The anxiety disorder had generally an early onset, before the onset of the eating disorder, thus raising the possibility of OCD as a eating disorder prone condition (Kaye, 2004). In another study, the dimensions of obsession and compulsion in a group of patients affected by AN were compared to a group of OCD patients. It was observed that the AN group did not differ from OCD controls when considered the frequency of obsession in the symmetry and somatic categories or in compulsion categories of ordering and hoarding suggesting a common brain behavioural pathway (Halmi, 2003).

The association between OCD and schizophrenia may be addressed by the overlap of structural and functional abnormalities, the involvement of dopamine/5HT neurotransmitter system and some demographic and clinical characteristics (Poyurovsky et al., 2004). The simultaneous presence of OCD symptoms and schizophrenia might identify a schizo-obsessive subtype of schizophrenia characterized by a more severe symptomatology and the co-occurrence of OCD spectrum disorders. In terms of pharmacological treatment this subgroup of patients showed a better response with either add-on SSRIs or clozapine (Poyurovsky et al., 2003).

Even the association between mood disorders and OCD has been widely reported. Some authors observed that resistant or severe OCD patients, not infrequently, suffer from a masked or hidden bipolar disorder, rising the hypothesis of a distinct form of OCD defined as "cyclothymic OCD" (Hantouche, 2003). Furthermore, OCD-bipolar patients showed a more episodic course with a greater number of concurrent major depressive episodes, more frequent abuse of substance and less positive outcome for mood symptomatology and general functioning (Perugi, 2002). It has been also reported a strong association between panic disorder and OCD which may raise relevant therapeutic implications (Torres, 2004). However, no biological markers for these conditions is available.

Taken together, the presence of such a wide phenomenological overlap associated with a substantial resistance to the conventional pharmacological treatments and the involvement of different brain areas, should be the basis for further investigation in terms of pathogenesis and neurobiology of OCD.

CONCLUSION

Throughout the last decade, considerable advances have been made in our understanding of the pathogenesis of OCD. A wealth of evidence in favour of abnormalities of the 5-HT system has, however, led to the notion that "the best is yet to come.."(Greden, 1998). That is, if the role of 5-HT is not debatable, there are a number of open questions related to the serotonergic system that await to be answered. Are the serotonergic disturbances primary or secondary? Are they involved in the pathophysiological chain or only in the phamacological response? In addition, the serotonergic abnormalities found in OCD have been reported also in other psychiatric conditions and, therefore, cannot be considered nosologically-specific, but rather linked to a dimension (or dimensions) cutting across different diagnostic entities. Although much research is still required, some authors have already highlighted relationships between the 5-HT transporter and personality traits (Lesch et al., 1996), aggressive features (Mazzanti et al., 1998), anxiety traits (Coccaro et al., 1996) and the overvalued ideation typical of the early, romantic phase of a love relationship (Marazziti et al., 1999). In addition, if the successful use of SSRI's has highlighted the key role of the 5-HT transporter, latest developments in the mode of action of these drugs suggest the involvement of different 5-HT receptor subtypes yet to be identified and, probably, of second messengers. Taken together, all these latest findings would suggest further possibilities in the treatment of OCD through the modulation of new therapeutic targets. Thus, compounds acting on specific on 5-HT receptor subtypes, such as the 5-HT_{2A}, 5-HT_{2C}, 5-HT_{5A} and probably others, or compounds which inhibit PKC or potentiate PKA or act on various G-protein subunits seem to represent potential antiobsessive drugs.

The role of other neurotransmitters has not been deeply explored, mainly for the lack of sensitive and reliable research tools, nevertheless the role of norepinephrine, dopamine and some peptides deserves further investigation.

Increasing evidences show disturbances of the immune system in some OCD subtypes, in particular in a chilhood form: however, data are also available of immune dysregulations in adult OCD. Immunological alterations appear to be different in children and adult patients and, probably reflect different pathophysiological mechanisms such as autoimmune and possibly primary processes in the first case, and perhaps secondary alterations in adulthood. The immunological disturbances may be also related to peculiar dimensions, as a correlation between the antigen D8/17 and repetitive behaviors in autistic subjects has been recently reported (Hollander et al., 1999).

In conclusion, the availability of research data from a number of sources has served to underline the complexities of OCD that appears to be heterogenous not only from the clinical point of view, but also in terms of pathophysiological mechanisms. Probably there exist multiple causes with the ability of triggering OCD symptoms, according to individual vulnerability (genetically based?) or exposure to certain agents (infections?), with prevalence of one or another in different ages. The involvement of various neurotransmitters/ neuroreceptors and circuitries and the balance between them might provide an explanation of the presence of more or less obsessions or compulsions or both, or of one type of obsessions and/or compulsions over another.

Alternatively, the neurochemical dysbalance can produce disturbances in dimensions yet to be identified that might explain the overlapping of symptoms and the common drug response observed in various psychiatric conditions. With no doubt, the identification of these common dimensions that certaintly constitute the "core" features of the disorder, will constitute an extremely intriguing area for future research.

REFERENCES

Allen AJ, Leonard HL, Swedo SE. Case study: a new infection-triggered autoimmune subtype of pediatric OCD and Tourette's syndrome. *J Am Acad Child Adolesc Psychiatry* 1995. 34: 307-311.

Altemus M, Pigott T, L'Hereux F, et al. Cerebrospinal fluid somatostatin in obsessive-compulsive disorder. *Am J Psychiatry* 1993; 15: 460-464.

Altemus M, Swedo SE, Leonard B, et al. Changes in cerebrospinal fluid neurochemistry during treatment of obsessive-compulsive disorder with clomipramine. *Arch Gen Psychiatry*1994; 51: 794-803.

Anderson G, Horne WC. Activators of protein kinase C decrease serotonin transport in human platelets. *Biochem Biophys Acta* 1992; 1137:331-337.

Asberg M, Thoren P, Bertilsson L. Clomipramine treatment of obsessive disorder: biochemical and clinical aspects. *Psychopharmacol Bull* 1981; 18; 13-21.

Ashendel CL. The phorbol ester receptor: a phospholipid-regulated protein kinase. *Biochem Biophys Acta* 1985; 822:219-242.

Barber Y, Toren P, Achiron A, et al. T cell subsets in obsessive-compulsive disorder. *Neuropsychobiology* 1996; 34: 63-66.

Bastani B, Arora RC, Meltzer HY. Serotonin uptake and imipramine binding in the blood platelets of obsessive-compulsive disorder patients. *Biol Psychiatry* 1991; 30: 131-139.

Bastani B, Nash F, Meltzer H. Prolactin and cortisol response to MK-212, a serotonin agonist, in obsessive-compulsive disorder. *Arch Gen Psychiatry* 1990; 47: 946-951.

Benkefalt C, Murphy DL, Zohar J, et al. Clomipramine in obsessive-compulsive disorder: further evidence for a serotonergic mechanism of action. *Arch Gen Psychiatry* 1989; 46: 23-28.

Berridge MJ, Downes CP, Hanley MR. Lithium amplifies agonist-dependent phospatidylinositol responses in brain and salivary glands. *Biochem J* 1982; 206: 587-595.

Black DW, Kelly M, Myers C, Noyes R Jr. Tritiated imipramine binding in obsessive-compulsive volunteers and psychiatrically normal controls. *Biol Psychiatry* 1990; 27: 319-327.

Blier P, De Montigny C. Possible serorotonergic mechanisms underlying the antidperessant and anti-obsessive-compulsive disorder responses. *Biol Psychiatry* 1998; 44: 312-323.

Brambilla F, Perna G, Bellodi L, et al. Plasma interleukin 1 beta and tumor necrosis factor concentrations in obsessive-compulsive disorder. *Biol Psychiatry* 1997; 42: 976-981.

Bronze MS, Dale JB. Epitopes of streptococcal M proteins that evoke antibodies that cross-react with human brain. *J Immunol* 1993; 151: 2820-2828.

Broock A, Pigott TA, Hill JL, et al. Acute intravenous administration ondansetron and m-CPP, alone and in combination, i patients with obsessive-compulsive disorder (OCD): behavioral and biological results. *Psychiatry Res* 1998; 79: 11-20.

Coccaro, E.F., Kavoussi, R.J., Sheline, Y.I., et al. Impulsive aggression in personality disorder correlates with tritiated paroxetine binding in the platelets. *Arch Gene Psychiatry* 1996; 53: 531-536.

De Vivo M, Maayani S. Inhibition of forskolin stimulation adenylate cyclase activity by 5-HT receptor agonist. *Eur J Pharmacol* 1985; 119 (3):231-234.

Delorme R, Chabane N, Callebertes J, Falissard B, Mouren-Simeoni MC, Rouillon F, Launay JM, Leboyer M. Platelet serotonergic predictors of clinical improvement in obsessive-compulsive disorder. *J Clin Psychopharmacology 2004*; 24: 18-23.

Denckla MB, Rapoport JL. Neurological examination. In Denckla MB, Rapoport JL, editors, *Obsessive-compulsive disorder in children and adolescents*, pp. 107-118. American Psychiatric Press Inc: Washington DC, 1989.

Duman RS. Novel therapeutic approaches beyond the serotonin receptor. *Biol Psychiatry* 1998; 44: 324-335.

Erzegovesi S, Ronchi P, Smeraldi E. 5-HT2 receptor and fluvoxamine in obsessive-compulsive disorder. *Hum Psychopharmacology* 1992; 7: 287-289.

Fineberg N. Refining treatment approaches in obsessive-compulsive disorder. *J Clin Psychopharmacol* 1996 (suppl. 5); 11: 13-22.

Frare F, Perugi G, Ruffolo G, Toni C. Obsessive-compulsive disorder and body dysmorphic disorder: a comparison of clinical features. *Eur Psychiatry*. 2004 Aug; 19(5):292-8.

Fux M, Levine J, Aviv A, Belmaker RH. Inositol treatment of obsessive-compulsive disorder. *Am J Psychiatry* 1996; 153: 1219-1221.

Garvey MA, Perlmutter SJ, Allen AJ, et al. A pilot study of penicciln prophylaxis for neuropsychiatric exacerbation triggered by streptococcal infections. *Biol Psychiatry* 1999; 45: 1564-1571.

Gibofsky A, Khanna A, Suh E, Zabriskie JB. The genetics of rheumatic fever: relationship to streptococcal infection and autoimmune disease. *J Rheumatol* 1991; 18 (suppl. 30): 1-5.

Goldsmith TD, Shapira NA, Keck PE. Rapid remission of OCD with tramadol hydrochloride. *Am J Psychiatry* 1999; 156: 660-661.

Greden JF. Serotonin: how much we have learned! So much to discover. *Biol Psychiatry* 1998; 44: 309-311.

Greist JH, Jefferson JW, Kobak KH, et al. Efficacy and tolerability of serotonin transport inhibitors in obsessive-compulsive disorder. *Arch Gen Psychiatry* 1995; 52: 53-60.

Halmi KA, Sunday SR, Klump KL, Strober M, Leckman JF, et al.. Obsession and compulsions in anorexia nervosa subtypes. *Int J Eat Disord*. 2003 Apr; 33(3):308-19.

Hantouche EG, Angst J, Demonfaucon C, Perugi G, et al.. Cyclothymic OCD: a distinct form? *J Affect Disord*. 2003 Jun;75(1):1-10.

Hollander E, De Caria C, Nitescu A, et al. Noradrenergic function in obsessive-compulsive disorder: behavioral and neuroendocrine responses to clonidine and comparison to healthy controls. *Psychiatry Res* 1991; 37: 161-177.

Hollander E, DeCaria C, Wong CM, Aronowitz B. Predictors of SSRI treatment response in OCD and autism. Paper presented at the XXI CINP congress, Glasgow (UK), July 12-16, 1998, pp. 191, Abstract book.

Hollander E, DelGiudice G, Simon L, et al. B lymphocyte D8/17 and repetitive behavior in autims. *Am J Psychiatry* 1999; 156: 317-320.

Hollander E, Fay M, Cohen B, et al. Serotonergic and noradrenergic sensitivity in obsessive-compulsive disorder: behavioral findings. *Arch Gen Psychiatry* 1988; 145: 1015-1023.

Hoyer D, Martin G 5-HT receptor classification and nomenclature: towards a harmonization with the human genome. *Neuropharmacology* 1997; 36: 419-428.

Hrdina PD. Differences between sodium-dependent and desipramine-defined ^{3}H-imipramine binding in intact human platelets. *Biol Psychiatry* 1989; 25: 576-584.

Husby G, van den Rijn I, Zabriskie JB, et al. Antibodies reacting with cytoplasm of subthalamic and caudate nuclei neurons in chorea and acute rheumatic fever. *J Exp Med* 1976; 144: 1094-1110.

Insel TR, Mueller EA, Alterman I, et al. Obsessive-compulsive disorder and serotonin: is there a connection? *Biol Psychiatry* 1985; 20: 1174 -1188.

Jenike MA. Obsessive-compulsive disorder. *Compr Psychiatry*. 1983;24:99-115.

Kaplan HI, Sadock BJ. Anxiety disorders. In: Synopsis of Psychiatry: Behavioral Sciences/Clinical Psychiatry. 8th ed. Baltimore, MD: Lippincott Williams & Wilkins; 1998:609-617.

Kaye WH, Bulik CM, Thornton L, Barbarich N, Masters K. Comorbidity of anxiety disorders with anorexia nervosa and bulimia nervosa. *Am J Psychiatry*. 2004 Dec;161(12):2215-2221.

Khanna S, Ravi V, Shenoy PK, et al. Cerebrospinal fluid viral antibodies in obsessive-compulsive disorder in an indian population. *Biol Psychiatry* 1997; 41: 883-890.

Kiessling LS, Marcotte AC, Culpepper L. Antineuronal antibodies in movement disorders. *Pediatrics* 1993; 92: 39-43.

Kikkawa U, Kishimoto A, Nishizuka. The protein kinase C family: heterogenity and its implications. *Ann Rev Biochem* 1989; 58:31-44.

Knesevich JW. Successful treatment of obsessive-compulsive disorder with clonidine hydrochloride. *Am J Psychiatry* 1982; 139: 360-365.

Leckman JF, Goodman WK, Anderson GM, et al. Cerebrospinal fluid biogenic amines in obsessive-compulsive disorder, Tourette's syndrome, and healthy controls. *Neuropsychopharmacology* 1995; 12: 73-86.

Leckman JF, Goodman WK, North WG, et al. Elevated levels of CSF oxytocin in obsessive-compulsive disorder: Comparison with Tourette's syndrome and healthy controls. *Arch Gen Psychiatry* 1994; 51: 782-792.

Lesch KP, Hoh A, Disselkamp-Tietze J, et al. 5-hydroxytyptamine$_{1A}$ receptor activity in obsessive-compulsive disorder: comparison of patients and controls. *Arch Gen Psychiatry* 1991; 48: 540-547.

Lesch KP, Wolozin BL, Murphy DL, Riederer P. Primary structure of the human platelet serotonin uptake: identity with the brain serotonin transporter. *J Neurochem* 1993; 60: 2319-2322.

Lesch, KP, Benge D, Heils A, et al. Association of anxiety-related traits with a polymorphism in the serotonin transporter gene regulatory region. *Science* 1996; 274: 1527-1531.

Maes M, Meltzer HY, Bosnan E. Psychoimmune investigation in obsessive-compulsive disorder: assay of plasma transferrin, IL-ß and IL-6 receptors, and IL-1ß and IL-6 concentrations. *Neuropsychobiology* 1994; 30: 57-60.

Mann CD, Hrdina PPD. Sodium dependence of ^{3}H-paroxetine binding and 5-^{3}H-hydroxytryptamine uptake in rat diencephalon. *J Neurochem* 1992; 59: 1856-1861.

Marazziti D, Dell'Osso L, Presta S, Pfanner C, et al.. Platelet [3H] paroxetine binding in patients with OCD-related disorders. *Psychiatry Res* 1999 Dec 27;89(3):223-8.

Marazziti D, Hollander E, Lensi P, et al. Peripheral markers of serotonin and dopamine function in obsessive-compulsive disorder. *Psychiatry Res* 1992; 42: 41-51.

Marazziti D, Masala I, Rossi A, et al. Increased inhibitory activity of protein kinase C on the serotonin transporter in OCD. *Neuropsychobiology* 2000, 41: 171-177.

Marazziti D, Presta S, Pfanner C, et al. Immunological alterations in adult obsessive-compulsive disorder. *Biol Psychiatry* 1999; 46: 810-814.

Marazziti D. Predictors of response. *Eur Neuropsychopharmacol* 1997; 27 (suppl. 2): 101-102.

Marazziti D., Akiskal HS, Rossi A., Cassano G.B. Alteration of the platelet serotonin transporter in romantic love. *Psychol Med* 1999; 29: 741-745.

Marazziti D., Ori M., Nardini Met al.:mRNA expression of serotonin receptors of type 2C and 5A in human resting lymphocytes. *Neuropsychobiology* 43: 123-127, 2001.

Marazziti D., Perez J., Cassano G.B.: Is obsessive-compulsive disorder caused by a second-messenger imbalance. *CNS Spectrums* 2001, 6: 206-209.

Marazziti D., Rossi A., Masala I., et al. Regulation of the platelet serotonin transporter by protein kinase C in the young and elderly. *Biol Psychiatry* 1999; 45: 443-447.

Marazziti, D., A. Rossi, A. Gemignani, G., et al. Decreased ^{3}H-paroxetine binding in obsessive-compulsive patients. *Neuropsychobiology* 1996; 34:184-187.

Marcusson JO, Fowler CJ, Hall H, et al. "Specific" binding of ^{3}H-imipramine to protease-sensitive and protease-resistant sites. *J Neurochem* 1985; 44: 705-711.

Mazzanti, C., Lappalainen, J., Long, J.C., et al. Role of the serotonin transporter promoter polymorphism in anxiety-related traits. *Arch Gen Psychiatry* 1998; 55: 936-940.

Mc Dougle C J. Update on pharmacologic management of OCD: agents and augmentation. *J Clin Psychiatry* 1997; 58 (Suppl 12):11-17.

McDougle CJ, Goodman WK, Leckman JF, et al. Limited therapeutic efficacy of addition of buspirone in fluvoxamine-refractory obsessive-compulsive disorder. *Am J Psychiatry* 1993; 150: 647-649.

McDougle J, Goodman WK, Price LK, et al. Neuroleptic addition in fluvoxamine-refractory obsessive-compulsive disorder. *Am J Psychiatry* 1990; 150: 647-649.

Mellerup ET, Plenge P, Engelstoft M. High-affinity binding of ^{3}H-paroxetine and ^{3}H-imipramine to human platelet membranes. *Eur J Pharmacol* 1983; 96, 303-309.

Meyerson LR, Ieni JR, Wennogle LP. Allosteric interaction between the site labelled by ^{3}H-imipramine and the serotonin transporter in human platelets. *J Neurochem* 1987; 48: 560-565.

Montgomery SA. Pharmacological treatment of obsessive-compulsive disorder. in: Hollander E, Zohar J, Marazziti D, Olivier B, eds. *Current insights in obsessive-compulsive disorder*, 215-226, Wiley & Sons: Chichester, 1994.

Moreno FA, Delgado PL. Hallucinogen-induced relief of obsessions and compulsions. *Am J Psychiatry* 1997; 145: 1037-1038.

Murphy TK, Goodman WK, Fudge MW, et al. B Lymphocyte antigen D8/17: a peripheral marker for childhood-onset obsessive-compulsive disorder and Tourette's syndrome? *Am J Psychiatry* 1997; 154: 3: 402-407.

Nestadt G, Samuels J, Riddle M, Bienveniu OJ III, Liang KY, LaBuda M, et al.. A family study of obsessive-compulsive disorder. *Arch Gen Psychiatry* 1998;155:1592-1598.

Nishizuka Y. Studies and perspective of protein kinase C. *Science* 1986; 233: 305-312.

Perez J, Tardito D, Ravizza L, Racagni G, Mori S, Maina G. Altered cAMp-dependent protein kinase in platelets of patients with obsessive-compulsive disorder. *Am J Psychiatry* 2000; 157:284-287.

Perugi G, Toni C, Frare F, Travierso MC, et al..Obsessive-compulsive –bipolar comorbidity: a systematic exploration of clinical features and treatment outcome. *J Clin Psychiatry.* 2002 Dec; 63(12):1129-34.

Pian KL, Westemberg HG, Van Migen DJ, Den Boer JA. Sumatriptan (5-HT_{1D} receptor agonist) does not exacerbate symptoms in obsessive-compulsive disorder. *Psychopharmacology* 1998; 140: 365-340.

Piccinelli M, Pini S, Bellantuono C., Wilkinson C. Efficacy of drug treatment in obsessive-compulsive disorder. *Br J Psychiatry* 1995;166: 424-443.

Pigott TA, Zohar J, Hill JL, et al. Metergoline blocks the behavioral and neuroendocrine effects of orally administered m-chlorophenylpiperazine in patients with obsessive-compulsive disorder. *Biol Psychiatry* 1991; 29: 418-426.

Pitman RK. Animal models of compulsive behaviour. *Biol Psychiatry* 1989; 26: 189-198.

Poyurovsky M, Kriss V, Weizman G, Faragian S, Kurs R, et al.. Comparison of clinical characteristics and comorbidity in schizophrenia patients with and without obsessive-compulsive disorder: schizophrenic and OC symptoms in schizophrenia. *J Clin Psychiatry.* 2003 Nov; 64(11):1300-7.

Poyurovsky M, Weizman A, Weizman R. Obsessive-compulsive disorder in schizophrenia: clinical characteristics and treatment. *CNS Drugs*. 2004;18(14):989-1010.

Rauch SL, Jenike MA. Neurobiological models of obsessive-copulsive disorder [Review]. *Psychosomatics* 1993;34:20-32.

Rausch JJ, Hutchinson J, Li X. Correlations of drug action between human platelets and human brain 5HTT. *Biol Psychiatry* (suppl.), 1995; 137: 600.

Rosenberg DR, Keshavan MS. AE Bennett Research Award. Toward a neurodevelopmental model of obsessive-compulsive disorder. *Biol Psychiatry* 1998;43:623-640.

Sallee FR, Richman H, Beach K, et al. Platelet serotonin transporter in children and adolescents with obsessive-compulsive disorder or Tourette's syndrome. *J Am Acad Child Adolesc Psychiatry* 1996; 35: 1647-1656.

Sasson Y, Zohar Y. New developments in obsessive-compulsive disorder research: implications for clinical management. *J Clin Psychopharmacology* 1996 (suppl. 5); 11: 3-12.

Shapira NA, Goldsmith TD, Keck PE. Open label study of tramadol hydrochloride in treament-refractory obsessive-compulsive disorder. *Depression and Anxiety.* 1997; 6: 170-173.

Stern L, Zohar J, Hendler T, et al. The potential role of 5-HT_{1D} receptors in the pathophysiology of obsessive-compulsive disorder. *CNS Spectrums* 1998; 3(8): 46-49.

Swedo SE, Leonard HL, Garvey M, et al. Paediatric Autoimmune Neuropsychiatric Disorders associated with Streptococcal Infections (PANDAS): a clinical description of the first fifty cases. *Am J Psychiatry* 1998; 55: 264-271.

Swedo SE, Leonard HL, Kiessling LS. Speculations on antineuronal antibody-mediated neuropsychiatric disorders of childhood. *Pediat* 1994; 93: 323-326.

Swedo SE, Leonard HL, Mittleman B, et al. Identification of children with paediatric autoimmune neuropsychiatric disorders associated with streptococcal infections by a marker associated with rheumatic fever. *Am J Psychiatry* 1997; 154: 110-112.

Swedo SE. Sydenham's chorea: a model for autoimmune neuropsychiatric disorders. *JAMA* 1994; 272: 1788-1791.

Thoren P, Asberg M, Cronholm B. Clomipramine treatment of obsessive-compulsive disorder: a controlled clinical trial. *Arch Gen Psychiatry* 1980; 37: 1281-1289.

Torres AR, Dedomenico AM, Crepaldi AL, Miguel EC. Obsessive-compulsive symtoms in patients with panic disorder. *Compr Psychiatry*. 2004 May;45(3):219-24.

Vitiello B, Shimon H, Behar D, et al. Platelet imipramine binding and serotonin uptake in obsessive-compulsive patients. *Acta Psychiat Scand* 1991; 84: 29-32.

Wang HY, Friedman. Central 5-hydroxytryptamine receptor-linked protein kinase C translocation: a postfunctional postsynaptic signal transduction system. *Mol Pharmacol* 1989; 37:75-79.

Weiss S, Ellis J, Hendley DD, Lenox RH. Translocation and activation of protein kinase C in striatal neurons in primary culture: Relationship to phorbol dibutyrate actions on the inositol phosphare generating system and neurotransmitter release. *J Neurochem* 1989; 52:530-536.

Weizman R, Carmi M, Hermesh H, et al. High-affinity imipramine binding and serotonin uptake in platelets of eight adolescent and ten adult obsessive-compulsive patients. *Am J Psychiatry* 1986; 143: 335-339.

Weizman R, Laor N, Barber Y, et al. Cytokine production in obsessive-compulsive disorder. *Biol Psychiatry* 41996; 40: 908-912.

Wilkinson SE, Hallam TJ. Protein kinase C: is pivotal role in cellular activation over-stated?. *TIPS* 1994; 15: 53-57.

Zabriskie JB. Rheumatic fever: a model for the pathological consequences of microbial-host mimicry. *J Clin Exp Rheumatol 1*986; 4: 65-73.

Zohar J, Insel TR, Zohar-Kadouch RC, Hill J, Murphy DL. Serotonergic responsivity in obsessive-compulsive disorder. Effect of chronic clomipramine treatment. *Arch Gen Psychiatry* 1988; 45: 167-172.

Zohar J, Insel TR. Obsessive-compulsive disorder: psychobiological approaches to diagnosis, treatment and pathophysiology. *Biol Psychiatry* 1987; 22: 667-687.

Zohar Y, Sasson Y, Chopra M, Groos R. Predictors of response in OCD. Paper presented at the XXI CNP congress, Glasgow (UK), July 12-16, 1998, pp. 191, Abstract book.

INDEX

A

D

K

L

M

P

T

U

V

W

Y

Z